THE BIBLE LOOKS AT FATHERS

The Bible Looks at Fathers

Annemarie Ohler

Translated by Omar Kaste

A Liturgical Press Book

This book was originally published in German under the title *Väter. Wie die Bibel Sie Sieht,* © 1996 by Verlag Herder, Freiburg im Breisgau. All rights reserved.

Cover design by Greg Becker. Illustration: "Isaac Blessing Jacob" by Rembrandt, ca. 1652.

1 2 3 4 5 6 7 8

Library of Congress Cataloging-in-Publication Data

Ohler, Annemarie.
[Väter. English]
The Bible looks at fathers / Annemarie Ohler ; translated by Omar Kaste.
p. cm.
Includes bibliographical references.
ISBN 0-8146-2541-X (alk. paper)
1. Fathers in the Bible. 2. God—Fatherhood—Biblical teaching. 3. Fatherhood (Christian theology)—Biblical teaching. I. Title.
BS579.F303713 1999
220.8'3068742—dc21 98-22835
CIP

In memory of my father
Karl Hoguth (1900–1965)

Contents

Introduction xvii

Fatherhood after the end of patriarchy xviii

Comparing modern and biblical ideas about fatherhood is triply difficult xix

Objectives and organization of this book xxiii

Chapter One: Fathers among God's People 1

1. *Acts 16: A prison official becomes a good father in his house* 1

A miracle that liberates for life 1
A man undergoes a change 3
A dream becomes reality 4

2. *Fathers find salvation for others* 5

"You will be saved, you and your household" (Acts 16:31) 5

The different children of Abraham 5
Hope for the renewal of the People of God 7
Daily reality as a support for hope 8

3. *Believing fathers of a faithless world* 10

"Customs that we cannot accept" (Acts 16:21) 10

Jeremiah's letter to the fathers among the exiles 11
Why does Jeremiah address only the fathers? 12

The revised version of the flood story
in postexilic times 13

4. *Tobit: a believing father alone in a hostile world* 15

Tobit believes himself to be
the only righteous man 16
Tobit's righteousness gets him into trouble 17
Tobit opens his heart to his son 18
What do clan and family mean
when God wills to help? 18
A father needs brothers 20

5. *Fathers as hosts* 21

"He brought them up into the house" (Acts 16:34) 21

Genesis 18: Criticism of Abraham's hospitality 21
Exodus 2:15-22: Moses as a needy guest 23
Hospitality as a trace of God in everyday life 24
Genesis 19: Hospitality in Sodom 25
Hosts in the New Testament 26

6. *Fathers celebrate with their families* 28

"He and his entire household rejoiced that he had become
a believer in God" (Acts 16:34) 28

Family fathers organize religious festivals 28
What religious authority did fathers possess? 29
The People of God composed of both men and women:
a Jewish ideal 30
Fathers and mothers serve God together 32
The People of God composed of both men and women:
a Christian ideal 33

7. *In retrospect: fathers, not "patriarchs"* 34

A good family father maintains an open house 34
A good family father practices brotherliness 35
The house of a good father is a portrait of hope
for all humanity 36
How fathers are to live out their fatherhood is a question
to be decided within the world 37

Faith in the God who loves life protects us from expecting too much from fathers 38

Chapter Two: Fathers in Their Political Responsibility 42

1. *1 Samuel 22: Saul's massacre of the priestly clan* 42

The historical and literary context of the story 42
Is Ahimelech guilty ? 43
Saul's guilt 43
The guilt of Doeg the Edomite 45
Why David takes the guilt upon himself 45
A story about the significance of the "father's house" 46

2. *A strong paternal house: hope for Israel* 47

"Eighty-five men who wore the linen ephod" (1 Sam 22:18) 47

The massacre of the priestly clan: an act of madness 47
The deliverers of Israel, their paternal houses, and their fathers 48
What is the basis for the paternal house's strength? 50
The solidary house of the father as an endangered ideal 52

3. *Tensions between fathers and sons endanger Israel* 52

"My son has stirred up my servant against me" (1 Sam 22:8) 52

Fathers and sons among a politically unstable people 53
1 Samuel 20: Why Saul tries to kill his son 54
1 Samuel 14:24-46: Does the curse of the father kill the son? 55

4. *Responsibility for the solidarity of the father's house* 58

"You shall surely die, Ahimelech, you and all your father's house" (1 Sam 22:16) 58

2 Samuel 21: Saul's sons are executed for the bloodguilt of their father 58

Must Joab's descendants atone for his atrocities? 60
Why does God avenge the sins of the fathers on their sons? 61
How the disastrous continuity of fathers and sons can be broken 63
Genesis 4: Sons of a murderer 63

5. *The heritage of the fathers entrusted to the sons* 65

"Will the son of Jesse give every one of you fields and vineyards?" (1 Sam 22:7) 65

Fatherhood and prosperity 65
Inherited property and remembrance 66
The son and the memory of the father 67
Inherited property and daughters 68
Luke 15: The wealth and inheritance of the merciful father 70

6. *Men without fathers* 71

"Doeg the Edomite . . . was in charge of Saul's servants" (1 Sam 22:9) 71

The fatherless in the king's service 72
"Father": a title of respect for the man willing to serve 73
"Fatherless" soldiers 74
David's crimes against Uriah the Hittite 75
The suicide of a grandfather 76
The resistance of a fatherless man 77

7. *A king like his father David* 78

"Saul was sitting at Gibeah under the tamarisk tree on the height . . . and all his servants were standing around him" (1 Sam 22:6) 78

Israel's deliverer must be more than just the son of a father 78
Ahaz cares nothing for the traditions of his father's house 79
Isaiah 7:14: The father of the Immanuel can be forgotten 80

Matthew 1:23: Why Joseph must not be forgotten 82

8. *Prophets are signs of admonition for a people proud of its families* 83

"You conspired against me . . . by inquiring of God for him" (1 Sam 22:13) 83

The son leaves his father's house 84
Elisha is "father" of the king and "lord" of his disciples 85
Elisha gains a father 86
The "fatherless" man can become a father 88
Do the Elisha traditions project a particular "father-image"? 88

9. *In retrospect: fathers need sons* 89

Fathers apply their strength for Israel 89
Fatherhood alone does not guarantee Israel's survival 92
When God wishes to give life, God needs no fathers 94

10. *The disciples of Jesus: a family in which there is no father* 96

Matthew 8:18-27: To follow Jesus is to meet "the Lord" 96
Leaving one's father: a prophetic sign 97
A society without fathers 98
Polemic against fathers 99

Chapter Three: The Father in His House 108

1. *A new paternal house arises* 108

"I served you fourteen years for your two daughters, and six years for your flock" (Gen 31:41) 108

Foundations on which a man can build his family 109
Only a free man has paternal rights 110
Separation from the father's house is a precarious venture 112
God's blessing builds a house even for a guilty father 113

2. *Fathers give away their daughters* 115

"If you illtreat my daughters . . . or . . . take wives in addition to my daughters . . ." (Gen 31:50) 115

Why does the father receive the bride price? 116
Judges 19: A father fails to protect his daughter's rights 116
Deuteronomy 22 and 1 Samuel 13: Rape is like murder 118
Judges 11: Jephthah sacrifices his daughter for the victory 120

3. *Paternal authority* 122

"The same night [Jacob] got up and took his two wives, his two maids, and his eleven children, and crossed the ford of the Jabbok" (Gen 32:22) 122

Fathers recognize their responsibility 122
1 Kings 12: Solomon's son despises his father 123
Genesis 9:20-27: When a father is despised, brotherliness dies 125

4. *Fathers teach their sons* 126

"When Jacob ended his charge to his sons, he drew his feet into the bed, breathed his last, and was gathered to his people" (Gen 49:33) 126

Fathers and sons constitute the chain of bearers of tradition 126
The issue of a father's authority to teach 127
Should fathers discipline their sons? 128
The "strong hand" of mothers 129
Fathers, do not provoke your children to anger! 130

5. *How fathers love their sons* 132

"His life is bound up in the boy's life" (Gen 44:30) 132

Fathers and little children 132
The father and the only son 134
The very image of his father 134
The son set free 136

6. *How fathers love their daughters* 137

"Afterwards [Leah] bore a daughter, and named her Dinah" (Gen 30:21) 137

A poor man loves his lamb like a daughter (2 Sam 12:3) 138
Job's daughters have the right of domicile with their father 138
Jairus loves his daughter 139

7. *Abraham binds his son (Genesis 22)* 142

A provocative story 142
The literary context of the narrative 143
The historical placement of the story 144
A story about a father's difficult journey of faith 146
A story about the saving name 147

8. *Fathers without power* 149

"Then Jacob said to Simeon and Levi, 'You have brought trouble on me'" (Gen 34:30) 149

Genesis 34: Jacob is silent 149
2 Samuel 15: David flees 150
Genesis 27: Isaac trembles 151
1 Samuel 2:29: Can a father do more than reprimand his wicked sons? 152
Deuteronomy 21:18-21: The rebellious son must die 153
Even as "judges," fathers were in need of help 154

9. *In retrospect: fatherhood and fatherliness* 156

Why the Bible speaks so often about fathers 156
To what extent is the priority of fathers self-evident for biblical authors? 157
How biblical texts encourage an examination of long-held ideas about the preeminence of fathers 159
Why fatherhood and fatherliness are not always easy to reconcile 161

Chapter Four: Our Father in Heaven 169

1. *Jeremiah's message of the fatherhood of God* 170

Jeremiah 12:7-8: God surrenders paternal rights 170
Jeremiah 3:4, 19: God yearns to be called "My Father" 172
Jeremiah 31:9, 20: God wants to be a motherly father 174

2. *The biblical message about God the Father within the framework of the history of religion* 177

The kinship group of YHWH 177
The universal fatherhood of God 177
God, our Father 178
God, my Father 180
Matthew 6:32: Your Father knows that you have need of all these things 182

3. *The will of the Father: the Law of God* 183

Matthew 21:28-29: A parable about the will of the Father 183
Deuteronomy 1:31: The father carries the son to the place of the renewal of the covenant 184
Deuteronomy 32:6, 11: Israel's creator behaves like a father bird 185
Isaiah 63:16 and 64:8: Israel's ultimate hope lies in its Father and Creator 187
Malachi 2:10: Have we not all one father? 189
Once again: The parable about "the will of the father" 190

4. *The Lord's Prayer: Testimony to Jesus' message about the Father* 190

The prayers of children to the incomprehensible God 190
The childlike requests of responsible people 191
The father who is ready to forgive 193

5. *God, a Father with daughters* 195

A remarkable expression in one of Paul's epistles 195

Two ways in which God is the Father
of the sons of David 196
The "Abba" cry of the early Christians 198

6. *God, the Father of Jesus* 199

The "Abba" cry as a witness to Jesus' message
about the Father 199
Mark 14:36: Jesus alone with the Father 200
Jesus seeks successors 201
The Father of Jesus is the incomprehensible God 202
Father, for you all things are possible 204

7. *Fragmentary images of the Father* 205

Fragmentary images of the father's heritage 206
Fragmentary images of divine sonship 208
Father and son work together 210
The hearts of father and son are close to one another 211

Index 217

Introduction

It is the objective of this book to ask of biblical texts what they have to say on the subject of fatherhood. Is it worth the trouble? The question is unavoidable in an age when it is no longer possible to ignore the participation of women in the shaping of our common life, for the Bible speaks a great deal about fathers—far too much, many would say. Word statistics furnish some impressive numbers: the word "father" appears in the Bible more than 1,200 times, while "mother" is not mentioned more than 220 times. The most frequently used word, "son," occurs more than 5,000 times, especially because men are constantly being presented as sons of fathers.[1]

It is not the patriarchalism of the biblical era alone that must bear responsibility for the strangeness that clearly appears in the Bible's manner of thinking and speaking about the theme of fatherhood. Mothers are able at least to some extent to recognize in mothers of other times what they themselves have experienced. Such things as pregnancy, giving birth, and nursing a baby give concrete guidance toward understanding what it means to be a mother. Experiencing fatherhood in the flesh, however, is never a given. For a man that happens naturally only when mother and child mean something to him. Not until he has discovered something of himself transformed in the child can he concretely experience that he has fathered the child. Fatherhood exists only when people make it visible to one another, that is, when they give it form. The nature of fatherhood can be perceived only in the historically changing forms that human beings give it.

Fatherhood after the end of patriarchy

Modern society hardly assigns specific tasks to fathers any longer. Men and women are continuously becoming more like one another in their training and professions, and what the father does is increasingly being assumed just as much by the mother. There is no longer at hand any established concept of fatherhood into which a man could step as the founder of a family, especially because the ancient conceptions of fathers as the heads of families have fallen into disrepute.

Contemporary criticism of patriarchy directs itself also against biblical testimony. In protest, it asserts that paternal authority based on the Bible has been decked out with an almost sacrosanct holiness. This book accepts this criticism insofar as it shows that the Bible by no means establishes privileged rights for fathers. Many a sharp rejection of "biblical" patriarchy would be more appropriately directed against other patriarchal remnants that, persisting down to the present day, make little sense in themselves and shadow and obscure the patriarchal order of life into which people have settled in the past.

The broad aftereffect of the Freudian hypothesis about the "Oedipus complex" has contributed in no small measure to the darkening of the image of the father. Citing the Oedipus story, it declares that the son can only win a life of his own by "killing" his father. In these ancient myths about overpowering fathers is said to be reflected an archetype that works deep within every person, something like a timeless law of nature to the effect that sons, in order to be able to live, must stand out in contrast to their fathers. Biblical texts, which praise the unity of father and son, seem against this background to be deceptive propaganda for a paternal power that prefers to destroy the son rather than surrender anything of itself.[2]

A few generations ago the image of the father who did not permit his son to prosper in his presence often corresponded to actual experiences. In many places the ruins of patriarchy still stood high and tottered dangerously, so that many sons—but also daughters—were not able to find room to live among them. While Freudian analysis may indeed help such people to understand their situation and so be better able to cope with life, is its image of fathers always and everywhere correct?[3]

If Freud had felt any interest in democratic America he could have learned of an entirely different form of fatherhood. In the year 1830 Alexis de Tocqueville, a young Frenchman of aristocratic background, observed from outside and with the eye of an ethnologist the day-to-day affairs of "democracy in America." Among other things he describes with what naturalness American fathers release their grown sons from obedience. He is struck by how much more personal affection grows when, in contrast to the practice among the aristocratic families with whom he was familiar, the son does not need to wait until his father retires in order to be able to assume independent responsibility, nor does the father need to insist that his son be both able and willing to carry out the tasks imposed by his father.[4]

More justice can be done to biblical texts by the application of Tocqueville's style of investigation than by the search for "archetypes" of fatherhood, for precisely the Bible's foreignness attests how deeply biblical faith is rooted in the history of a certain little group of people, and thus also in the forms in which this history was present. Against the background of his aristocratic heritage, Tocqueville's attention was attracted to characteristics of daily life in a democratic land. Similarly, an examination of the strangeness of biblical concepts of fatherhood can sharpen our perception of contemporary experiences of and with fathers.

There are three reasons, however, why the task of examining biblical "father texts" is more complex.

Comparing modern and biblical ideas about fatherhood is triply difficult

(a) Modern society possesses no distinctive concept of fatherhood. It provides no sharp image, as clear as those Tocqueville imbibed from the European nobility, with which biblical concepts could be contrasted. Tocqueville was already describing inconsistencies: He applauds the progress in personal freedom and mutual affection that result when fathers have no rights beyond those possessed by all adults. Yet, because his own experiences had acquainted him with the consciousness of a responsibility for a family heritage that is passed on from fathers to sons, he also keeps his eyes open to perceive how readily democratic freedom can lead a person into isolated detachment. He deplores the man for whom neither ancestors nor descendants any longer have meaning, and who is concerned with his contemporaries only to the extent that they serve him in bringing his own life under control.

It seems as if Tocqueville anticipated contemporary conditions. The less families are bound together by material obligations the more freely they are able to base their lives on inner solidarity, yet the greater also is their vulnerability to certain corrosive forces. First to be affected was the bond between fathers and sons. In 1963 Alexander Mitscherlich described the "fatherless society" that comes into being as a result of the separation that occurs between family and profession in the modern world of work.[5] Children know little about their father's work, only that at home he demands to be left in peace. As a countermove men are with increasing frequency seizing what is almost the only chance that the modern division of life functions still leaves them in order to experience themselves as fathers, that is, becoming "new" fathers, "motherly" fathers. In other words, they share with their wives the concern for the inner space of the family and live in friendly relations with the children. Just as the only support for a friendship is the friendship itself, so also the family is held together almost entirely by the personal ties its members build up and cultivate among themselves. The insecure nature of this support is indicated as much by the number of fathers who live separately from their families as by the fact that there are fathers who raise their children alone. Fatherhood today takes many forms, none of which, however, is clearly distinctive.

The reason why biblical ideas about fathers cannot simply be contrasted with modern ones can be found also in the Bible itself.

(b) There is no consistent father-image in the Bible. The community in whose midst the Bible came into being repeatedly experienced profound and radical changes that altered even its ideas about the rights and duties of fathers. In the sagas about Israel's fathers and mothers—Abraham and Sarah, Isaac and Rebecca, Jacob with Rachel and Leah—there is a reflection of a stateless world in which the family constituted the broadest community to which people felt they belonged. Stories from the book of Judges contain recollections of the time of transition when Israel was becoming a people. Groups of peasants who had created a homeland in the mountains organized themselves into defensive tribes and tribal leagues in which fathers and sons together defended their homeland against other groups in search of land. It was under this pressure that the nation eventually came into being. Israel then lived for several centuries in two states that existed side by side and in which families could hope for protection. One can also imagine that fathers were again assigned an entirely different significance when Israel lost its political freedom, and then once more when Judah consolidated itself as a border province of the Persian Empire. The concept of fatherly duties and rights changed anew when opposition to the political lords of the land became so sharp that Jewish life retreated steadily more into the inner space of the family. Early Christian congregations, whose ideas of fatherhood found expression in the New Testament, accommodated these changes.

Nevertheless, the fact that the Bible in itself knows no clearly consistent image of fathers cannot be attributed solely to the fact that it was shaped over more than a thousand years. The differing ideas about fatherhood that came into being during these historical epochs cannot be clearly separated from one another in the Bible. This is not to be explained solely by the side-by-side persistence, continuing even to our day, of ideas that originated at different times. Still greater are the consequences of the fact that biblical authors neither define the essence of fatherhood nor describe in which forms it appears at any given time, but rather describe how human beings deal with one another and with the structures and institutions that exist. Rather than what is usual and normal, they tell about events so shocking that they cannot simply be accepted as a matter of course. They argue and discuss what they communicate, provoking those to whom they write to deal with what they have reported.

The discussion about the person, rights, and duties of fathers occurs on the basis of a criterion that must be tested ever anew, that of Israel's faith. The original experience of this faith was the Exodus from Egypt, when God stood on the side of the oppressed and against the stronger forces of the great nation Egypt. It is thrilling to note how this works itself out in biblical father-texts. In every epoch in which biblical faith was developing, the authority of fathers was very important, but biblical texts ask how paternal authority can be so applied as to promote faith, or even whether it can be so applied at all.

The conviction that fathers do not deserve authority just because they are fathers has in our days become merely a commonplace and a platitude. If the "critique of patriarchy" that appears in the Bible were nothing but a confirmation of this, we could confidently forget it. Yet these critical words do not appear in the Bible without any relation to other texts that project bright images of paternal authority. Also, where the dialogue centers on the theme of fathers the Bible witnesses to a great discussion, continuing through the centuries and involving many voices who have, ever again and in constantly new ways, dialogued with those who earlier had done so. How can this be made a reality: living through changing times with the God who does not will that human beings should oppress one another? That cannot be established definitively and once and for all. And thus it is that the Bible sets up neither examples simply to be imitated nor rules simply to be followed. It keeps open questions that can never be finally settled as long as human beings exist.

With this we address the third reason why current ideas about fatherhood cannot simply be juxtaposed to those of the Bible:

(c) Biblical conceptions about fatherhood are still alive: the fathers of the French aristocracy and those of Tocqueville's *Democracy in America* were separated by more than just the Atlantic; there was also a clearly definable social and spiritual distance. Biblical conceptions of fatherhood are by no means so easily distinguishable from one another. As the book of the questions about life the Bible has been uninterruptedly a living book since it came into existence. Its images of fathers have long influenced ideas about how fathers should live, and continue to have their effect even today. Dealing with the Bible texts about fathers includes confronting the later history of the Bible.

Of course, what is still known in post-Christian society often does not amount to more than certain reminiscences of biblical ideas that, having solidified into clichés, not infrequently actually distort the perspective of the Bible itself. That is especially true of the widespread misconception that in "God the Father" the Bible contains the original image of fatherly authority.[6] In the fourth section of the book it is nonetheless demonstrated that only extremely late, seldom, and very reservedly do the biblical texts speak of God as a father, and that it is thereby by no means the authority of the father that stands in the foreground.

The Church keeps watch over the Bible as the living charter of its faith. Are outlines of the biblical father tradition there being more faithfully drawn out into the present? Nowhere do elements of patriarchalism live on more strongly than in the Church. There is above all one element of the patriarchal form of life to which it still holds fast: in the past, the role of intermediary between family and public was attributed to fathers. What a father decided was decisive for where and how the family lived. In public matters it was sufficient to speak to the heads of families, who then saw to it that the essential was accomplished in relation to their people. In the Church, decisions about the nature of the common life are made and passed on in this same way down to the present, that is, through representatives whom the community of faith can no more choose than children can select their own fathers.

That is one of the concerns that motivated the beginning of work on this book.

Objectives and organization of this book

Does the Bible speak about fathers in such a way that biblical faith can remain alive only in a Church that lags behind society in the manner in which people within it treat one another? The first section of the book deals with the question by introducing biblical texts that speak of the significance of fathers within the people of God.

It is true that the texts examined there do not distinguish between the secular duties of fathers and their importance for the community of faith. This reflection introduces the second motive that became steadily more important during work on this book because it is more relevant to the question of the biblical authors' intent than the mere issue of Church patriarchalism. For the texts, the day-to-day world and the world of faith self-evidently belong together. In contrast, today faith seems to live exclusively in a special world of religion. Can it continue to do so?

Biblical authors have something to say to this question that merits serious consideration, for faith in the God who is present for human beings moves them to observe how people live. That people deal humanly with each other has, in their view, intrinsic value because this is the earthly realm in which faith must be rooted if it is not to wither away. Though in many ways biblical texts portray how faith is the divine gift that cannot be manipulated, it is the responsibility of the human being to care for his or her own roots. How do people live as fathers and with fathers? Where do the chances lie within this area of experience to promote humane behavior, and what are the corresponding dangers? This book will employ biblical texts in the pursuit of these questions. Both are questions that contain meaning and are questions of faith.

Texts stemming from ancient times do not disclose themselves without the help of historical methods. Historical curiosity, too, is a part of the motivation behind this book. But if biblical texts are also to be "understood in the spirit in which they were written,"[7] then one may not use them merely as material with the help of which one can determine what importance fathers once had in earlier times. Therefore it is much more important to discover those questions that keep alive the inner-biblical discussion of the theme of "fathers" in order in this way to heighten attention to questions that people will continue to confront as long as fatherhood has meaning in their lives.

The immense abundance of biblical comments on the theme and the variety of perspectives from which it is seen should be put in order, but if possible not inserted into a system imposed from outside. The guidelines for the investigation are therefore extracted from the Bible itself. For the first two parts of the book they are found in two narratives with very divergent father-images appearing in widely separated spheres of the Bible: the jail officer from Philippi who appears in the book of Acts, and King Saul. Both stories portray with the help of numerous motifs how these fathers understood themselves and were understood by others. The organization is structured according to these motifs. Each section deals with one of the motifs, and shows what questions arise in various historical and life contexts when fatherhood is thus lived and experienced.

Two narratives, each of which pursues one of these questions in a subtly different manner, are introduced at the respective locations and in individual sections: the Tobit story, which asks how long a father can remain righteous when no one stands beside him, and the story of Abraham's readiness to sacrifice, which considers whether there is any justification possible for a father who decides whether his child shall live or die.

The series of motifs from the two narratives about the prison officer and King Saul lead into texts that inquire about the public significance of fathers. What do fathers contribute to the life of the community of faith? What political rights and duties do they have? There is no other text to be found in the Bible that at the same time tells so much about the life of a father within the interior space of his family. That should not surprise anyone, for the Bible did not originate as a book for the faith of the individual, but as the book of the two communities who have lived with the God of Israel, the God of Jesus Christ.

Yet the question of the importance of fatherhood for the private life of the individual cannot be simply passed over, because fatherhood is today experienced almost exclusively in the private realm. It must be asked also because biblical traditions often reveal how much of the strength of fathers and sons who bear responsibility for the shaping of the common life flows to them from their own personal feelings for their own families, and, on the other hand, because of how deeply the entire people of God is affected when there is a general low opinion of "private" fatherly love. Even though no individual text takes the daily life of the family as such for its theme, the biblical record contains impressive images and scenes from family life. In the third part of this book they are arranged along a "biographical" principal connecting thread. The stations in a father's life, from the establishment of the family to the leave-taking of the dying father, are thereby first visualized by means of scenes from the Jacob tradition.

As a follow-up to each of these three chapters, features of each of the individual texts examined are brought together to form one larger image. The unifying center point is not any special father image, but rather faith in a God who is friendly to human beings and who also acts in and through them. In the Christian faith and teaching about God, what is said about God the Father has profound meaning, but the Bible exercises great restraint with respect to this Father God. The final chapter shows that it adopts only a few fragmentary individual elements in order to speak about the God who is both near and inscrutable.

In consideration of the fact that Jews do not speak aloud the name of God, it is written in this book only by means of its consonants: YHWH. Occasionally, as in the NRSV, it is expressed as LORD to remind us that it indicates a personal name and not a title. Translation of biblical texts is based on the NRSV, but is continually compared with the respective Hebrew or Greek texts. Some divergences were necessary in order to emphasize more clearly important individual aspects of the text. Significant departures from the published text are individually explained.

Notes: Introduction

[1] Ernst Jenni, ed., *Theologisches Handwörterbuch zum AT* (Munich, 1971) 1, articles *ʾab, em, ben.*

[2] V. E. Pilgrim, *Vatersöhne* (Hamburg, 1993) 229–230 cites as example for this Gen 1:27: The "forefatherly behavior" of "created him in his image" has burdened sons for hundreds of generations. For the interpretation of the text within its biblical context see below, chs. 3 and 4.

[3] The psychoanalyst H. Tellenbach came to the conclusion, from his experiences with patients, that the Freudian hypothesis is passé; as editor of an anthology he initiated sweeping reviews of the history of fatherhood: *Das Vaterbild in Mythos und Geschichte* (Stuttgart: Kohlhammer, 1976); *Das Vaterbild im Abendland* (Stuttgart: Kohlhammer, 1978).

[4] Alexis de Tocqueville, *Democracy in America,* 2nd ed. (Chicago: Encyclopedia Britannica, Inc., 1990).

[5] Alexander Mitscherlich, *Auf dem Wege zur vaterlosen Gesellschaft* (Munich, 1963); cf. G. Corneau, *Abwesende Väter—verlorene Söhne* (Düsseldorf, 1993).

[6] See notes 2 and 3. W. E. Fthenakis, *Die Psychologie der Vater-Kind Beziehung* (Munich, Vienna, and Baltimore, 1985) 1:10, projects an unbroken line from the "early Hebrew agrarian culture" to the "Judaic image of God." "God is a paternal figure, almighty, demanding, often incomprehensible, but also caring and illuminating. He demands absolute obedience." Y. Kniebiehler, *Les pères aussì ont une histoire* (Paris, 1987) 41, knows how seldom biblical texts speak about God as "Father," but explains: "Even though he is rarely described as a father, the God of Israel presents an ideal image of paternity."

[7] Vatican Council II, Constitution on Divine Revelation *(Dei verbum)* 12.

Chapter One

Fathers among God's People

1. Acts 16: A prison official becomes a good father in his house

Luke tells about a jail keeper who one night receives into his prison two men who have been badly beaten and is ordered to keep them securely locked up. He "throws" them into the jail, puts their feet in the stocks, and goes to bed. The condition of the two men imprisoned on the first floor of his house clearly does not bother him. What kind of life does this man lead, earning his living with such employment, and even living at the location of his job? The question is soon answered in the telling of the story.

A miracle that liberates for life

During the night the jailer is startled by an earthquake. Noting that the doors of the prison are open, and believing that the prisoners have escaped, he wants to kill himself. His suicide attempt reveals something about how he had lived until that time. He is sure that his supervisors will not even consider that he might be innocent. Up to that point it had made little difference to him that he had played his part in the prisoners' miserable suffering. Now he sees the same terror descending over himself, for he understands that to the Romans he is worth no more than the prisoners. He does not want to go on living.

Luke does not take the trouble to tell everything just as it could have happened. An earthquake had broken open the prison doors and even the prisoners' shackles. Can we imagine that it caused no additional disturbance? In fact, if the nocturnal episode had not been mentioned in the report of Paul's stay in Philippi, no one would have noticed it. That evening the jailer took Paul and Silas into custody as he had been instructed, and next morning he obeyed the new orders to free them and send them on their way (Acts 16:23, 35).

In other instances Luke is concerned to portray the Romans as equitable rulers and the Christians as a community at home in the Roman Empire. He would hardly have told about Paul's imprisonment and dismissal if something of the kind had not really happened. In 1 Thess 2:2 Paul himself speaks of his suffering and of the shameful treatment he had received in Philippi. Also credible is what Luke says about the reason for the subsequent banishment: the authorities were obliged to follow up on a complaint about propaganda for "Jewish customs" (16:20-21). The Jews were not to bother the general population, which was well-disposed to the Romans, with their strange customs. By means of a quick proceeding that would discourage the return of the troublemakers the Roman commanders hoped to avoid further annoyance of that kind.

Fitted into this intrinsically straightforward report is the story of the nocturnal events in the jail that surround Paul and Silas with such legendary splendor. Though beaten and bound, about midnight they are still singing songs of praise. Luke is here depicting exemplary forms: faith gives joy that even pain and humiliation cannot erase. Even when in chains, the believer is free.[1] The earthquake that smashed the door of the prison and the bonds as if in response to the songs of praise is a powerful demonstration of the liberating power of faith. But Paul and Silas do not understand the earthquake as a sign that God means to free them from prison. For the sake of the jailer they relinquish their freedom. In this Luke sees a miracle that is just as great as that of the earthquake. He had called the earthquake "great." Now he says that Paul "shouted in a loud voice" to save the jailer from suicide: "Do not harm yourself, for we are all here."

The double miracle produces double freedom. On his own responsibility the jailer leads the prisoners out of the prison. The fear of the unknown power that fills these two men makes him forget his dread of his superiors. What kind of people are these, who choose to reject freedom? They must be acquainted with something immeasurably better. The jail officer hopes that they will let him share in it: "he fell down trembling before Paul and Silas. Then he brought them outside and said, 'Sirs, what must I do to be saved?'" (Acts 16:29-30).

A man undergoes a change

The apostles' response unexpectedly reveals something new about the jailer: "And they said, 'Believe in the Lord Jesus, and you will be saved, you and your household'" (Acts 16:31). The apostles remind the man that he is a father. What would have become of his family if he had killed himself? What would have been the result for them if he had continued his present life, which, as he had now comprehended, was worse than death itself?

How do the apostles actually know that the jailer has a family? Did those living in the house perhaps come running because of the earthquake and Paul's loud cry? Luke does not concern himself with such questions, nor is he concerned that both of the apostles could hardly have spoken the same answer and with one voice. Luke wants to speak correctly about faith. For faith is not proclaimed by one person alone, nor does anyone receive it for himself or herself alone. It is for this reason that the apostles speak as if with one voice and address the jailer as the father of a family.

The jailer understands this. Immediately he proves himself to be a good father in his house, giving help to those most in need of it: "At the same hour of the night he took them and washed their wounds." Life had been given to him, and he passes it on. Real life is realized in mutual giving and taking. So the jailer, who had now been transformed, gets back what he had given the injured men: "he was baptized at once." Clearly it must have happened at the same place where he had taken the water to care for the prisoners. Once again Luke emphasizes that the jailer is a father: he is baptized "with all his family" (Acts 16:33).

Fragmentary as is Luke's account of these nocturnal events, so much more eloquently does he make clear that from that point on the jailer conducted himself like a real father, head of the household and host: "Then he brought them up into his house, and set food before them . . . and rejoiced with all his household that he had believed in God" (Acts 16:34).

A dream becomes reality

It was not solely the pleasure of telling a story that moved Luke to insert this legend into the account of Paul's activity in Philippi. Philippi is the first European city to which Paul goes, encouraged by a dream in which a Macedonian had pleaded with him: "Come over to Macedonia and help us" (Acts 16:9). Thereafter, however, no Macedonian had wanted anything to do with Paul. He had preached at a Jewish place of prayer in the house of a woman from Lydda who was friendly to Jews: a woman of Asia Minor, therefore, around whom a congregation had come into existence. Thus the first Christian congregation in Europe was in the house of a woman. The native residents, nonetheless, had arranged with the Roman authorities for Paul's expulsion.

Just before he is about to be expelled, he meets this prison official who needs his help. Did Paul notice immediately when he met the man that his dream was becoming reality? Was this why he knew that the earthquake was not intended to help him personally? In any case, it is when Paul does not seize upon the chance to escape that his dream suddenly becomes reality. A Macedonian man asks for help: "What must I do to be saved?" Luke tells how wonderfully faith in Jesus Christ set roots in Europe.

With the scene of the apostles' expulsion the report of Paul's stay in Philippi is resumed. Only the jailer's words of farewell remind us once again of the nighttime episode: "go in peace" (Acts 16:36). On the previous evening he had "thrown" Paul and Silas into prison without any regard to their condition. Though now he still obeys his employers, faith has made him free to take friendly leave of them. During the night he had fearfully addressed Paul and Silas as "Sirs," but now, as a friend who shares their faith, he sends them on their way with the greeting of peace.

Luke describes how faith transforms a person. To the supervisor who had treated the prisoners cruelly it gives the courage to treat them humanely; on the man who had fallen trembling to the floor it bestows the dignity of a hospitable father of the house.

From a modern perspective it seems strange that the whole family comes to faith with the father. Did the family in that "patriarchal" time have no other option than to follow the father's decision? Is Luke here simply telling, without devoting any deep thought to it, what was self-evident in those days? Probably that is not the case, for he underlines much too clearly that the jailer did not find faith by himself. For him the former life ends at the moment when he decides to kill himself. He takes the first step toward a new life when he allows himself to be reminded that he is not just a servant of the Romans but a man responsible for a family. His suicide would not be without consequences for those who were his. Then Luke piles up expressions that reveal this convert as a father. He shares his faith with his family and celebrates a feast of rejoicing with them and with his guests. Four times in four verses Luke repeats "he and his entire family/household."

Luke had a good reason for emphasizing the father-motif in this way. He is telling about the beginning of the Christian faith in Europe and wishes to cite a much older story of beginnings. The jailer is a man like Noah. Because Noah trusted in God, he and his family with him were saved from the flood, so that humanity was created anew. Because at the word of the apostles the jailer believed in Jesus, a new epoch begins for Europe. Luke's dependence on the Noah story is reflected in his choice of words. The apostles say, "You will be saved, you and your household" (Acts 16:31). God had said to Noah, "Go into the ark, you and all your household" (Gen 7:1).

At the beginning of the history of the Church in Europe a dream of all humanity is realized, the vision of the house of the father in which a family finds life. The following sections will trace additional biblical traditions from which Luke draws his conception of a good father.

2. Fathers find salvation for others

"You will be saved, you and your household" (Acts 16:31)

There is no way in which parents can better contribute to their children's coming to trust in life than that they themselves live in this way. An Old Testament proverb says solemnly: "In the fear of the LORD one has strong confidence, and one's children will have a refuge" (Prov 14:26). In this New Testament idiom especially dear to Luke there is a hint of the same experience, that is, when a man comes to faith "his whole household" finds salvation with him. Does it not depend at least as much on mothers whether or not a family thrives? A comparison of two stories will show that when Luke speaks thus about fathers he does so only after careful consideration, and not in thoughtless acceptance of a patriarchal pattern of thinking about fathers.

The different children of Abraham

Luke 13 tells how a woman whom Jesus had healed of her bent back raises her voice in praise of God in a synagogue service. When the leader of the synagogue council is indignant, Jesus defends her and calls her a "daughter of Abraham." As a member of the family of God's people she has the right to witness honestly and publicly to her faith. Thereby Luke gives the miracle a remarkable meaning, that is, that Jesus wishes to heal all his people, not one individual alone. As God's people they are to be a family in which the "daughter," too, is honored.

In Luke 19 the evangelist tells how Jesus demands the same recognition for a man. In the joy of an encounter with Jesus the tax-collector Zacchaeus promises to share his riches with the poor. His joy would soon turn sour if the neighbors interpreted this as nothing more than the long-overdue restitution of a man who, as a tax-collector, had grown rich at the expense of his own people. For this reason Jesus replies to Zacchaeus' joyful promise by saying publicly: "Today salvation has come to this house, because he too is a son of Abraham" (Luke 19:9). Along with Zacchaeus, all are obliged to change their way of thinking, to recognize that even a tax-collector belongs to the family of Abraham and that when he shares his money with the poor he is doing no more than anyone would expect of him.

In these two narratives Jesus promises their birthrights, each in his or her own manner, to the "daughter" and the "son" of Abraham. To the man he guarantees a good place in his family, to the woman a place of public honor. The criteria that still today often determine the place of men and women are here reversed. Jesus understands the people of God as a family in which women possess the right of domicile even when they are mothers[2] and in which men understand themselves as fathers. The narrative motif that a man experiences salvation "with his entire household" is the expression of the hope that through Jesus a new and different people of God will come into being.

Hope for the renewal of the People of God

This hope is given powerful expression at the very beginning of the Gospel of Luke. An angel promises the birth of John the Baptist and announces what he will do: "With the spirit and power of Elijah he will go before him, to turn the hearts of parents to their children, and the disobedient to the wisdom of the righteous, to make ready a people prepared for the Lord" (Luke 1:17).

Luke certainly did not understand the word of the angel as a prediction of what the child John would one day accomplish, for the Baptizer never addressed himself in a special way to fathers and sons. Whoever in those days told about the message of an angel could be sure that he would be understood in a different way: angels appear when human history nears its end and God comes to renew the world.[3] Luke reports the word of the angel because he is convinced that John had contributed to making the people "well-prepared" to meet their God. In addition, this is a quotation: Luke is repeating the last words of the last book of prophecy, the book of Malachi.

That book establishes how severely Israel was being destroyed by its offenses. God speaks the final word, and only knows one more way by which to avoid treating the corrupted land as God had once done with the earth in the deluge: by sending the great man of God, Elijah, the one whom not even death could harm, so that Israel might again come to life. After the deluge life could begin again with one single father and his family; but if Elijah helps his people, such a sharp break will not be necessary: "Lo, I will send you the prophet Elijah before the great and terrible day of the LORD comes. He will turn the hearts of parents to their children and the hearts of children to their parents, so that I will not come and strike the land with a curse" (Mal 4:6).

At the beginning of his gospel Luke takes up this closing word of Israel's Holy Scriptures.[4] He is convinced that the final hope of the Jewish people will spring powerfully to life again in the new people of God, the hope that fathers will take heart to be fathers.

Luke is moved by the same concern that had, centuries earlier, moved the prophet Malachi: How can God's people survive? He also remembers the ancient answer: it is not enough that individual members of the people—a woman freed from her bent back, a one-time exploiter—find the recognition they deserve as descendants of Abraham.

In order for the people to prevail before God, the family must also hold together. How that happens is told by Luke's examples. When God sends Jesus, Zacchaeus' family stands with him, and a jailer thinks about the fact that he is a father and that his suicide would bring his family into the worst kind of want.

This conception of the people of God is remarkable. It consists of families in which people devote themselves to one another, not of individuals who turn to God. There is neither egalitarian uniformity nor does each person vouch for himself or herself alone. A multiplicity of small communities in which people "turn their hearts to one another" has a home in the People of God. Just as remarkable is how Malachi and Luke think of a proper family. It does not depend on the rank of the father but on this, that "fathers and sons" have a heart for one another. Families who already live in this mutual understanding have no reason to be proud of it, and families who do not possess it cannot simply take it by force. Peace in the family is a gift of Israel's mighty helpers. Elijah brings it; faith in Jesus makes it present.

Daily reality as a support for hope

The hope that renewal of the people could begin among families was nourished in everyday Jewish life. After the loss of national independence the life shared by the family became for many Jews the most important content of existence. No longer in possession of freedom in their own land, pious Jews were able to experience in their families what it meant to be a Jew. Especially for Jews living outside of Palestine, the family was the place where they lived out their faith and customs.

The New Testament attests that such families existed. Luke tells, for example, about the Roman centurion Cornelius who was so fascinated by the Jewish faith and lifestyle that he imitated them as well as he could in his profession: He was "a devout man who feared God with all his household" (Acts 10:2). Along with many other treasures, the young Christianity inherited from the Jews also their conception of the family. Families participated in their fathers' decisions of faith: Cornelius was baptized "with all his household" (Acts 11:14). Lydia, the dealer in purple cloth whose affinity with Judaism Luke mentions in Acts 16, had apparently lived in such good agreement with her fellow lodgers that they received baptism with her. In Europe, faith in Christ took hold in Philippi, first in the house of a woman, Lydia, and then in that of a man, the jailer.

In Corinth the official of the synagogue, Crispus, comes to faith in Christ "together with all his household" (Acts 18:8). As mentioned in 1 Cor 1:16, Paul there baptized "the household of Stephanas." In Philemon 2 he sends greetings to a family, a father, mother, and son, as his coworkers. The apostle considers it so natural that believing parents receive salvation also for their children that, in 1 Cor 7:14, he draws the bold conclusion that just as children are "made holy" through their believing parents, so also the unbelieving marriage partner is sanctified through the believer as long as the unbelieving partner is brought to the point of not wanting to separate.

There is reflected in these reports a bit of early Christian reality. Very often, because synagogues and other public buildings were not accessible to the messengers of the faith, the gospel could be proclaimed only in private dwellings. The instruction that Jesus gives his disciples when they are sent out takes this for granted: "As you enter the house, greet it. If the house is worthy, let your peace come upon it" (Matt 10:12).

People who shared their daily life also heard the message of Jesus together and belonged together in faith. That such harmony did not always prevail is hinted by Luke, who is otherwise so concerned about the communality of the home, through a minor modification of this word of Jesus: "And if anyone is there who shares in peace, your peace will rest on that person" (Luke 10:5). Thus far, at least, it cannot be assumed that one will find "peace" with those of his or her own household.

Happier, of course, is the one who shares faith with those who are one's own. The Fourth Evangelist once called attention to this greater happiness by telling of the royal official who, having asked Jesus to heal his son, begins his more than daylong return journey without being able to take along more than the word of Jesus, "Your son lives." John is right when he says of this father, "he believed" (4:50). The evangelist is not satisfied with this representation of the nature of faith, however. He continues the story. The next day the official's servants come to meet him and to say that his son has become healthy, calculating that this took place at the very hour when Jesus had promised him life. In comment, the evangelist repeats: "So he himself believed, along with his whole household" (John 4:53). The evangelist is certainly not thereby denying that the official had already proved himself in the faith, but now he experiences for the first time the complete joy of faith, that is, that his next of kin, too, are convinced that Jesus' word saves and that he can now also share his faith with those with whom he shares his life.

The story motif so beloved in the New Testament, that of the "father and his household," testifies to how impressive Jewish family life was. Only once does it appear in the story of a man for whom Judaism meant nothing: the jailkeeper in Acts 16 saw no problem with mistreating Jews. Yet he, too, embarks on the way to faith when he allows himself to be reminded of his paternal responsibilities: "you will be saved, you and your household!" Luke shows the place where faith can find fertile ground also outside of Jewish influence, that is, with a man who recognizes his responsibility for his own.

The most impressive of the biblical images of the house of a righteous father, that of the ark, had long ago told of a hope of humanity. After the flood humankind begins anew with the family that had been saved along with their father, Noah. Must there not still be present in all of humanity something of the legacy of righteous Noah? This picture was able to help the tiny community of Jews and Christians scattered among all the peoples to see others not just as strangers with whom they had to contrast favorably, but as descendants of the same Father. For fathers who feel responsible for those who belong to them, life in a foreign country presents certain difficulties. Both of the following sections present biblical texts that consider this fact.

3. Believing fathers of a faithless world

"Customs that we cannot accept" (Acts 16:21)

It is not easy to live in an environment that does not value customs to which one is attached, and yet Luke seems to see no problem in this. In Roman-friendly Philippi Paul is accused of causing trouble with Jewish customs. But Luke proves how false this accusation is. For instance, the jailer converted by Paul obeys the Romans seemingly without a second thought, even when he must expel his own brothers in the faith.

Will not the father who earns the life support for his family sometimes find himself forced to do worse things than merely to expel his brothers and sisters in the faith? During the night this overseer had, against the orders of his masters, brought the prisoners into his own house. Will he now as a believer continue just as unconcernedly to serve an authority that orders unwelcome foreigners to be whipped? Luke says nothing about such things, yet the confrontation with such problems had long been urgent. Ever since Israel had lost its political freedom, believers were obliged to live under rulers for whom their faith and customs were alien. How can faith remain alive under such conditions? The first biblical writer to deal with this question was the prophet Jeremiah, in a letter to deportees from his own nation. Though the horrors of war and deportation were still fresh in their minds, he no more laments the rule of the victorious Babylonians than Luke does that of the Romans. What is the basis for such composure?

Jeremiah's letter to the fathers among the exiles

In Jerusalem, Jeremiah had heard that there were prophets who were painting in glowing colors for the exiles the picture of a speedy homecoming. Would not God crush the Babylonians? Jeremiah warns: "Do not listen to the dreams that they dream" (Jer 29:8). In place of the splendid visions of future well-being he gives simple suggestions: "Thus says the LORD of hosts, the God of Israel . . . build houses and live in them; plant gardens and eat what they produce. Take wives and have sons and daughters . . . multiply there, and do not decrease. But seek the welfare of the city where I have sent you into exile, and pray to the LORD on its behalf, for in its welfare you will find your welfare" (Jer 29:4-7).

When illusions collapse, exhausted people are left even more disheartened. Jeremiah wishes to empower a strength that nourishes a sustainable hope: he addresses the exiles as fathers. Moved by responsibility for their own, human beings often accomplish what they would not have managed to do for themselves alone. Jeremiah is not thereby preaching a retreat into private contentment. Families can only prosper when their surroundings are peaceful. It is for this reason that the prophet challenges the exiles to work for Babylon's welfare. Love your enemies! Jeremiah anticipates the command of Jesus in such a way that every person of good will understands that only if things go well in Babylon will the exiles live there in peace.

While Jeremiah speaks humanly to human beings, he speaks about God with great astringency. Though it was the Babylonians who carried off the Jews, the prophet declares in the name of God, "I have led you away." As long as the exiles are obsessed with the fact that Babylon is to be blamed for their misery they will not escape from their evil past, and will only wait for compensation and revenge. If they accept Jeremiah's word that God accepts the blame for their misery they can, freed from their hatred for Babylon, work for their revivification.

However, the prophet does not speak the "I" of God only in this harsh dependent clause. Building houses, planting gardens, living with wife and children, striving for the public welfare—all these suggestions, so says Jeremiah, God has thought out. Israel may believe in the proximity to human beings of this incomprehensible God who is at work even there where disaster happens. God, so says the prophet, can imagine how fathers like to live, and encourages them to do so even in an unfriendly and alien world.

Why does Jeremiah address only the fathers?

Jeremiah writes "to all the exiles" (29:4) and yet addresses his instructions only to men (v. 6: "take wives"). Does he forget that it is especially mothers who are made inventive by need? Do not women also need a word of encouragement? Living in a foreign country is still more difficult for them than for men, and what is considered seemly at home can endanger them in foreign parts.[5] Yet it is precisely this that may have convinced Jeremiah to speak directly only to men. His most difficult demand is to work on behalf of the enemy city. He could not demand of women that they engage themselves in public matters. Nevertheless, his letter is meant for the whole congregation, for one of his exhortations is a promise for all. It cancels a threat that he himself personifies. God had commanded him, "You shall not take a wife, nor shall you have sons or daughters in this place" (Jer 16:2). By adopting what was for those days the very unusual lifestyle of an unmarried man the prophet was to be a constant image of exhortation to his people. In the war and deportations many would die without being able to console themselves with the hope of a new life in a coming generation. Even more impressive is the fact that it is this man, not permitted to be a father, who now orders in God's name that new families be established. The threat of death, which he himself personified, is no longer in effect, and Israel will live. In order not to load the women with unbearable burdens Jeremiah challenges only the men to continue their everyday life in the foreign country just as they had at home. Because this contains hope for all the people, he speaks to the "whole congregation."

What Luke depicts centuries later with the figure of the jailkeeper who expels his brothers in the faith is shown in a historical situation reflected in Jeremiah's letter: what is expected of believing fathers who must guarantee life support for their families is a difficult balancing act between faith, on the one hand, and, on the other hand, a life in surroundings that are both hostile to faith and inhuman. Still, there exists no justification for trying to isolate oneself from this fact. Jeremiah warns that faith would become a mere illusion if it should retreat into a kind of special space in which believers believe only for themselves. There are times and situations in which it can be the special task of men to affirm the courage of their faith when they as fathers keep in sight the connection between the internal affairs of their family and that which is external to families.

Life in a world inimical to faith does not leave believers untouched, however. A postexilic revision of the Noah narrative, clearly discernible as an inserted stratum in Genesis 6–9, deals with this fact.

The revised version of the flood story in postexilic times

During the epoch in which Israel lost its political freedom, great turmoil had come upon the entire Near East. The two empires whose efforts at attaining great-power status were to blame for the destruction of many smaller peoples, Assyria and, soon thereafter, Babylon, were themselves dragged into the turmoil and disappeared. The ancient image of the flood came to possess contemporary relevance.

For survivors who had come from Israel, the image of the ark must have been very pleasing. In the midst of the destroying waters the family of Noah and the animals are rescued. Although all around them the world may perish, in the house of one just man the unspoiled creation still exists. What can be said about this presentation of the pious family? How important this question is to the authors of the new revision of this story is revealed by a conspicuous style of expression. While the older version speaks only once about Noah and his "household" (Gen 7:1), the new authors describe repeatedly and ponderously the makeup of Noah's family: Noah and his sons, his wife and the wives of his sons.

All the members of the family are defined in relation to the father. This is correct in the narrative context, for they owe their very survival to his piety. But why are the sons named even before the mother? The narrators themselves provoke this question, because for once they alter the sequence at a striking place. God commands Noah to leave the ark: "Go out of the ark, you and your wife, and your sons and your sons' wives with you" (Gen 8:16).

The family of the just man is not to remain for long withdrawn from the world in the ark. God personally calls Noah out. He is not called into a world washed clean by the flood. As a sign of how ugly it looked outside, the new version supplies the picture of the raven that flies in and out instead of the pleasant image of Noah's dove. As an eater of carrion, the raven finds an abundance of food outside after the flood. Noah is called out into a world marked by death and ruin. How will it be possible for a pious man and his family to live in a ruined world?

The answer is given by the authors in the two long discourses by God that they append to the story. In the process they suddenly alter the image of Noah's family: "God blessed Noah and his sons, and said to them, 'Be fruitful and multiply, and fill the earth'" (Gen 9:1). In the course of the narrative the women are five times elaborately enumerated, but they are missing precisely in the blessing of fertility, where all is impossible without them. The narrators certainly did not forget them inadvertently, for they repeat here the blessing that in Gen 1:28 applies to man and woman: "God blessed them, and God said to them, 'Be fruitful and multiply . . . .'"

A comparison of the two texts shows how ironically the authors of 9:1 are speaking. God's blessing of creation is spoiled when men think that God has spoken to them alone, and to the women only through the men's mediation. How foolish that is becomes clear when one imagines such a thing as possible even in the blessing of fertility. With this the new version of the saga of the flood reacts to a development of the postexilic period. Among a people ruled by foreigners it was reasonable to leave public responsibilities to the men. But are they for this reason to be permitted also to claim a special position in the community of faith?

The second discourse of God in Gen 9:8-17 is also directed to men alone. "Noah and his sons" receive the confirmation of the covenant with God. How can anything of the creation miracle, that is, that the one God created men and women as a double reflection of God's very self (see Gen 1:27) still remain visible where God is said to covenant only with men? The depravity of the world "after the flood" had left its imprint on the family of the just father.

The Old Testament, too, is the Holy Scripture of the Church. The questions about the flood narrative apply to the Church also. The "flood" continues to manifest itself in the Church when men claim that they are the primary ones to whom God has entrusted the covenant. Noteworthy, however, is the composure of the biblical narrators. God blesses these people even though their rules contradict the divine plan. God cannot, after all, continually be sending deluges.

How well does the mutual life of believers succeed in a world hostile to faith? Both the texts introduced at this point direct this question inward, to the people of God and to the very family of the righteous. Believers may not barricade themselves as if in an ark; they must seek well-being for the "outside world." Nevertheless, they are to know that the corruption of the world affects them also. There is no neat distinction between "internal" and "external."

How can people live by faith in a faithless world? In the later Old Testament period that was primarily a question for the fathers because it was they who felt themselves primarily responsible for the faith. The Tobit story describes with such subtlety the difficulty that thereby ensued for a father that the next section is dedicated to it alone.

4. Tobit: a believing father alone in a hostile world

The book of Tobit posits the situation of a believing man and his family living in surroundings alien to faith and as isolated as they can possibly be. Living in heathen Nineveh,[6] Tobit is convinced that he is the only just man among his people. The fact that the book of Tobit was repeatedly revised reveals that many Jews recognized their situation in it. The story certainly also shows that a pious man in such a situation could definitely live with great style. Historical sources document how true this was. The Jews living in Babylon had already attained prosperity soon after their deportation.[7] The book of Tobit transcends even this: as purchasing agent for the heathen king Tobit became fabulously wealthy and, when on a business trip, entrusted a fortune (ten talents, or sixty thousand drachmas; according to Tob 5:15 a drachma represented a day's wages) to a friend from among his own people for safekeeping. But accounts of bad experiences with foreigners were also entered in the book. It is always possible that a ruler will come who will persecute the Jews. Tobit remains true to his people in that he gives honorable burial to those executed. When a neighbor denounces him, he is forced to flee. But, according to the description of the book, that is only a passing scare, and an evil ruler can also be replaced by a good one. Although after the change of power Tobit does not return to his lucrative post, a friend helps him at least to go home to his family (1:15-22).

Tobit believes himself to be the only righteous man

The first three chapters introduce the book as a personal report of Tobit himself. As soon as the narrator has him speak, one begins to wonder if he is not exaggerating when he calls himself the only just man. It was not just the exile—so he claims—that had seduced "everyone of [his] kindred and [his] people" into a heathen manner of life (1:10-11). All the others were said to have been unfaithful already at home: "I alone went often to Jerusalem for the festivals, as it is prescribed for all Israel by an everlasting decree" (Tob 1:6). In addition, Tobit does not admit that it is difficult to do alone what "all Israel" ought to do. His righteousness beams even more brightly when seen against that dark background. His people are untrue to their God, but Tobit remains true to them. To the poor of his people he gives alms, and by his burial of those executed he puts at risk both his own life and the happiness of his family.

One could be of the opinion that it was only an unhappy accident when one day bird feces get into his eyes, making him blind and impoverishing him. But biblical piety does not see "the will of God" only in God's commandments, which Tobit followed to the letter, but includes everything that happens to a person. Even in the case of an accident one should ask, "What does God want me to do in this situation?" A Wisdom saying from the later Old Testament could have explained to Tobit what this evil coincidence was supposed to make clear to him: "Do not be too righteous, and do not act too wise; why should you destroy yourself? Do not be too wicked, and do not be a fool; why should you die before your time?" (Eccl 7:16). Tobit had really ruined himself because he had held strictly to the Law. Before a festive meal he had sent his son to invite a poor person. But Tobias found a corpse that no one dared to bury. The joy of the festival was gone. Tobit buries the dead, and in the evening lies down to sleep outside in order not to infect the house with the uncleanness he has now contracted. And then it happens: bird dung falls into his eyes, and he becomes blind. The Jewish readers for whom the story was told could only approve that Tobit slept outside, while Christian readers who did not see the sense of the law of purity would at least agree that in this way Tobit spared his family the effort of "purifying" the house.[8] The narrators also consider it correct that Tobit let his festive meal be canceled because of a dead man, and the angel later expressly states, "it was I who brought and read the record of your prayer before the glory of the Lord, and likewise whenever you would bury the dead" (Tob 12:12). Another "good deed" was that he had sent out his son. Tobit had seen the "abundance of food" that had been served up in his honor. The son should learn that a good father shares such honors with the poor.

Tobit's righteousness gets him into trouble

That Tobit's blindness is no pure happenstance that strikes down the wrong person is shown at another place in the narrative. Tobit's wife earns money as a weaver in order to feed her family. Although it is she who bears the principal burden, Tobit continues to feel himself responsible that his family live piously and justly, and he keeps watch, full of mistrust. When Anna one day receives the gift of a young goat from one of her customers, Tobit hears the animal bleating. He accuses her of having stolen it, doubts her protestations, and "became flushed with anger against her over this." Anna replies bitterly that, though Tobit has helped many people, he has never received any blessing for it.

Anna's outburst is understandable. She had worked hard to feed the family, but now, when her husband could have rejoiced with her in the kindness of other people who had given her a useful present, she is overwhelmed by unjust accusations. Must she not feel herself mocked when Tobit calls her a liar and a thief?

At this point one understands why the authors chose the form of the personal report. Tobit confesses the sin of his life. He describes how it happened that he unjustly accused his wife. Too long he had lived with the illusion that he alone was just. Now he is blind to the goodness of his fellow men and women. He would rather believe that his wife is lying to him than that others, too, are magnanimous.

In his confession of sin Tobit also quotes the prayer he prayed at that time. It is the prayer of a person embroiled in guilt. Tobit speaks in formulas about "my sins . . . and those that my ancestors committed" (3:3-5). That he is guilty in relation to his wife is not something he recognizes. He does not blame his family, but only himself. He even wishes to die because he cannot "listen to undeserved insults" (3:6). Yet he is the one who, as he admitted, covered his wife with unjust accusations.

Nevertheless, Tobit's prayer is heard, not because he recognized his guilt, but because in his hopeless trouble he cries out to God, "do not . . . turn your face away from me!" (3:6). The book of Tobit begins with a personal report for "theological" reasons as well. Not until Tobit has been saved can he tell how blind his own righteousness had made him. God first saves, and only then is a person able to recognize his or her own sin.

Tobit opens his heart to his son

Salvation begins in the most mundane fashion. Tobit remembers that he left behind a fortune in the far country. He sends his son on a journey to fetch it. The mother is afraid of losing her last support, but fortunately she does not get her way. If the father, too, had wanted to spare his son all danger, what would then have happened to the family? Life can only be won when it is risked once in a while. Tobit, when he buried the dead, had done what was right without regard to mortal danger. Now the old daring comes alive in him once more.

He does not, however, act thoughtlessly. His son is to seek out a reliable traveling companion. In the guise of a young man, the angel Raphael offers himself as one who is prepared to accompany Tobias. Only briefly mentioned is that young Tobias' dog goes along, being present at both departure and homecoming (6:2; 11:4). This detail lends surprising color to the image of the father, Tobit. This man who chose to sleep outside in order not to contaminate his house now allows his own son to befriend an unclean and contemptible animal.[9] However strictly Tobit observed the laws, his son's enjoyment of friendship with an animal, at that time still very unusual, was even more important to him.

What do clan and family mean when God wills to help?

In every other respect, however, Tobit holds exactly to the Law. His marriage, too, had been lawfully contracted, and he admonishes his son to do just the same.

Teachers of the Law in the late Old Testament period warned zealously against mixed marriages with heathen women.[10] From the report of Nehemiah, who in the fifth century B.C.E. reorganized Judah at the behest of the Persians, it can be seen that they had good reason to issue this warning. Children of mixed marriages, so he reported, could no longer speak "the language of Judah." Must not a tiny subjugated people be careful not to mix promiscuously with the peoples of neighboring lands? On his own initiative the governor Nehemiah initiated legal action against fathers who permitted their children to enter into mixed marriages:

> I contended with them and cursed them and beat some of them and pulled out their hair; and I made them take an oath in the name of God, saying, "You shall not give your daughters to their sons, or take their daughters for your sons or for yourselves" (Neh 13:25).

At this point, too, Tobit exaggerated his fidelity to the Law. His wife is not only a Jew, she actually came from his immediate kindred (Tob 1:9). The narrators are probably alluding to a rule that had been meaningful as long as Israel lived in its own land, that is, that daughters of a man without male heirs who were entitled to inherit from him should be given in marriage only to near relatives, so that the inheritance would not fall to aliens (Num 27:5-6).[11] Perhaps Anna had been such an heiress: after all, Tobit had taken her as his wife when they still lived in their land. In exile the marriage to relatives no longer retained any meaning. In inflexible fidelity to the Law, Tobit nevertheless adjures young Tobias to marry only a close relative (4:12-13).

The angels, however, know how to turn even this to a good end. In the course of the journey young Tobias meets a woman closely related to him who could be a good wife, but does not dare to ask her hand in marriage. Then Raphael reminds him, "Do you not remember your father's orders when he commanded you to take a wife from your father's house?" (6:16). That does not mean, however, that Raphael endorses Tobit's exaggerated supervaluation of the near relationship. When Tobit had asked this unidentified young man (the angel in disguise) about his origins, Raphael had answered with his own question: "Why do you need to know my tribe?" (5:12). In other words, are you concerned about tribe and family, or about having a man who, in consideration of payment, goes with your son on the journey?

Among this folk so proud of their families it must certainly have been noted how much irony lies in this question. However, the angel contents himself with this rebuke. He has more important things to do than to correct a closed-hearted person. He must convince people who in their hopeless need have asked God for death that God does not give death, but life. Certainly if Tobit had paid attention he would have had to recognize that he had exaggerated ideas about his own righteousness. "I alone," Tobit had said, have done as all Israel should have done (1:6). Raphael reminds him of people from among his kindred who were also on the right path (5:14). Yet Tobit notices nothing, and when his son departs he remains at home in his blindness.

A father needs brothers

Paternal responsibility goes bad when a father insists on always bearing it single-handedly. That is the principal theme of the book. Tobit had become narrow-hearted because he considered himself to be the only just person, which may have been a compelling conclusion. He finally comes to the point of no longer trusting his own competent wife. His deliverance begins when he notices that his son can help him by bringing back the money that the family needs. How good it is when a father encounters "brotherly" help from his own son, says a word that the narrators place in the angel's mouth. When young Tobias does not dare to take Sarah as his wife, Raphael encourages him thus: "[Sarah] will go with you. I presume that you will have children by her, and they will be as brothers to you" (Tob 6:18).

Real fatherly joy is experienced by the man whose sons one day become like "brothers" to him. As a brother among brothers, he is protected from the self-righteousness of the one who thinks that everything depends on him alone. This image of the family was so attractive to young Tobias that "his heart was drawn to [Sarah]." In the language of the Bible the heart is the residence of rational decisions; Tobias has a heart to begin such a family together with Sarah.

At the end of the narrative even old Tobit, now healed from his blindness, finally notices that he is not alone. At his son's wedding he experiences that he has "brothers" in Nineveh: "on that day there was rejoicing among all the Jews who were in Nineveh. . . . With merriment they celebrated Tobias's wedding feast for seven days" (Tob 11:17-18).

That is a feast different from the earlier one at which Tobit's misfortune began. On that occasion, not wishing to celebrate only with his family, he had sent his son out to find a guest. Now he has no need to seek guests, for "brother" Jews celebrate the festival along with the family.

Because two festivals frame the story of the blinding and healing of this much-too-righteous father, its theme is illuminated from yet another side. A "father's house" is not the dwelling of a private family, isolated and cut off from the outside. Families flourish when they have "brothers" and "sisters" all around who participate in their life, as Tobit finally discovers on the occasion of the marriage feast. A real father opens his house for guests. In its description of the first feast the book of Tobit stresses that that does not always go well. The next section of this book reviews biblical texts that deal with the theme of hospitality.

5. Fathers as hosts

"He brought them up into the house" (Acts 16:34)

The prison warden of Philippi did not really live in much more freedom than did his prisoners, and his baptism had changed nothing in this regard. Nevertheless, Luke is able to reflect onto this newly baptized man a little of the splendor of a lordly householder. The warden led Paul and Silas to the baptismal feast in his house and "set food before them." As a host, even a pathetic minion of the Romans becomes a "master of the house" who takes the direction of the feast into his own hands.

The serving of the guest also belongs to the image of the good host. With his own hands the jailer "washed their wounds" (Acts 16:33). The book of Ruth tells about the rich man Boaz who had servants and maids, but at dinner time personally served his guests, and so abundantly that Ruth had enough left over to bring her mother-in-law a meal (Ruth 2:14).

Genesis 18: Criticism of Abraham's hospitality

A good host is not stingy. Genesis 18 portrays this effusively. Abraham had invited the three men who appeared before the door of his tent to eat "a little bread," but on the table he laid out a whole calf with bread from three measures of flour—almost forty pounds. The narrative shows Abraham as the exemplary host. Out of consideration for the three strangers he immediately leaves his place at the entrance to the tent, where a breeze could make the noonday heat more tolerable. With great courtesy he invites them in and hurries to serve them. Genesis 18 is the only instance in which one can see Abraham running. The guests are seated and he stands to serve them. Others, of course, work harder: the servant slaughters the calf and prepares it; Sarah bakes bread in the midday heat. Abraham does the honorable service, and Sarah, though she remains invisible, the heavy work.

Clearly the three divine emissaries do not accept this attitude as the most natural thing in the world. They ask Abraham: "'Where is your wife Sarah?' And he said, 'There, in the tent'" (Gen 18:9). Volubly, with an easy flow of words, Abraham had invited the three. Why, then, does he answer their question about Sarah so tersely as to be almost impolite? He does not need to protect her from covetous looks, for Sarah, as she herself says, is already "worn out." Is he ashamed of his old wife? The divine messengers, however, honor her. They do not promise their visitors' present to Abraham, but solemnly, speaking in the "I" of God, to the invisible Sarah: "I will surely return to you in due season [literally, 'in the time of life,' that is, after nine months, the time of gestation], and your wife Sarah shall have a son."

The promise of a son is not just compensation for the hospitality, it is also a reprimand for Abraham. The narrators imitate human conduct far too accurately to present Abraham as merely the exemplary host. "Make ready quickly three measures of choice flour," he calls to Sarah. So speaks a man who knows his wife well enough to be sure that she considers the choice flour, laboriously won by sifting, to be too good to offer to strangers. The narrators not only know that the tent entrance is the most pleasant place at noon, they also hint that Abraham liked to act as if Sarah did not exist.

Many biblical texts reflect a loving interest in the strengths and weaknesses of human beings. How people treat each other is just as important as their life with God. One of these texts, precise in its observations in spite of its brevity, tells how a father of seven daughters comes to host Moses. Not a word about God is spoken in the process.

Exodus 2:15-22: Moses as a needy guest

While in a rage, the young Moses had killed an Egyptian. Having to flee, he comes to the plain of Midian. Fortunately he finds a well, where he can count on meeting people, one of whom might take him in. In fact, seven young women soon appear to give their herds to drink. At the same time there is a chance for Moses to win the girls' gratitude, for other shepherds come and attempt to drive them away.

Water is precious in the steppe. That is revealed, for example, by the place name Beersheba, "seven wells." Seven oaths protected the well against unrightful use, but at this well to which Moses came what predominated was clearly the right of the fist. The young women are allowed to draw water only after the men, when the water level has sunk. But this time the shepherds meet resistance. A sense of justice had moved Moses to kill the Egyptian; now his anger at the shepherds gives him incredible strength. He keeps them in check and at the same time alone undertakes the work that at other times had been done by the seven young women: he gives water to their animals.

He receives neither thanks nor admiration. The young women go away and leave him sitting there. Their experience seems so unimportant to them that they say nothing about it at home until their father asks them why they have come home earlier than usual. Now it appears that they had not even asked Moses where he had come from and where he was going, for they explain only that an "Egyptian" had defended them against the shepherds and even watered their animals. Their arrogance is almost incomprehensible. It is true that Moses, too, had erred. If he had limited himself to reprimanding the shepherds, the young women might perhaps have seen in him a distinguished man traveling through the country. But now he had actually given their flocks to drink. A man who makes himself a servant of women is of little importance.[12] But their father Raguel rebuked his daughters: "Where is he? Why did you leave him there? Invite him to break bread" (Exod 2:20).

Raguel is not really interested in the stranger either. He neither goes himself to invite him nor orders his daughters to do so in his name. He is not happy with the conduct of his daughters, for whoever receives help should not consider himself or herself too refined to eat with the benefactor. And so it is that Moses finds himself at table with young women who had not conceded him even a single word after he had helped them. One understands that Moses wishes to stay with this family because of the father, not because of the daughters. It would be possible to live with a man who was concerned that his daughters be grateful to a stranger.

Though the narrative sketches only the external order of events, at this point (Exod 2:21) it deviates. Moses must himself decide to stay, for no one presses him to do so. Moses appears in this story as a man who can exercise power in his actions. With the decision to stay with Raguel, he gives up his freedom. From that point on, the Midianite will make his decisions for him: "he gave Moses his daughter Zipporah in marriage."

Though Abraham's three guests were guests of honor, he himself was a "foreign worker." Though a strong helper, he himself was dependent on help. Guests of honor are given full freedom: After a little refreshment you can go your way, Abraham says to the three men. A good host does not detain his guests, and he is happy when they can return strengthened to their own affairs. Moses cannot permit himself such freedom. Because he urgently needed a place to stay he had done a servant's work for the young women, and as a servant he will now take care of his father-in-law's sheep. The name that Moses gave his son with Zipporah reveals how bitter the experience of a foreign worker can be: Gershom, meaning "foreign guest of the desert."

Hospitality as a trace of God in everyday life

Although God is not mentioned in the story of Raguel and his daughters, this is nonetheless a story of God's activity. A Midianite helps the God of Israel. Raguel deserves credit for the fact that Moses did not die in the steppe, so that "after many years," while he was still herding his father-in-law's sheep, God could call to him from the thornbush to lead Israel out of Egypt (Exodus 3).

This story, which does not mention God, is like a word introducing the provocative and "worldly" New Testament parable about the judgment of the world. The judge of the world invites people into the reign of God who cannot even imagine that it has been prepared for them. Raguel, too, would be able to ask with them, "Lord . . . when was it that we saw you a stranger and welcomed you?"[13] A father who is concerned only that his daughters conduct themselves well in relation to a refugee, and who gives this capable stranger one of them as a wife in order to keep him as a servant, is nonetheless also one who cooperates in doing God's work. Matthew's parable explains: It is enough that human beings be humane. They need not know whether or not they are thereby engaging themselves for God, for the judge of the world knows it for them.

In everyday life, differently than in the judgment, it is admittedly not so easy to distinguish "the sheep from the goats." Abraham does not permit Sarah to share the honor of the visit of the distinguished guests. Moses receives as his wife one of the young women who had ignored him. The Old Testament tells about the guest of honor and the foreign worker, about the host as lord and servant, about the foreigner who becomes a member of the host's family while still remaining a stranger. It does not set up examples, but teaches the art of making a distinction.

Genesis 19: Hospitality in Sodom

The author of Genesis 19, who is concerned with the art of making a distinction, links the saga of the destruction of Sodom with a story parallel to the one about the hospitality of Abraham. As zealous as was Abraham to serve his guests, just so nasty were the inhabitants of Sodom. The Sodomites refuse to shelter the messengers of God, and when Lot takes them in they want to rape these strangers. In order to protect his guests Lot offers to hand over to the Sodomites his virgin daughters. When Sodom is destroyed, only Lot and his people survive. Is this a story about the reward of hospitality?

When the divine messengers urge Lot to leave the city they call his attention to how shameful his attitude had been in relation to his daughters: "Get up, take your wife and your two daughters who are here."[14] In their fright the young women have hidden themselves, and have to be sought so that they do not remain in the city about to be destroyed. The continuation of the story shows what the Bible narrators think of this father. Though Lot is saved, it is as a man loaded down with shame. He agreed to give up his own daughters to defilement, and soon thereafter *himself defiled them*. Thinking that after the destruction of Sodom they will be uselessly alone with him in the world, they get him drunk so that he will sire children by them.

Hospitality is a "public" virtue. To give shelter to strangers could have been rewarding at that time, if for no other reason than that one could perhaps in this way receive important bits of news from far places. The domestic virtue of paternal love was of even less value to Lot. Something of Sodom had rubbed off on him. When a person lives too long in an evil place, even a virtue can go bad. A father believes that he has to send two young women out into the street in order to protect the security of three men in the house. Lot was not saved because he was such a good man, but because he heeded the divine messengers.

In our present age it is often believed that goodness is genuinely good only when it brings no benefit to the one who does good. In Moses, Raguel gains a capable hired man; Boaz invites the young grain-gleaner to dinner because she pleases him so well; and Abraham and Lot recognize as distinguished lords the three men whose visits honor them. Do these facts really diminish the value of the hospitality they offer?

The Old Testament was formed among a people who had lived free in their own land for only a few centuries. It is no wonder, then, that it speaks about hospitality also from the perspective of the homeless person in need of help. It is good for a refugee to be able to prove to the host that he or she remains a capable human being. For biblical narrators it is a part of satisfying hospitality to give aid to the host as well. Although Moses knows how bitter it is to be a "foreign guest of the wasteland," he also gains a friend in his father-in-law, and in the daughter a good wife. According to Exodus 18, Raguel the priest later helped him give Israel its system of laws, and according to Exod 4:24-26 Zipporah later saved Moses' life. Hospitality is spoiled when a father tries to appear a good host at the expense of his family, but virtue suffers no harm when it benefits the host, for rather the contrary is true: The dignity of the stranger who needs help is best preserved when he, too, gains thanks for himself.

Hosts in the New Testament

In early Christianity, congregations and messengers of the faith had to depend on private hospitality. Thus it is understandable when the critical differentiation practiced by Old Testament witnesses comes off badly in the New Testament. Jesus Sirach (three centuries before Christ) is still advising fathers to consider that hidden virtues that bring in little honor outside the family can suffer damage from hospitality: "Receive strangers into your home and they will stir up trouble for you, and will make you a stranger to your own family"

(Sir 11:34). The letter to the Hebrews, on the other hand, mentions Abraham's hospitality only to support an exhortation: "Do not neglect to show hospitality to strangers, for by doing that some have entertained angels without knowing it" (Heb 13 2).

In one respect, however, the New Testament is more varied, for it is aware of more than just fathers of families as hosts. In the Old Testament there is only one story about a hostess. Having the agreement of her husband to do so, a woman from Shunem hosts the prophet Elisha. In the New Testament, four traditions immediately take this up: women open their homes to Jesus or to the apostles.[15] It is characteristic that it is always unmarried women who do so. A single woman was better able to offer the congregation her house than was the prison officer who, because of his family, could not afford to offend the Romans. Also characteristic is the fact that a man's house offered more protection. In Philippi, where he lived at the house of Lydia, Paul was put in prison, while in Thessalonica he was left free because his host Jason vouched for him (Acts 17:9).

In the second Christian generation the congregations still depended on hospitality in private houses, but in the meantime they had become able to seek out the house that offered the best possible protection. At the head of the congregation there was to be a respected family father. In 1 Timothy this development is reflected when it is expected of the "bishop" that he be "hospitable," "manage his own household well," and "be well thought of by outsiders" (1 Tim 3:1-7). In today's Church, of course, this counsel is no longer being observed. For a long time now leadership offices in some churches have been assumed by unmarried clerics who can call themselves "fathers" only in a figurative sense.

In the New Testament it is principally Luke who tells of hospitable women and men. As did the Old Testament narrators, he also calls attention to the fact that good hospitality is based on mutuality. In the prison officer, in Zacchaeus, and in the host Martha he introduces us to people who are both in need of help and "rulers in their own house."[16] And whenever he speaks of hospitable fathers he keeps in mind what Jesus Sirach and, even more so, the Sodom story advise, namely, that hospitality does not cancel responsibilities for one's own family. The next section will now show what varied traditions Luke has in mind when he talks about fathers who celebrate with their families and with strangers.

6. Fathers celebrate with their families

"He and his entire household rejoiced that he had become a believer in God" (Acts 16:34)

As long as the emerging Church was dependent on private hospitality its worship services were like celebrations in which a family opened its house to guests. The nocturnal celebration in the dwelling of the jailkeeper, too, is both a religious service and at the same time a family festival in which the apostles celebrate with the father and his family, giving thanks for their baptisms.

Family fathers organize religious festivals

The Christian religious services held in houses were no mere expediency, for they were simply a continuation of what had long been a custom in Judaism. The Passover festival, for example, was celebrated in families as the "Festival of Unleavened Bread." Because the Passover lamb could only be slaughtered in the Temple, many people traveled year after year to Jerusalem for Passover. But here, too, it was the fathers of families who organized the festivity, as the order for the festival in Exod 12:3-4 prescribes: "they are to take a lamb for each family, a lamb for each household. If a household is too small for a whole lamb, it shall join its closest neighbor in obtaining one; the lamb shall be divided in proportion to the number of people who eat of it." The father of the house is to take care of getting the lamb and inviting the guests. He directs the paschal feast. "In the night of the Passover," says Philo, a Jewish writer of the first century C.E., "all Jewish fathers are priests" (*Vit. Mos.* II, 224).

Ancient traditions from a prenational society in which the kinship group was the largest societal unit to which a person belonged live on in such festivals. How well that was understood can be noted in Job 1:5. The authors understand Job to be one of the fathers of early times and a man like Abraham. They tell how he regularly brought sacrifices on behalf of his children. Food offerings in Israel belonged for hundreds of years to family life, if for no other reason than that every slaughter was a cultic act. Not until shortly before the downfall of the state of Judah did religious reformers declare every slaughter undertaken outside of the Temple to be profane.[17]

At the holy places where all Israel gathered, families also presented themselves as cultic groups. According to 1 Samuel 1, Elkanah went regularly with his wives and children to Shiloh. Luke 2 relates that the parents of the twelve-year-old Jesus traveled with him and with relatives and acquaintances to Jerusalem. Though the stories are separated by hundreds of years, they take into account the same custom, namely that pilgrimages were made by families. At home it was certainly the strongest person, generally therefore the father, who butchered the cattle, and to whom corresponding duties fell in connection with the sacrificial celebrations led by the professional priests. An example could be Elkanah, who, according to 1 Samuel 1, distributed to his wives and children in Shiloh the meat that had been offered. According to Lev 1:5-9 a "man" is himself to butcher the animal of offering before the priests perform the blood rituals.

The law of offerings in Leviticus 1 has good reason to speak of "a man" and not of "a father," for not every father is strong enough at all times to be able to do the slaughtering. It is probably also in this sense that the story about the festival of the Davidic clan is to be understood: the young David goes home in order to see his "brothers," nothing being said about his father. For the narrator it is clearly self-evident that old Jesse celebrates with his sons like a brother among brothers. He had handed over the management of the celebration to one of his sons, who had probably summoned David to the festivities.[18]

What religious authority did fathers possess?

All of this would be no more than at best historically interesting were it not for the continuing explosive nature of the question about the religious authority of fathers. Can one appeal to the Bible for help in this question?

An ideal is projected by Judges 6:25-26. The narrative begins with God ordering a son to take action against his own father: "Take your father's bull, the second bull seven years old, and pull down the altar of Baal that belongs to your father." Gideon is told to sacrifice on a new altar to the God of Israel that animal from his father's herd that is the most important for field work and cattle breeding, and he obeys. Violent conflict is expected, and the whole relationship is already shaky. But the father defends his son's deed, saying, "if he (Baal) is a god, let him contend for himself, because his altar has been pulled down" (6:31). A father can learn even from his son how God wishes to be honored.

Things happened differently when the worship of God went bad. In Exodus 32 it is told how Israel, out of pure anxiety, was celebrating its worship in exaggerated splendor. Moses had been absent for a long time, and Israel feared that they would be abandoned by God also. Then Aaron, speaking in coarse words, shows the people an evil way out: "Take off the gold rings that are on the ears of your wives, your sons, and your daughters, and bring them to me" (Exod 32:2). Out of this gold Aaron casts the "golden calf," or, more precisely, a young bull. The irony of the story is inescapable. Young bulls do not belong in the desert; what is the sense of an agricultural cultus in the middle of the desert? It is the fathers who have the principal role in these senseless services of worship. With violence they are to compel their wives and children to bring an offering.

The biblical narrators imagine the construction of the legitimate temple of the wilderness in quite different terms: "So they came, both men and women; all who were of a willing heart brought brooches and earrings and signet rings and pendants, all sorts of gold objects" (Exod 35:22). This conception of the construction of the wilderness temple comes from the time of the arduous new beginning after the end of the nation-state. Just that much brighter seemed the memory that in the wilderness Israel had raised a tent that had all of the splendor that the poor new temple did not have. During the dangerous times of foreign rule women had retreated to the private realm, hardly ever appearing at public worship. In the wilderness, however, where Israel had been alone with its God, there they had been coworkers at the shrine: "and they came, everyone [= every man or woman] whose heart was stirred, and everyone whose spirit was willing, and brought the LORD's offering to be used for the tent of meeting, and for all its service, and for the sacred vestments" that God had commanded through Moses (Exod 35:21). That is how the People of God ought to look. Men and women follow willingly together the orders of their God.

The People of God composed of both men and women: a Jewish ideal

This ideal was not simply projected back into the distant beginnings of Israel. Another story from the beginnings tells how Judaism, faithful to the Law, was reborn in the time of the Second Temple. On their own initiative the people requested the priest Ezra to "bring the book of the law of Moses." He brought it and "read from it facing the square before the Water Gate from early morning until midday, in the presence of the men and women and those who could understand" (Neh 8:3). In order that all might understand, Levites went around and explained what had been read. At the end the people wept, understanding how lawlessly they had lived. Ezra comforted them, saying "do not be grieved, for the joy of the LORD is your strength." The reading of the Law ends with a festival: "and all the people went their way to eat and drink and to send portions and to make great rejoicing, because they had understood the words that were declared to them" (Neh 8:12). In many ways this is a model for that celebration of the converted jailer that Luke tells about. Families celebrate and invite guests, for the People of God has come to life again.

But after this initial festival things suddenly begin to go differently: now the Law has to do only with fathers: "On the second day the heads of ancestral houses of all the people, with the priests and the Levites, came together to the scribe Ezra in order to study the words of the law" (Neh 8:13). The contradiction remains unresolved. For whom is God's law intended? For everyone who can understand? Or for the fathers alone? Do the authors of Nehemiah 8 perhaps lay out the contradictions so uncompromisingly in order to make clear how little consistent with its initial ideals is the Jewish life they know?

The authors of Nehemiah 8 extracted from an earlier tradition this beautiful picture of a people in which men and women learn the Law together and families celebrate with their guests. At the time when the state of Judah was perishing, the teachers of the Law had presented a great outline for how Israel's life could be renewed from its very beginnings. Their document, the book of Deuteronomy, presents itself as Moses' farewell speech in which, once more before his death, he lays the Law upon the peoples' hearts. Again and again it gives a detailed accounting of those to whom Moses gives the Law: "You stand assembled today, all of you, before the LORD your God—the leaders of your tribes, your elders, and your officials, all the men of Israel, your children, your women, and the aliens who are in your camp" (Deut 29:10-11). Moses ordered that there be just such gatherings in the future: "Assemble the people—men, women and children, as well as the aliens residing in your towns" (Deut 31:12).

Once, however, Deuteronomy seems to project a different image of the People of God, when only men are addressed: Three times a year all the men are to go to the place God chooses to see the face of the Lord. Other instructions specify that "sons and daughters, male and female slaves" accompany the pilgrimage. Widows and orphans are to be invited when the people "rejoice before the LORD, your God." Why does this law of pilgrimages address only the men? Are women out of place where the question is who may "see the face of the Lord"?[19]

Fathers and mothers serve God together

On the basis of the Elkanah narrative, a story influenced by deuteronomistic ideas about a man who each year makes a pilgrimage with wives and children to Shiloh, a differing interpretation of this conspicuous change is possible. Elkanah's wife Hannah herself mentions a convincing reason why she does not wish to go along. She has a little son whom she is still nursing (1 Sam 1:22-23). The life of a wife in those days offered few enough occasions when she, free from her concerns for a child, could consider undertaking the strains and risks of a pilgrimage. The deuteronomist teachers of the Law may have thought of such things when they charged only the men with the responsibility for pilgrimages. The Law is not to furnish overzealous fathers any occasion for inconsiderately pushing through their religious demands, thus weighing down their wives with intolerable burdens.

The narrators, influenced by Deuteronomy, present Elkanah as a good father and husband. He agrees with Hannah that she should not accompany him on the pilgrimage as long as she has duties with the little child. But he himself has an important reason for undertaking the journey, and says: "Do what seems best to you, wait until you have weaned him; only—may the LORD establish his word" (1 Sam 1:23). The fact that even after the birth of the child Elkanah continues to be concerned about whether God really wants to give the promised child is easily understandable in the context of the high infant mortality of that time. For this reason he leaves his wife and child at home, but goes himself to the shrine to ask blessing for them.

Hannah did not care for her child in order to be able to keep it for herself. As soon as he was old enough to live without her she gave up this son for whom she had wept and prayed so that he could serve God. Again Elkanah participates in her decision: "Then they slaughtered the bull, and they brought the child to Eli" (1 Sam 1:25). It was certainly the father who did the slaughtering. However, the narrator attributes well-considered words to the mother when she delivers the child to the priest. The story itself does not specifically assign functions to either parent, and they share functions at both the slaughter of the sacrifice and at the giving over of the child. "With her husband," says 1 Sam 2:19, Hannah began coming to the shrine "to offer the yearly sacrifice." Admittedly, the priest speaks only to the father: "May the LORD repay you with children by this woman for the gift that she made to the LORD" (1 Sam 2:20). It can nevertheless be assumed that with this Eli was blessing both Elkanah and his wife.

The People of God composed of both men and women: a Christian ideal

Is it correct to read the words of the story of Elkanah and Hannah in the way we have done here? Luke did so, projecting an image of the parents of Jesus based on the example of Hannah and Elkanah. According to Luke 2:21-24, Joseph and Mary not only undertook together the journey of offering to the Temple, but the father even participated in the "purification" that Leviticus 12 prescribes so that, after bleeding at the birth, the mother can again be admitted to worship. "When the time came for their purification according to the law of Moses, they brought him up to Jerusalem to present him to the Lord" (Luke 2:22).

Married couples who lent their houses for the use of early Christian congregations and jointly promoted faith in Jesus Christ[20] could well have taken encouragement from this story of how the parents of Jesus fulfilled their cultic duties together. Early Christian worship services in which men and women celebrated together and without class distinction, Christian congregations in which, following the example of Jesus' disciples, men and women learned the faith together were signs that through Christ was becoming reality what holy tradition had told about the true Israel.

Nevertheless there soon appears—already in the New Testament and against the authority of Jesus—a developing Church in which, just as had become customary among the first People of God, men claimed the managerial functions. At first they were still fathers of families from whose public image the congregations could profit: "He (the bishop) must manage his own household well, keeping his children submissive and respectful in every way—for if someone does not know how to manage his own household, how can he take care of God's church?" (1 Tim 3:4-5). "You . . . should appoint elders . . . someone who is blameless, married only once, whose children are believers" (Titus 1:5-6).

Finally, against the authority even of these texts, the Church came to reserve tasks of leadership for celibates alone. The time during which the New Testament came into being was too brief for it to have been able to reflect on this development in the many ways evident in the Old Testament, and yet from the very beginning the Church had recognized the Old Testament as its sacred Scripture. The warning in the story of the "golden calf" applies also to the Church, and in following Jesus it must exert itself to transform into reality the hopes that are expressed in the Old Testament's ideal images of a People of God composed of men and women.

7. In retrospect: fathers, not "patriarchs"

However brief the story about the prison officer in Acts 16 may be, just as many-faceted is its reflection of biblical ideas of fatherhood. What these ideas are remains now to be briefly stated and clarified; abbreviated reference will be made to the texts consulted in each case.

A good family father maintains an open house

What probably attracts the most attention in our days is an idea about fathers that is missing in the biblical texts to which one is led by Acts 16. The fathers that appear in them are not in the first instance heads of families, but rather people in need of help. It is when a father feels an obligation to guests that he is most likely to present himself as a master who has the say in his house. The prison official escorts his guests to the table (Acts 16). Raguel admonishes his daughters to invite the stranger (Exodus 2). Boaz orders his servants to treat the foreign woman well (Ruth 2). Abraham orders the meal for the guests to be prepared by his wife and servant (Genesis 18).

But a good host also takes upon himself personally the work for his guests, and no humble task is too lowly for him. The jailer washes his prisoners' wounds. Abraham stands up at the meal to serve his visitors. Boaz himself serves the poor foreigner her midday meal.

Nevertheless, even stories of rewarded hospitality are not inserted as good examples to be followed, serving instead the purpose of describing human behavior, including its darker aspects. They tell of the father in the house who, wishing to appear the good host before his exalted guests, neglects to honor the people to whom he is committed in the daily life of the family. The narrators do not themselves say what is to be thought of this, preferring to reveal it by what results for such a father: In Genesis 18 the heavenly messengers give Sarah the honor that Abraham has denied her. In Genesis 19, Lot, who in order not to be considered a bad host is ready to abandon his daughters to dishonor, himself ends up in shame.

A good family father practices brotherliness

For biblical authors, the dignity of every person is more important than any abstract virtue of "hospitality." For this reason they describe what a great gift even a poor guest can give his host: Raguel is convinced that even a miserable refugee deserves thanks for his help. In the stranger whom he receives he gains an able son-in-law who becomes his friend and counselor (Exodus 2 and 18). A poor foreign woman brings blessing for Boaz and even for all Israel (Ruth).

In many ways the biblical writers emphasize how greatly the success of a family depends on the readiness of all its members, including the father, to give mutual help. Elkanah endorses his wife's decision (1 Samuel 1). A father can learn even from his son (Judg 6:25). A young man hopes to have sons who will be "brothers" to him (Tob 6:28). The community of the worship service of a kinship group remains a community of "brothers" even when an old father is part of it (1 Sam 20:29). A prophetic picture of hope tells of an Israel in which fathers and sons understand one another (Mal 3:24). The New Testament tells of fathers who, with their families and supported by them, live by faith (Luke 19; Acts 16; John 4).

The house of the good father is a portrait of hope for all humanity

Biblical ideal images often present the People of God as a company of many families who, because fathers receive guests, do not wish to close themselves off each in its private space. The deuteronomistic plan for the renewal of Israel speaks of joyful services of worship that fathers celebrate with their families and with the poor (Deuteronomy 12). The story of the renewal of the Jewish people through Ezra ends with a festival in which families take in guests (Nehemiah 8). The happy conclusion of the Tobit story is sealed with a festival at which Tobit finally notices that his companions in faith are "brothers" (Tob 11:18). Such salvation pictures contrast with the image of downfall personified by the prophet who lives alone, without wife and children (Jeremiah 16).

Biblical authors know how worldly this idea about the ideal People of God is. They know that people live with one another in peace and justice also in the houses of non-Israelite fathers: a Macedonian experiences the same family solidarity that characterizes Jewish families (Acts 16). A Midianite is concerned that his daughters act humanely (Exodus 2). All humanity stems from a family that owes its deliverance to its righteous father (Genesis 6–10). Many Jewish and Christian fathers were obliged to earn a living for those who belonged to them while living in a heathen world for which their faith and customs were foreign. They were able to stand up to this task in the conviction that there is not only in Israel but in all humanity, just as in Israel, the longing for the house of the father in which peace and justice rule. The People of God have no need to close themselves off from other peoples. Biblical authors hold to this insight even when they reflect on the dangers that confront believers. Even a miserable slave of Rome can live by faith with his family (Acts 16). In the book of Tobit, persecutions caused by evil foreign domination are considered to be temporary horrors. Jeremiah urges fathers for the sake of their families to work for the welfare of the state into which they have been deported (Jeremiah 29).

Can fathers live by faith together with their families? With this question the biblical authors are not thinking primarily about what foreigners have done to the People of God, but are asking the believers themselves if Israel is a people within which families can prosper. Will a father who desires nothing else but to live in piety and justice not finally become blind to the rights of others? The creation blessing becomes a joke in the house of righteous Noah because men are of the opinion that God speaks with them alone (Gen 9:1). Because Tobit feels himself all too responsible for the righteousness of his family, he becomes unjust to his wife (Tob 2:14).

How fathers are to live out their fatherhood is a question to be decided within the world

The biblical authors erect no models for fathers to imitate. What they do is, in the first place, teach how people should conduct themselves with wisdom and sympathy. Their faith in the God who is friendly to human beings moves them to this, and because they trust that God is specifically and individually concerned with the manner in which fathers apply their powers, they themselves pay precise attention to how people live. Announcing to them that God, too, knows how eager men are to prove themselves as fathers, Jeremiah encourages the exiles to dare a new beginning (Jeremiah 29). The heavenly messengers give attention to women about whose honor the father of the house is less concerned than he is about honoring the exalted guests (Genesis 18 and 19). Because God tests exactly how human beings treat one another, God does not overlook it when, at the cost of their families, fathers claim the greater honor for themselves.

But when fathers fail, that is no reason for those who believe in the God who is friendly to humanity to become fainthearted. Biblical texts tell how God is able to open the way to life even to those who have ruined their lives. God "gives blessing" even when men are of the ridiculous opinion that the blessing of fertility was meant only for them (Gen 9:1). Though Lot experiences shame, God will at the same time multiply his life when new peoples come into being through his incest with his daughters. Tobit's imperfect prayer is heard.

Conversely, fathers who experience that their family stands with them have no reason to become proud. Biblical authors call attention to the fact that when a father notes that his whole family is loyal to him, that cannot be attributed solely to his performance as a father. God must send powerful helpers so that hopes can be realized for a people within which families live in mutual agreement: Elijah, John the Baptist, Jesus, and Paul are such figures who render assistance (Mal 3:24; Luke 1:17; 19:9; Acts 16:31).

Faith in the God who loves life protects us from expecting too much from fathers

Not infrequently biblical voices state that, contrary to their own earliest traditions, the idea of the preeminence of fathers had come to prevail among the People of God: According to Nehemiah 8 there was just one day of public study of the Law, after which only "heads of families" came together to meet with the experts. The New Testament names only one woman, Lydia, the seller of purple cloth, who leads an "entire household" into the way of faith (Acts 16:15). By the second Christian generation only fathers of families were regarded as qualified to assume the administration of congregations (1 Tim 3:4-5; Titus 1:6).

Though the preeminence of fathers was recognized, it was never religiously justified. On the contrary, repeatedly and in differing ways biblical texts keep open the memory of the ideal of a people in which men and women are able to serve God together and to be present for one another. In the wilderness men and women worked together to erect the tabernacle (Exodus 35). The book of Deuteronomy demands with the authority of Moses that men, women, old people, and children assemble together to learn the Law (Deuteronomy 21 and 29). In such an assembly Ezra renewed the People of God. Jesus renewed the hopes of his people when he assures both men and women of their birthright in the family of Abraham (Luke 13:16; 19:9). A negative image is presented by the story of the "golden calf." A religious zeal dictated by anxiety permits fathers to be physically violent against their own wives and children (Exodus 32).

The biblical texts consulted to this point neither describe powerful father-figures nor speak about fathers as masters to whom other family members must always be subservient. Could these findings have resulted only because the story from Acts 16 concerning the pitiful prison official was chosen as the main theme? Or because in a New Testament father story the memory of Jesus, who always dismissed patriarchal prejudices, continues to have an effect? The second division of this book will follow another principal theme, namely that of an Old Testament narrative of an event from the early days of Israel. The story of the prison official occurred during the night. Without attracting public attention a man finds the way to life.

First Samuel 22 has to do with a bit of political history and tells about things that shook all Israel. Down to the present day "great history" has been made almost exclusively by men alone. In old Israel, among a people who resisted governmental institutions just as long as that was at all possible, it was men behind whom families stood. What does it mean that they were fathers and the sons of fathers?

Notes: Chapter One

[1] The episode is modeled on Jeremiah 20: Jeremiah, too, had to spend a night in the stocks after having been flogged and nevertheless sang songs of praise.

[2] Cf. Ps 113:9; on this whole subject see Annemarie Ohler, *Mutterschaft in der Bibel* (Würzburg, 1992) 234ff.

[3] Cf. the appearance of the angel Gabriel ("God's hero") in Dan 8:16.

[4] The modern Jewish Bible ends with the call to return to Jerusalem at the end of 2 Chronicles. In NT times there was also another Jewish Bible, differently organized, which in the NT is called "the law and the prophets" because of its beginning and end. It closes with a look into the end time. Cf. Annemarie Ohler, "Die jüdische Bibel" in eadem, ed., *Heilige Bücher* (Freiburg: Herder, 1995) 134–135.

[5] In a legendary motif from prenationalist times one recognizes experiences from one's own postnationalist age: Israel's ancestors had to fear for their women in alien lands. It is significant that these legends tell how the fathers of Israel treated the aliens unjustly, thus revealing themselves. Cf. Gen 12:10-20; 20:1-19; 26:1-11. The end of the saga in Genesis 34 (see ch. 3 below) about the endangering of Jacob and Leah's daughter Dinah in the non-Israelite city Shechem has a no less shameful outcome for Father Jacob.

[6] In 612 B.C.E. Nineveh, capital of Assyria, came to an end. For the author of the book of Tobit this event lies in the distant past. Although according to Tob 14:15 Tobit, on his deathbed, envisions the destruction of Nineveh, this seems to echo the image of the destruction of all the kingdoms of this world. Believers, so proclaims the dying man, may find only a temporary homeland in each of these world powers.

[7] In an archive of cuneiform tablets from Nippur that records transactions of the banking house of Murashu and Sons (established after 437 B.C.E.), seventy of the eighty-nine merchants who were clients of the house had Jewish names. G. Cornfeld and G. J. Botterweck, eds., *Die Bibel und ihre Welt* (1972) 473.

[8] "Unclean" means "ritually impure." Whoever stands before the living God is to do God honor by wearing no sign of death. Even the good deed of burying the dead makes unclean, and impurity "is contagious." The laws of purity (Leviticus 15) are God's good gift to the people. Mortals are never "pure" from signs of death. But it is enough for God if they observe certain periods of time and cleansings. Then they are "pure" enough for God.

[9] In the OT dogs are considered despicable (Prov 26:11; Job 30:1) and unclean animals (Exod 22:31). They were above all known as a hungry, abandoned, and roaming pack that goes after the ill, the dying, corpses, and spilled blood; cf. 1 Kings 16:4; 21:19; 22:38; Isa 56:11; Jer 15:3; Pss 22:16, 20; 59:6, 14-15; Sir 13:18.

[10] For a reason that can probably no longer be precisely explained, Deut 23:3-4 condemns marriages with the Ammonites and Moabites who, according to Genesis 19, do belong to Abraham's family of nations, as more abominable than those with other peoples, for instance the Egyptians.

[11] For more on the inheritance rights of daughters, see chapter 2.

[12] In Hos 12:12 the prophet declares that his people have no reason to be proud of their progenitor Jacob, arguing, among other things: "for a wife he guarded sheep."

[13] Matt 25:38.

[14] Gen 10:15. A comment in the German *Einheitsübersetzung* explains Lot's incredible behavior by saying that "the right of hospitality was sacred in the ancient Orient." By no means! It rather shows how a father who has lived too long in Sodom can go bad.

[15] According to the NT, hosts for Jesus, the apostles, and the congregations were not only fathers of families (cf. Luke 19:5; Acts 17:5-9, 18; 1 Cor 16:15) but married couples (cf. Mark 1:20; 1 Cor 16:19; Rom 16:5; Philemon), or single women (cf. Luke 10:38-42; Acts 12:12; 15:40; Col 4:15), or men (cf. Mark 14:3), or brothers (cf. Mark 1:29; Rom 16:14). In Acts 16:15 it can be noted that Luke alludes to the OT story. Lydia "urges" that the apostles stay at her house, just as the woman of Shunem "urges" Elijah; cf. 2 Kings 4:8.

[16] Cf. Luke 10:38-42: Jesus receives friendly hospitality from "Martha" ("Lady"). Like a lady, she believes that she must criticize her sister and Jesus; Jesus instructs her that service for the reign of God can only be successful when done without "worries."

[17] Cf. Deut 12:20-27. The Deuteronomic reform made it possible for exiled Jews to butcher and to eat meat also in the heathen lands in which they had no shrine for food offerings.

[18] Cf. 1 Sam 20:29; according to the conception of the narrators, the father participates at the festival of the "brothers" as an old man, for according to 1 Sam 22:3-4 he is still alive.

[19] Daughters, female slaves, and widows are named in the festival laws of Deut 12:12, 18; 16:11, 14, but married women are strangely never named.

Are they also addressed when the teachers of the Law say "you" (sing.) or "you" (pl.)? In Hebrew there are masculine and feminine forms for the second person. The laws continually address men. The Sabbath commandment (Deut 5:14; Exod 20:1) numbers all the members of a house with the exception of the wife; is she also included in the masculine "you"? The law condemning lust, at least ("you shall not covet your neighbor's wife") clearly addresses only the men. Is that different for the "you" of the other commandments? The lack of linguistic clarity at least left the text open to the interpretation that God's commandment is addressed first to the men, who then guide the women.

[20] Cf. Mark 1:29-31; 1 Cor 16:19; Rom 16:5-7; Philemon.

Chapter Two

Fathers in Their Political Responsibility

1. 1 Samuel 22: Saul's massacre of the priestly clan

In contrast to most contemporary portrayals of history, biblical authors repeatedly state that the men on whom the history of the people depends are fathers and sons of fathers. Why do they attach such importance to this fact ? What significance do they assign to fathers in the history of their people? Motifs from the story of Saul furnish the connecting thread in the examination of this question. Because Saul had been wounded in his fatherly honor, he annihilated an entire paternal house, the priestly clan of Nob. It is scarcely possible to know whether the incident really happened. There are, however, other questions that bring us further along, such as asking why such a story was told at all, as well as what historical situation it reflected.

The historical and literary context of the story

Saul, Israel's first king, was a failure. Had not David soon established a nation that lasted for about four centuries, Israel would have become an indistinguishable part of the mixture of populations in Canaan. In retrospect Saul's failure is only too comprehensible. Dependent on a retinue of voluntary supporters and willing to exercise power only in occasional instances, such a king could not hold his own against the Philistines, who were organized as a state and had professional soldiers.

Nevertheless, biblical traditions reveal how difficult it was to understand the downfall of the first king in Israel. Saul had been chosen by God and had become Israel's deliverer. The people had proclaimed him king. His son Jonathan was well loved. Where was the God of Israel when Saul's decline forced the people into ruin? This question is debated in many related narratives that appear between 1 Samuel 9 and 2 Samuel 1. The story that is more closely examined here (1 Sam 22:6-23) impressively describes the problem posed by Saul but offers no solution for it. Is it at all comprehensible that Israel's king should kill the priests of his God? Can something of this kind even be understood? The story responds with a number of answers.[1]

Is Ahimelech guilty?

It had all begun when David, who was fleeing from Saul, came to Nob, where Ahimelech helped him with bread, weapons, and priestly counsel. Because of one man's deed Saul summons not just him but all eighty-five men of his kinship group. In his dignified statement of defense Ahimelech says that he knows why Saul did this: the king suspects there is a whole group of conspirators in Nob: "Do not let the king impute anything to his servant or to any member of my father's house; for your servant has known nothing of all this, much or little" (1 Sam 22:15).

Ahimelech takes everything upon himself, pointing out that he had already helped David, the king's son-in-law and confidant, so many times that this time, too, he believed that he was acting as Saul would have wished. From a contemporary perspective it seems strange that Ahimelech did not protest against the summoning of his uninvolved relatives, yet in those days it was no doubt considered only right that Ahimelech's relatives accompany him and demonstrate what Saul was getting himself into when he accused a priest from Nob. Nevertheless, Saul responds with the order of execution: "You shall surely die, Ahimelech, you and all your father's house" (1 Sam 22:16). Ahimelech had certainly not reckoned with this. But Saul's incredible reaction does not come as a total surprise for the hearer of the story, for the narrators have prepared us for it.

Saul's guilt

The beginning of the scene prepares the stage on which everything takes place: King Saul presides over his court. His "audience chamber" is the tamarisk tree of Gibeah, his sign of majesty the spear, his "royal household" the members of his own strong, proud tribe. If the Saul tradition had not already revealed that Saul had hurled his spear at David and even at his own son[2] this could be an idyll from Israel's early days.

As soon as Saul speaks, one notices how dangerous he has now become. He calls the people of his retinue "Benjaminites" only to enrage them, insinuating that men proud of their lineage were after the fiefdoms that a young have-not, not even a member of the tribe of Benjamin, had to distribute: "Hear now, you Benjaminites; will the son of Jesse give every one of you fields and vineyards . . . ? No one discloses to me when my son . . . has stirred up my servant against me, to lie in wait, as he is doing today" (1 Sam 22:7-8).

The narrators know how to choose their words. Saul lashes out with words like a badly wounded person who rears up and strikes those who want to help him. He attacks his followers and actually begs for their sympathy. His son has hurt his feelings, and he wants someone else to "hurt" along with him. But whoever would want to support Saul in his baseless mistrust of Jonathan and David would have to be really sick. Therefore the men of Benjamin remain silent. They can remain true to Saul only by tolerating his hurtful words. Then a foreigner directs the king's anger against a reachable target. Doeg the Edomite reveals that Ahimelech has helped David.

Whoever hears Ahimelech's words of defense knows that they strike Saul's most sensitive point. Out of fury at David, Saul is already "sick" with rage at all who are close to him, and now Ahimelech reminds him that it was after all he himself who had made David his son-in-law and bodyguard. Saul is entirely beside himself.

The brothers of his tribe, however, prove themselves to be his "servants." Saul commands them to "turn and kill the priests of the LORD." The narrator refers to them here as "guards" whose only task is the speedy execution of the king's commands. But the Benjaminites refuse to carry out this unjust order, and the narrator again calls them "servants of the king." A servant does the work of the master, and the work of a king is to protect the defenseless. By their resistance to Saul his "servants" do what should be the task of the king.

The story then depicts how Saul does "what is not done in Israel": he carries out the murder with alien assistance. Doeg the Edomite kills the priests of YHWH.

The guilt of Doeg the Edomite

The narrator certainly does not mean to say that Doeg "encircled"[3] and killed eighty-five men all by himself while the men of Benjamin looked on. The Edomite was able to carry out the order to kill because he had enough followers at his disposal to prevent the Benjamites from simply intervening and allowing the priests to flee. The narrators do not speak about these followers of Doeg because they are nothing but an extension of his arm and receivers of his commands.

In contrast to Saul and his tribal brothers, the "sons" of Benjamin, Doeg bears the name of no father. He is called only "the Edomite." He needs no backing from a family or a tribe, and his power consists of the fact that he has at his disposal a group of unscrupulous people who are prepared even to murder the defenseless. Saul's guilt is, of course, not diminished by the introduction of this figure, for one can only wonder how the king could make use of such a man.

Doeg's behavior reveals why this Edomite put himself at Saul's disposal: he is seeking to gain personal power. He makes use of the king's offended anger to severely shake the basis of Saul's power, that is, Israel's trust in its king. When Saul's rule disintegrates, a man like Doeg becomes much better able to apply his power for his own advantage.

Why David takes the guilt upon himself

The story ends with David's words of greeting to the lone survivor of the massacre, Abiathar, the son of Ahimelech, who flees to David and is received with a surprising confession of guilt: "I am responsible for [or: have encircled] the lives of all your father's house" (1 Sam 22:22).[4] Thus the narrator attributes to David the conspicuous and really inappropriate word "encircle" with which Saul had ordered the murder and that was used to describe how Doeg carried out the command. The intention is to establish clearly that David takes upon himself the guilt of Saul and of Doeg. Soberly, and without seeking to protect himself, David explains why he is guilty. He had noticed that Doeg was in Nob when Ahimelech helped him. Already on that occasion it was clear to him that Doeg would betray the priest before Saul. He had, nevertheless, asked for and received help. Why had he not at least warned Ahimelech? David does not comment on the question with even a word, nor does he attempt to excuse himself. Yet precisely in this way he gains Abiathar's loyalty. From now on the priest will be a faithful ally.[5] David's confession shows how sharply he differs from the two principal offenders. In contrast to Saul, whose fury makes him incapable even of distinguishing his friends from his foes, David did not lose his ability to judge clearly, though he had certainly also experienced terrible things. He soberly recognizes how the massacre came about, though he must thereby blame himself.

Even more important is that David's confession shows how different he is from Doeg. In the report that immediately precedes the story we learn that David had not long remained alone after he had fled. He was joined by men who were "in distress, and everyone who was in debt, and everyone who was discontented . . . and he became captain over them. Those who were with him numbered about four hundred" (1 Sam 22:2). A mass of embittered men, threatened and homeless, can easily be provoked to deeds of violence. When someone like Doeg leads such people they do not shy away even from a massacre of priests. Did David, as the captain of a throng of homeless people, become a "fatherless" person of Doeg's kind? Just as the Edomite joined the servants of Israel, David will later enter the service of the Philistines (see 1 Samuel 27). If it had not really been so, certainly no one would have told that Israel's great king David had once served Israel's worst enemy. For the narrators it is just that much more important to show that David was never a man of Doeg's type. He knows that he should have protected the priests and that he failed to do so.

These reflections shed a little light on this grim story. The bitterly offended king who had lost his power of judgment and the unscrupulous foreigner are not the only forces who determined Israel's fate. David is also there, ready to take responsibility for what happens through him.

A story about the significance of the "father's house"

In contrast to Doeg, David is no "fatherless" man; Saul calls him "the son of Jesse." Coming as it does from the mouth of Saul that is certainly not meant as a word of praise. He also fails to address the priest with his own name, saying, "Listen now, son of Ahitub." For Saul, Ahimelech has not become his enemy for himself alone, but as a representative of the entire "house of Ahitub." He means the same thing when he calls David nothing but "the son of Jesse." Thus Saul severs a bond that he himself has doubly and triply tied. In the story David is called "servant of Saul," "his son-in-law," "foremost of his bodyguards," and "honored in the house of Saul." Saul cancels all of this when he calls him "the son of Jesse." For him, David is a man from an alien tribe.

In this way, too, the story comments on the account given above: People who, like the fugitive David, are in jeopardy have gathered around him. The first of these are "his brothers and all his father's house" (1 Sam 22:1). The destiny of the priestly clan demonstrates how necessary that was. If the entire house of Ahitub must die for one person's deed, then the kinship to which David belongs must really be in great danger.

This story presents a historical development, the transition from Saul's kingdom to the rule of David, as a confrontation between "fathers' houses." In the following sections individual motifs from the story will be sought out in other biblical traditions. Where and how do they speak about "paternal houses" that influence the fate of Israel? How and why is a publicly active man judged according to his father and his father's house? What do biblical authors think about an entire family's responsibility for solidarity with the deed of an individual? What kind of respect is accorded to men about whose paternal house nothing is known? What conceptions of a father's responsibility to his family and his people are reflected therein?

2. A strong paternal house: hope for Israel

"Eighty-five who wore the linen ephod" (1 Sam 22:18)

Before the king's judgment seat stands Ahimelech, surrounded by a great throng, each of whom wears the sign of priestly dignity. Yet this impressive demonstration of fraternal solidarity does not help the accused man in the least. On the contrary, they all fall prey to Saul's revenge. Is there any value at all in standing together as a family as did "Ahimelech son of Ahitub and all . . . his father's house" (1 Sam 22:11)? What do biblical texts say about this?

The massacre of the priestly clan: an act of madness

The story in 1 Samuel 22 describes how "un-Israelite" the murder of the priestly clan is. The members of Saul's tribe refuse obedience to their king, but an alien, Doeg the Edomite, carries out the command to kill. With this atrocity Saul turns a deaf ear to everything on which his rule is based. He had been chosen by the God whom the priests serve, and he had heeded priestly words in the exercise of his power.[6] Family solidarity as demonstrated by the "house of Ahitub" helps him to maintain his rule. The leader of the army, Abner, is his cousin. His most important ally is his son Jonathan, and he and his most loyal followers understand themselves to be sons of the same progenitor, that is, "sons of Benjamin."

To do justice to the difficult tasks of a king of a distressed people Saul might, of course, need more support, for "there was hard fighting against the Philistines all the days of Saul; and when Saul saw any strong or valiant warrior, he took him into his service" (1 Sam 14:52). It was probably in this way that Doeg, a man whose father and brothers were known to no one, had come into Saul's service. Still, according to 1 Sam 17:55-58 Saul did not summon to himself even the victor over Goliath until after he had learned whose son the young man was. Saul was no longer himself when he destroyed the priestly clan.

From a modern perspective the catastrophic end of Saul's reign can be explained only too easily. A people among whom power was based on personal ties and family and tribal loyalties was hopelessly inferior to the well-organized professional armies of the Philistines. Biblical traditions, however, look for the reason only in Israel itself, in its king and in its God. Already at the beginning of the stories about Saul's decline stands such a statement: "Now the Spirit of the LORD departed from Saul, and an evil spirit from the LORD tormented him" (1 Sam 16:14). Nothing is explained by this, of course; on the contrary, new questions arise, as illustrated by the narrative about Saul's insane attack on the house of Ahitub. How can a king sacrifice that on which his kingdom has been founded from the very beginning? He exterminates an entire paternal house even though he himself was called to be Israel's deliverer, not as an individual but as a member of a paternal house.

The deliverers of Israel, their paternal houses, and their fathers

Right down to the present day we like to hear and tell stories like that of the call of Saul. A young man goes out to look for straying she-asses and comes home as a prince. Though he is still young and unimportant it is already clear what will happen to him. But the narrators are not interested only in Saul's abilities. The prophet Samuel asks him: "on whom is all Israel's desire fixed, if not on you and on all your ancestral house?" (1 Sam 9:20). Nor does Saul concern himself with the question of whether he himself is as Samuel thinks, but rather whether his kinfolk are: "I am only a Benjaminite, from the least of the tribes of Israel, and my family is the humblest of all the families of the tribe of Benjamin. Why then have you spoken to me in this way?" (1 Sam 9:21).

Other biblical narrators speak very similarly. When all Israel is in great distress a messenger tells Gideon: "Go in this might of yours and deliver Israel from the hand of Midian." Gideon means something like "(old) warhorse." Even for a "warhorse," "this might of yours" is not his own talent and strength, and Gideon answers the messenger thus: "But sir, how can I deliver Israel? My clan is the weakest in Manasseh, and I am the least in my family" (Judg 6:14-15).

For Gideon, too, the question of whether he can save Israel depends on whether his father's house is strong enough. Also: will the tribe put its military power at the disposal of its youngest member? A troubled people needs strong heroes, but just as important is that they have a strong paternal house at their side. How will one who is not even able to encourage the men of his own family for the tasks that await him be able to bind other comrades to himself?

There are, of course, other narratives in the Bible about the origins of great men. It is the fathers who accompany the rise of Gideon, Saul, and David, while in the case of Moses, Samuel, Samson, and Jesus it is the mothers. Can we identify the reasons for this differing interest of the narrators?

Firmly rooted in the Moses tradition is the idea that Moses comes to the aid of his people with the power of prayer.[7] Because one who prays does not need the support of a strong paternal house, the interest of the narrators can be directed toward the women at the beginning of Moses' life story, toward wily sisters and the benevolent princess who saves the child's life. The only battle in which Samuel participates is decided by his prayer (1 Sam 7:8-10), but in 1 Samuel 1 it is said that Samuel has only his mother's insistent prayer to thank for his birth.

It is true that Samson is one of the energetic fighters for his troubled people, yet for a long time he wastes his strength on ugly pranks. Only once does he inflict decisive defeat on the Philistines and so provide real help for Israel, but when he is captured and taunted he kills himself along with the enemies. Samson the individual fighter survives without the help of a strong paternal house. According to Judges 13 it was his mother who first understood that God had entrusted her with a very special child.

Gideon, Saul, and David, on the other hand, gathered around themselves warriors for the liberation of the nation during times in which the people, hopelessly overpowered by their enemies, wanted to give up. The stories that tell of their beginnings are preoccupied with how these helpers of Israel got along with their fathers as young men. Gideon pulls down his father's Baal altar but manages to retain his support. David secures the safety of his father and mother before he takes up the dangerous life of the leader of an armed band.[8] It is not difficult to guess why such stories were told. Should care for a people be entrusted to a man incapable even of getting along with his own father? Would the people be safe in the hands of a man who is not even able to get along with his own father? The theme of father and son is handled most exhaustively in the saga of the secret anointing of Saul in 1 Samuel 9–10. Saul travels around in wide circles in search of his father's she-asses. Father and son are so close that their thoughts coincide even when they are far apart. Though the she-asses are in the end unimportant for the father, he is worried about his son, and the son knows this and wishes to spare his father this worry.[9]

What is the basis for the paternal house's strength?

The stories about the rise of Israel's heroic leaders do not portray their fathers as commanding heads of families. Saul's father is concerned about him, as is Saul about his father. Gideon's father defends his self-sufficient son even though he himself has suffered loss. According to 1 Samuel 16, Jesse's conception of the ranking order of his sons does not prevail, and 1 Samuel 22:3 shows that David's father and mother are dependent on their son's protection. These fathers were not famous for having smoothed their sons' paths to power.

A man on whose activities the peace and unity of a people depend needs another kind of background, namely a paternal home in which this unity is already a reality because one person stands up for the other, the father for the son as well as the son for the father. The strength of a father's house is not based on a powerful father who always achieves his will, but rather on this, that many active men are prepared to help one another. The father recedes, so to speak, into the series of his adult sons. The narratives of the rise of Israel's deliverers project ideal images: when fathers and sons in Israel's families stand together in the way experienced by these young men, then the people have no need to be anxious about their freedom and peace.

These narratives also reflect the historical situation of a people that was still without definite governmental structures. In a political landscape in which areas of sovereignty had not yet been clearly defined either geographically or organizationally, islands of peace first appear where individuals stand by one another because they have grown up together in the same family, kinship group, locality or, ultimately, in the same landscape. The saga of the victory over Goliath contains a descriptive example of how nets of family solidarity were combined into a network that united Israel as one people. David's older brothers were serving in King Saul's army; the father was at home because he was too old and David because he was too young. Even so, both made their contribution to the army's ability to fight. David is not too young to take over the work that guarantees the welfare of his brothers, and old Jesse is not concerned only with the welfare of his sons, but also with that of the whole army. When he sends David with sustenance for his brothers he sends along a special gift for the commander of the army. The conception, formed in early times, of the "brotherly" house of the father remained alive in impressive narratives, thus contributing to Israel's ability to keep its identity alive even when it could no longer continue as an independent nation. The book of Malachi ends with the hopeful image of an Israel in which fathers and sons open their hearts to one another. Luke later takes up this theme again, and in the book of Tobit the image of a family in which the sons become "brothers" to their father prompts a young man to take heart and establish such a family. That fathers decide to live out their fatherhood in such a "brotherly" way is just as little a private concern in these traditions as in the narratives about the rise of Israel's rescuers. The continued existence of the People of God rests on the inner stability it receives from the many small communities within which people take a stand for one another without extensive questions about who has either an elevated or a lowly social position.[10]

The solidary house of the father as an endangered ideal

The narrators of 1 Samuel 22 have no need, in their description of the highly prestigious paternal house of the eighty-five priests, "all his (Ahitub's) house, the priests who were at Nob," to ask specifically about the whereabouts of the father for whom all of them were named. It is really not important whether old Ahitub (his son Ahimelech already had an adult son, Abiathar) is still there, for the strength of the father's house is not based on the fact that all subject themselves to one father who makes all the decisions for them, but rather on the fact that brothers of the same rank ("all who wore the ephod") stand up for one another. What is so shocking about the destruction of the house of priests is that so many reputable sons of one father had no chance against the violent actions of someone like Doeg.

A time of upheaval is reflected in the traditions about the decline of Saul and the rise of David. Israel had learned that the strength based on fraternal solidarity was not sufficient. The tribes would not have survived if David had not founded a new state that had other instruments of power at its disposal. Things that are taken for granted during tranquil times become questionable at such turning points. Therefore traditions of Saul and David become appropriate even as a point of departure for the question as to what biblical traditions saw as dangers to which family solidarity was exposed. The following section deals with this question.

3. Tensions between fathers and sons endanger Israel

"My son has stirred up my servant against me" (1 Sam 22:8)

Before the eyes of the public Saul accuses his son of being a coward who is able to satisfy his desire to revolt against his father only with the help of the father's servant. This reproach is so absurd that one can more easily hear it as an expression of Saul's "evil spirit" than of his own spirit. Jonathan remained faithful even to the point of dying loyally at his unhappy father's side. David's song for Jonathan praises the brotherhood in arms of father and son:

Saul and Jonathan, beloved and lovely!
In life and in death they were not divided (2 Sam 1:23).

For all its distortion there is, nevertheless, some truth in Saul's accusation. From a modern perspective it is a historical reality that David's kingdom came into being on the ruins of Saul's rule. Biblical narrators imagine how Saul must have experienced it. It is terrible to watch one's impending destruction, and even worse to know that a stranger will be the beneficiary. It is also possible to understand that the narrators describe Saul's conduct as it really was, namely that of a man persecuted by misfortune who can only with great difficulty tolerate a successful person in his proximity, especially when the latter is his subordinate. Beyond all this David had also befriended his son, and it is precisely this fact that has really made clear to the king how lonely his misfortune has made him. Saul's accusation is therefore directed at the right person after all. By his friendship with David, Jonathan had wounded his father deeply.

Fathers and sons among a politically unstable people

A conspicuously large number of biblical narratives focus on contrasts between fathers and sons. Central to the voluminous complex of narratives that describe David's power is Absalom's rebellion against his father David. In Genesis, the story of Joseph derives its impetus from the fact that his father treats one of his sons in such a privileged manner that his brothers sell the father's favorite into slavery. With the help of his mother, Jacob deceives his blind father. Samson's father has trouble with his son, who chases after foreign women.[11] These father-son conflicts vary greatly among themselves: Saul threatens his son and Absalom his father; Jacob provokes his sons against their brother, while Samson's father is unable to persuade his son to adopt an orderly style of life. Why were such stories told?

When tensions appear between fathers and sons in our day we think first about the conflict between generations. Is the son able to build up his own sphere of life? In the biblical narratives we do not have powerful fathers who do not permit their sons to prosper in their presence. Only too easily does David let himself be induced to give the fratricide Absalom a fatherly kiss, thus once more giving his worst enemy a place of honor in Israel. Samson's father honors his son's wife with his visit, although he did not approve of the marriage. When the marriage fails Samson returns to his father's house as if this were only a matter of course. Saul is angered by his son's friendship with David because he sees in David a rival for the throne that he wants to secure for his son.[12]

There is but one perspective from which all of these stories can be viewed together, namely, how vulnerable fatherly love made those called to safeguard Israel's continued existence. In this situation we get a glimpse of some of the troubles that beset a politically unstable people who must depend on the solidarity between fathers and sons for their security. We introduce here in more detail two of the narratives that deal with this question most vividly, stories about Saul and Jonathan that tell how the son is threatened with death by his father. If something like this can happen even between those who fight together for Israel, on what else can a frail people still depend?

1 Samuel 20: Why Saul tries to kill his son

At the beginning of the story Jonathan is convinced that he stands closer to his father than anyone else. He wants to convince his friend David not to be fearful of Saul. If Saul were up to something bad he, Jonathan, would have to know about it: "My father does nothing either great or small without disclosing it to me" (1 Sam 20:2).[13] David, too, was convinced that Saul was fond of Jonathan, but drew the opposite conclusion: because Saul loves his son he is concealing from him his hatred of his friend. For this reason David devises a bit of cunning meant to induce Saul to reveal his genuine attitude. Jonathan is supposed to put the plan into action, and he reacts with vehement words: "By the LORD, the God of Israel! When I have sounded out my father . . . shall I not then send and disclose it to you?" (1 Sam 20:12).

Should a son sound out his father?—a son whose help his father so desperately needs in his struggle for Israel's survival? Will the God of Israel permit this to go unpunished? Jonathan pushes aside such misgivings. The life of his friend is more important for him. Let God do with him as God wills!

The cunning plan succeeds, and yet in a way different from what the friends had planned. Jonathan realizes that his father would rather have David dead than alive. But when he asks how David has come to deserve death, Saul reacts in an unexpected way: "Saul threw his spear at him to strike him [Jonathan]" (1 Sam 20:33). Though it is David whom Saul considers his deadly enemy, he wants to kill his own son. How could that come about?

The narrative makes clear how inadequate are the images that human beings have of one another. Not only must Jonathan alter his image of his father, but David certainly had not imagined that Saul could attempt to kill his own beloved son. As for Saul, did he come to understand himself? In his gloomy heart his love of his son had darkened and revealed itself unexpectedly as hate.

Fatherly love can reverse itself like this because it lives in the images that father and son hold of one another in their hearts. Powers secretly at work within the human heart can be recognized and guided only with great difficulty. Saul had long controlled his hatred of David in Jonathan's presence. Only with the pressure of the intrigue does it burst out, but now in another terrible form: as hatred against his son. The narrative prompts sympathy for this lost man. The power that is changing him is almost too strong for him. Is it the power of YHWH, in whose name Jonathan had cursed himself? Had Saul noticed that his son had put him to the test for David's sake? Did Jonathan in this way prepare the ground for "the evil spirit from the LORD" that plagued Saul? The narrators do not here neatly assign blame to the people involved in this conflict between father and son. They show how God, too, is involved. But when God plays a part, no judgment can be established about human beings.

The motif of Jonathan's being endangered by his father appears a second time. Even in the time of his successes, when he did not yet know David, Saul is said to have brought deadly danger upon his son. This is an exciting story with surprising turns. By means of a curse Saul brings God into the action, and the priests are involved by drawing the holy lot. But the narrators show that to the degree that people try to restrict and define God it is that much less certain where God is at work.

1 Samuel 14:24-46: Does the curse of the father kill the son?

Saul, who has gotten into desperate straits in his battle with the Philistines, is aware of only one solution: He will direct the war like a worship service. The warriors are to fast. The situation is so desperate that Saul "laid an oath on the troops," threatening with death anyone who breaks the oath. Radical piety is to remedy extreme trouble. But Jonathan discovers a simpler source of help, bee nests, whose honey he eats, and "his eyes brightened" (1 Sam 14:27). Israel is victorious, the soldiers are allowed to eat, and Saul wants to be on his way to take advantage of the victory.

Everything seemed to have gone well, but then the priests delay Saul. The oracle is to speak. Saul obeys, but the oracle is silent. A lot is drawn to reveal who is responsible for the oracle's failure, and it falls on Jonathan. Is God speaking through the lots drawn? Jonathan is convinced of it, and confesses his violation of the command to fast, adding "here I am, I will die" (14:43). Saul, too, believes that God has spoken against his son: "God do so to me and more also; you shall surely die, Jonathan!" (1 Sam 14:44).

There is an extreme of violent expression in Saul's words, characteristic of a person in the gravest of trouble. Saul had taken an oath in order to force his own deliverance, and has been successful. And he is just that much more certain that his oath will be fulfilled. The father is appalled to realize that he has cursed his own son. It is not stated how Saul imagined Jonathan's death. And how can he know how his oath will be fulfilled? Yet he is just as convinced as his son that the curse kills.

Then the people intervene, instructing their king and saying, "Shall Jonathan die, who has accomplished this great victory in Israel? Far from it! As the LORD lives, not one hair of his head shall fall to the ground; for he has worked with God today" (1 Sam 14:45).

The radical change at the time of Saul is reflected also in this story. Saul places his confidence in an archaic "sacred" style of combat that is ineffective against an enemy like the Philistines. When Jonathan hears about his father's curse, he says: "My father has troubled the land" (1 Sam 14:29). In the context of the narrative this statement indicates how much more highly the son respects a modern conduct of war, in which it is not holy rites but the rational application of power that is decisive. The narrators present this graphically: skillfully, and without causing any delay, Jonathan had made use of the trove of honey.

The conflict of generations was not then resolved, however. Both son and father allow themselves to be convinced by the holy rites of the priests that they must accept the disaster that Saul has set in motion with the curse. The end of the story does not say that Saul and Jonathan are right, but rather the people, who are convinced that God will not fulfill Saul's curse but instead is at work when Israel experiences deliverance.

It would be a misunderstanding of the narrative to suppose that it was a rationalistic rejection of ritual piety. The narrators do not see it as mere chance that the lot falls upon Jonathan, yet neither do they claim that it was God who intervened through the people. The question of who was right, Saul, Jonathan, or the people, remains unresolved. Although the ritual of the curse, too, is considered correct by the narrative, it is nevertheless canceled. Even a holy rite does not give the father any power over the life of his son.

The fact that the narrators knew Saul's end lends still another tone to Jonathan's complaint that his father had brought disaster upon the land. When Saul lost his kingdom and his life in the battle on Mount Gilboa and Israel came under the might of the Philistines, Jonathan also had to die; but this came about because he remained true to his father until death, not because his father's curse had to be fulfilled.

The story in 1 Samuel 14 does not establish where God can be found, but shows how varied are the ways human beings seek and know God. The priests do it differently from Saul, Saul differently from Jonathan, and the people differently from any of them. Because the story safeguards the secret of God's activity it also fails to define the human being. Is it Jonathan who acts correctly in being ready to die, or the people, who protect his life? Was Jonathan right in refusing ever to oppose a father who "troubles the land"? When he violated his father's orders and ate honey he helped the people to gain the victory. There is no eternally valid lesson for fathers and sons to be garnered here. The story "only" calls attention to how difficult it is for father and son to be "in life and in death . . . not divided."

Many other narratives show similar engagement and precision when they ask where the harmony between father and son is at risk. The question is important because in Israel the protection of peace and justice was not entrusted to the individual, but rather to the man together with his paternal house. But there are also deep shadows that fall upon the biblical ideal of family solidarity. Biblical texts that deal with the responsibility of the solidarity of the kinship group for the deeds of the individual tend to be repulsive. The next section seeks to understand such statements within their historical and literary context.

4. Responsibility for the solidarity of the father's house

"You shall surely die, Ahimelech, you and all your father's house" (1 Sam 22:16)

Though Ahimelech had taken upon himself the sole responsibility for David's having found help, Saul killed the entire kinship group. Saul's deed is a grave crime. He does violence to the priests of his God, and does not care a whit for the fact that Ahimelech is innocent. But Saul also includes uninvolved relatives in the issue. How was that judged at the time?

Three additional biblical texts communicate dryly and succinctly that a man's family was executed for his deeds. Was that considered "normal" in those days?

This motif appears once in each of the books of Daniel (cf. 6:24) and Esther (cf. 9:13), later books that reflect experience of the persecution of the Jews. The description of the destruction of the wicked here sounds almost like a fairytale. The power to carry out such excessive revenge against their torturers was not possessed by the Jews even in the narratives themselves.[14] The third text, Joshua 7, is self-contradictory. It is remarkable what difficulty was caused for the narrators by the thought that in Israel innocent people could be executed along with their guilty father.[15]

Only a single story intimately addresses the troubling question of whether it is right to execute sons for the guilt of their fathers. It has to do with an ancient legend about David, but it deals with two problems that continue to concern people down to this day. That is, may a crime committed by the state—in those days it would have been the king—remain unatoned because the guilty one is dead? And do the dead still need to be honored?

2 Samuel 21:
Saul's sons are executed for the bloodguilt of their father

Famine had held sway for three years in David's kingdom, and David questioned God about it. The answer was ambiguous. "The

LORD said, 'There is bloodguilt on Saul and on his house, because he put the Gibeonites to death'" (2 Sam 21:1). This much is clear: the Gibeonites, alien residents of the land, are, in the narrator's opinion, so important to God that God reminds David of an unatoned crime of his predecessor against them. Is it not often the case that unpunished national crimes hinder a nation from achieving peace even when another regime has long been in power? The narrators assume that God thinks just as they do, that is, that Saul's guilt rests on his entire family. Yet it remains unclear why God does this. Are Saul's sons to be punished for the deed of their father? How is that to come about?

David hopes that he can satisfy the Gibeonites with "silver and gold from the house of Saul," but they want to execute seven sons of Saul. The land was suffering so terribly that David gave in, willing to do anything that might help. "Before the LORD" two sons and five grandchildren of Saul were executed. The Gibeonites are certainly not concerned to honor God with this, for they allow the bodies to hang in the shrine for months.

To deny a burial was monstrous. According to Deut 21:21 criminals are to be buried on the day of their execution so that the land does not become "unclean." The Gibeonites even defile a shrine.[16] By means of two time designations the story explains why they do this. The execution occurred in April, "at the beginning of barley harvest," and was probably bad enough in itself. The dead lay "until rain fell on them from the heavens," that is, until the fall rain in November. The stench of the corpses is to show the Deity, which has sent no rain over the land for three years, what it is doing. Is God impressed? In any case, the fall rains begin.

Nevertheless, the story has another objective. Its principal figure is Rizpah, the mother of the two sons of Saul, who defended the corpses from vultures and hyenas during the whole summer. It is only after the beginning of the rains that David hears of Rizpah's deed. Can it be that he did not want to hear earlier? Finally he does what up to that point only Rizpah has done as well as she could: he gave honor to the dead. He gathers the bones of the seven who had been executed. He also remembers that Saul and Jonathan have not yet had an honorable burial, and makes up for what had long been neglected. Only then has the saga reached its objective: "After that, God heeded supplications for the land" (2 Sam 21:14).

Is it right to execute sons for the deeds of their fathers "before the LORD"? The narrator puts the question differently: did David need to take this terrible detour to remind himself of the king's duty? He had avoided two problems: he had neither taken care of Saul's burial nor concerned himself that Saul's guilt be atoned for. Would the atonement have been different if David had thought of it by himself?

For the narrators there is no doubt that in Israel only the culprit himself may be legally pursued. It is no accident that these were foreigners who demanded the execution of Saul's sons.[17] If it had depended on him alone, David would have delivered only "silver and gold from the house of Saul" to the Gibeonites. The narrators are moved by another concern, namely whether God can be left out of play when evil deeds bring dire consequences for the descendants of the perpetrators. Let the example of the traditions of the atrocities of Joab, David's general, once more demonstrate how precisely biblical narrators distinguish between the judicial pursuit of an offender and the consequences of his misdeeds, which also affect his descendants.

Must Joab's descendants atone for his atrocities?

David has just been reconciled with Abner, the dead Saul's field commander, when Joab, David's general, lures Abner into a trap and kills him because he is a possible rival. David, not possessing enough strength to punish Joab, curses him: "May the guilt fall on the head of Joab, and on all his father's house; and may the house of Joab never be without one who has a discharge, or who is leprous, or who holds a spindle, or who falls by the sword, or who lacks food!" (2 Sam 3:29). Teachers of the Law advise that criminals who are out of reach of human punishment are to be cursed.[18] However, David curses not only Joab but his unborn descendants. Do the narrators concede to David the right to curse in this way?

Joab is a sinister figure. He will also kill a second rival (2 Sam 20:8-9). David is even less able to act against him this time because in the meantime, in order to hush up his adultery with Bathsheba, he has made him his accomplice in murder. Only Solomon is strong enough to punish Joab at the first opportunity. He orders his general, Benaiah: "Strike him down and bury him; and thus take away from me and from my father's house the guilt for the blood that Joab shed without cause" (1 Kings 2:31). In the biblical tradition Solomon is the ideal of the wise judge.[19] In the case of Joab, too, he proves his ability to judge. He carries out the judgment of death only on the guilty. On the other hand, he has not forgotten that his father shared in the guilt of Joab's atrocities, and that he himself is responsible for the guilt of his father. Within the lengthy story about the national crisis provoked by David's adultery and murder the judgment on Joab belongs to the final section, which describes how Solomon tries to restrain the evil results of David's sin.

A saying from the wisdom literature attributed to Solomon praises the skill of judging: "The Righteous One observes the house of the wicked; he casts the wicked down to ruin" (Prov 21:12). It is right to condemn a villain to destruction before he accustoms his children, too, to evil, and it is wise to distinguish between a wicked person and his family. In the same collection of proverbs is the reminder that "no wisdom, no understanding, no counsel, can avail against the LORD" (Prov 21:30). This applies also when people try to understand how God judges.

Why does God avenge the sins of the fathers on their sons?

When seven sons of Saul were required to die for their father's guilt God did nothing, even though God had gotten things moving through the drought and an equivocal answer to David's question. How can believing people live with the kind of experience captured in this legend? One biblical narrative—fortunately only one—seems completely to disregard such questions. According to Numbers 16, Moses called God's judgment down upon rabble-rousing priests: "As soon as he finished speaking all these words, the ground under them was split apart. The earth opened its mouth and swallowed them up, along with their households" (Num 16:31-32). "Their households" means their wives, adult offspring, and little children. Because they had not heeded the appeal to separate from the rebels the natural catastrophe strikes them, too, suddenly and indiscriminately.

The narrators connect this story with the kinds of experiences people actually have, but even biblical narrators may not then call them a just punishment of God. Such offensive conceptions of God's activity must be contradicted, in the case of other biblical texts as well.[20]

Where is God when catastrophes strike the guilty and the innocent indiscriminately? Those who most often had to deal with this question were the prophets who had accompanied Israel during the time when it lost its freedom to the fearsome great powers. They did so especially by showing that Israel is not simply the abject prey of radical historical change. They warned that the evil ways that children learn from their parents can hardly be overcome. They called attention to how much harder they are to stamp out when a people has lived with them for a long time. Israel could not escape from the sins of its ancestors. Its disastrous history began with the fathers of the tribes and came to a calamitous end with the catastrophic downfall of the free states.[21]

When the prophets thereby consistently accuse "fathers and sons," that does not mean that they are forgetting the women or that they are of the opinion that mothers could not teach their children anything bad.[22] They speak of the men because it was they who decided the fate of the people.

A famous proverb briefly summarizes what many words of the prophets divulge. In Exod 34:6-7 it is said that God calls out before Moses the ten divine names. The last of these describes the God who takes seriously the guilt of the fathers:

> yet by no means clearing the guilty,[23]
> but visiting the iniquity of the parents [Heb.: "fathers"]
> upon the children
> and the children's children
> to the third and the fourth generation (Exod 34:7).

When evil customs continue to predominate publicly for three and four generations of "fathers and sons" no one is any longer able to imagine what a good common life would look like, and a change for the better becomes ever more unlikely. God does not simply observe impassively when God's people condemn themselves. When fathers incur guilt, God pays persistent attention to whether sons, grandchildren, and great-grandchildren continue in the bad example.

But when nothing at all has changed? what then? Because God takes seriously the office of guardian over the generations God is not continually able to reveal divine goodness as forbearance. Wicked forms of life that have been too long passed from fathers to sons can sometimes be broken up only by a catastrophic change. One notices in the saying of Exodus 34 how haunting this thought is. There is something here of the terror of the wars in which the first People of God almost perished, when God was seen as "visiting the iniquity of the parents upon the children."[24]

How the disastrous continuity of fathers and sons can be broken

People who find themselves hopeless victims in dire need often condemn their parents, saying that from the very beginning they gave them no chance at all to have a good life. Just so was the case of those who suffered the deportations by which Israel lost land and freedom. Ezekiel quotes a proverb that circulated among the exiles: "The parents have eaten sour grapes, and the children's teeth are set on edge."[25] The proverb reveals how disheartened the exiles are. The fathers could perhaps have prevented the worst of it, but the sons are so sunk in misery that they can do nothing. Those who do nothing more than make others—especially the dead—responsible for their bad situation take from themselves the last bit of courage to live. Therefore Ezekiel repeats for his fellow sufferers in exile the old sermon about "the guilt of the fathers," that is, that deportees have no right to absolve themselves at the expense of their fathers, for in doing so they fail to free themselves from their sins (see n. 21 above). But the prophet carries the story of faith a decisive step beyond this. He forbids the repetition of that proverb, for it speaks falsely of God. Speaking solemnly in the name of God, he explains what is right: "A child shall not suffer for the iniquity of a parent, nor a parent suffer for the iniquity of a child" (Ezek 18:20). What is told of Solomon's skill in judgment is just that much more true of God, for God, too, is wise enough to distinguish between the guilty person and his or her family.[26] When Israel accepts this message even the recollection of the "guilt of the fathers" will become the beginning of new blessing. Ezekiel was sent out by God to tell Israel its history. "Then let them know the abominations of their ancestors" (Ezek 20:4). As soon as sons begin to be ashamed for their fathers the unholy continuity that links fathers and sons is broken, for then there is hope that the sons will no longer allow themselves to be seduced into imitating their fathers.

One amazing text leads one step further beyond this prophet of the Exile, namely the genealogy of Cain in Genesis 4.

Genesis 4: Sons of a murderer

The story of Cain is astonishing enough in itself. In contradiction to the opinion of ancient Israel's sense of justice it states that God does not will the death of a murderer.[27] God rather says that Cain's deed contains its punishment in itself. The criminal can no longer live where the crime was committed. The land that Cain plants no longer yields him any fruit.

But is there no possibility for Cain to live in other places? The information that follows about Cain's generation recounts that Cain initiated the construction of cities, as his great-grandchildren began living in tents and keeping cattle, as well as inventing the playing of zithers and flutes and developing skill in ironwork. When God shelters a life, be it even that of a murderer, strong new life then comes into being. The genealogy calls two of these inventors "fathers"—that is, of the tent-dwellers and the flute-players. Who is more zealously concerned to open new possibilities of life than fathers who do so for their children? While founders of cities like to perpetuate themselves by naming the cities after themselves, Cain names the city after his son. Unencumbered by the tainted name of his fathers, the son is to begin anew. The story of Cain ends when Cain "went away from the presence of the LORD" (Gen 4:16). The Cain genealogy adds that even some fathers who wanted to know nothing about God did good to their children. A word of Jesus sounds like a commentary on this: "If you then, who are evil, know how to give good gifts to your children . . ." (Luke 11:13).

The genealogy of Cain does not, however, conceal that the crime of the father can have its evil effects among his descendants. Vainly Cain attempts to block the remembrance of his name. The name of Cain appears again, for the inventor of wrought iron is Tubal-cain. This is, in the first place, a further indication of the admirable creative power that lives on also in the sons of Cain. Cain means "smith." In Tubal-cain is realized a possibility that lived also in the progenitor, yet Tubal-cain's father Lamech had another reason for naming his son as he did. Lamech boasts before his wives that he is even a greater murderer than Cain. The institution of blood vengeance that protects Cain becomes for Lamech a frenzy for blood. The Cain genealogy knows the power of a father's love by means of which even guilty people seek new life for their sons, but also the power of the evil example.

The Bible portrays both good and bad generation-spanning connections as father-son lines. Mothers, and especially daughters, seem to have been forgotten. That the fathers are not glorified thereby can be seen from the many texts that speak of the continuity of guilt that links fathers and sons. How a people lived was decided in those days, as it largely still is today, by the men. Thus one can understand the many accusations against the "fathers" also as an indication of the extent to which an order of common life in which the public responsibility lies on the men alone asks too much of them. Can erroneous decisions not better be avoided when the experiences and thoughts of women are also considered in the resolution of important questions?

The following section will suggest a historical reason why the continuity of generations throughout the years is presented in the Bible almost exclusively as the history of fathers and sons. The awareness of history was formed in the milieu of mountain agriculture, in which the land was the "heritage of the fathers."

5. The heritage of the fathers entrusted to the sons

"Will the son of Jesse give every one of you fields and vineyards?"
(1 Sam 22:7)

Saul offended his followers in two ways. He accused them of already secretly acknowledging David as king, and also of expecting lands in payment for it. A proper Israelite does not serve for wages. Biblical conceptions of fatherhood originated among a people whose men were proud when their family property yielded not just enough for the family, but enough also to permit them to invest time and strength in free responsibility for their people.

Fatherhood and prosperity

The aged Barzillai, according to 2 Sam 19:37, was rich enough to provide for David and his army, demanding nothing more in return than to "die in my own town, near the graves of my father and my mother." The prestige of a man in Israel was based on the fact that his inherited land prepared him for both life and death. That can be perceived also in the warning that the prophet Amos holds out to one of his opponents: When Israel perishes he will lose everything that lends him respect, his wife, his sons and daughters, his farm land and his expectation of a grave in his homeland (Amos 7:17). To whom will he then still mean anything?

In a song about the destruction of Jerusalem the people complain that this fate has struck all their men. They are no longer able to intervene for the rights of their families, and the inheritance from which they had lived with their own had been lost. "Our inheritance has been turned over to strangers, our homes to aliens. We have become orphans, fatherless" (Lam 5:2-3). A people whose men can only helplessly observe how their enemies seize their land becomes a "fatherless society."

For people who think as do those witnessed by these texts, a man is a father not because he has begotten children, but because he provides protection and help. Among Israel's neighboring people the king understood himself as "father of the widows and orphans."[28] Biblical texts, on the other hand, emphasize that among a people that assumes responsibility for itself there must be enough individuals who not only take care of their own families but also accept public tasks and become "fathers" for the poor.[29] Israel's farmers acquired the affluence that was necessary for this by means of inherited ownership of land, and yet the inherited land had a meaning beyond the merely economic one.

Inherited property and remembrance

First Kings 21 tells of a man named Naboth who refused to sell his vineyard to the king: "The LORD forbid that I should give you my ancestral inheritance" (1 Kings 21:3). The king summons him before the court and arrays false witnesses against him. Naboth is executed and the vineyard confiscated. What made inherited land so precious that a man would prefer to risk his life rather than sell it?

In the mountains of Israel preparing good tillable land required heavy work. Stones had to be removed, terraces and paths built, wells constructed, and trees planted. Such work projects tended to be done for children and grandchildren rather than for oneself, for a long time had to pass before orchards and vineyards produced respectable yields. Proverbs demonstrate how greatly concerned people were with the idea that a father must try to leave a good inheritance. The capable man, promises one of these parables, will leave an inheritance for "[his] childrens' children." Whoever brings down disaster on his house, another proverb remonstrates, will hand down only "wind." This was meant more seriously than it sounds. When strangers possess the land no one who uses wells, paths, and gardens will think about the one who laid them out.[30] If Naboth had sold his inheritance he would have subjected his fathers to this shame. In vineyards and fields lies the work of the ancestors. One lived from this and hoped to live on in the same way in the memory of one's own descendants.

A sign of life that united the generations beyond the death of the individual was the "grave of the fathers" that lay in the inherited property of the family.[31] It reminded the living to keep up the land for their children in the same way their ancestors had done for them. A dead person united with the living members of his or her family in the same inherited property would not be so quickly forgotten. It was a terrible curse to say: "your body shall not come to your ancestral tomb" (1 Kings 13:22).

The son and the memory of the father

How strongly the idea of the continuity of generations established by inherited land influenced conceptions of fatherhood is shown by the curious institution of levirate marriage. Even a man who died without heirs was to be able to pass on inherited property and a name to a son. To this end a son sired with the widow by a brother of the deceased was considered to be legally a son of the dead man.

In the biblical traditions, however, the widow generally had to push through the marriage with the brother-in-law against resistance. What was displeasing to the men about this arrangement? The book of Ruth describes in detail a legal process concerning a levirate marriage. Elimelech dies without heirs. A relative can inherit his field and would like to do so, even though he must in return care for Elimelech's old widow. But then it turns out that he must also sire a son with the young daughter-in-law, who is also a widow, "to maintain the dead man's name on his inheritance" (Ruth 4:5). Thereupon he refuses the inheritance. Should he raise a child who will have a legal claim on a piece of inherited land that is perhaps better than what he can give his own sons? It is nonetheless honorable that he openly admits how little he is interested in supplying his dead relative with a son and heir.

Genesis 38, on the other hand, tells the story of a revolting fraud. Judah brought the widow of his oldest son to his second son Onan. But Onan did not wish to sire any child with her: "he spilled his semen on the ground whenever he went in to his brother's wife, so that he would not give offspring to his brother" (Gen 38:9). Onan's offense is not that he wasted male semen,[32] but that he treated his sister-in-law with contempt and refused a son to his dead brother. The legend holds up a mirror before men who, though they belong to a people of brothers, forget their brotherliness as soon as there is anything to be inherited. Whoever had no son had to fear that there would remain for him "neither name nor remnant on the face of the earth" and that his name would be erased from his father's house.[33] As soon as he died his brothers could take over his land and pass it on to their sons in their own names. Every trace of his life would then be entirely lost.

When there are enemies to be fended off it is good to know that one has brothers at one's side; and yet, when the objective is to guarantee oneself a place in the memory of those who come after, brothers very easily become enemies. Judges 11 tells about this. Jephthah gets into such a dangerous quarrel with his brothers about inheritance that he had to fear for his life: "You shall not inherit anything in our father's house; for you are the son of another woman" (Judg 11:2-3).

One should not, of course, infer from all this that acquisitive greed was an especially widespread vice in Israel. The patches of fertile cropland were often very small in Israel's hill country. How much land could a father who "set his house in order"[34] give each of his sons? According to Deut 21:15-17 the firstborn was to receive twice as much as his brothers. Would every share remain large enough to support a family? The ideal of the proper Israelite who had made enough profits on his inherited land to be a father to all of his people, a fatherly protector of the widows and orphans and a helper for the people was probably not often realized.[35]

Biblical conceptions of fatherhood are shaped by having originated among a people of farmers who had to defend their agricultural land with human strength against "thorns and thistles" (Gen 3:18). The chain of fathers and sons who attended to this should not be severed. And how did it go with the daughters?

Inherited property and daughters

Not until a later text will the line of succession be settled for the case of a man who has only daughters. The law is presented in the story of how the daughters of Zelophehad bring their complaints to Moses: "Why should the name of our father be taken away from his clan because he had no son? Give to us a possession among our father's brothers" (Num 27:4). What is significant here is that the argument is exactly like that about a man who died without children, that is, that the name of the man is not to "disappear." Therefore in an emergency his daughters' sons are to count as his sons before the law. Thus here, too, the concern is only that the chain of fathers and sons not be broken in the inherited land. The daughters themselves are fundamentally ineligible to inherit.[36] In Egypt daughters and wives were just as able to inherit and bequeath as the men.[37] In a land whose farmland was newly measured each year after the flood of the Nile and belonged largely to the government one could experience the passing on of private property as a sign of affection and security. In Israel, on the other hand, it was necessary to ensure that men cared for the land. But at least one solitary note reveals that here, too, fathers gave their daughters gifts out of love and concern. In Judg 1:15 complicated ownership conditions in the dry south of Judah are discussed. The kinship group of Othniel is permitted the use of watering places that belong to the inherited property of the kinship group of Caleb. A brief story tells how this came about. Achsah, Caleb's daughter and wife of Othniel, is said to have pressured her father into giving her a present, a "gift of blessing," and to have received those watering places. A father can give his daughters "gifts of blessing."[38] Inherited land would be given to sons of the daughters only if there were no sons.

Against this background we can see how revolutionary the end of the Job story is. At the beginning Job was living just as would be expected of a rich and happy man in Israel: his sons took turns holding banquets in their houses, to which the daughters came as guests (Job 1:4). The new happiness with which the book closes is visibly different: To Job was granted everything in double measure, except that he received sons and daughters in the same number that he had lost, seven and three. The dead children are not simply forgotten, for the number reminds the father of them. Yet the newly given children are more than just "substitutes."[39] Before the sisters only came to visit the brothers, but now Job gives them "an inheritance along with their brothers" (Job 42:15). It is no mere literary ornament when the names of the daughters are now included: Jemimah ("Turtledove"), Keziah ("Cassia"), and Keren-happuch ("Mascara"). The names speak of Job's delight, which he will never again lose, in his daughters, who now have the right of domicile in the inheritance of their father. These are exotic names appropriate to the "land of Uz" in which Job lives (Job 1:1). Israel can also learn from foreign peoples what a joy it is when daughters, too, have the right of inheritance.

Job 42:15 is one of the texts that show that the high regard for women in early Christian congregations had roots in the Old Testament. Women had the same right as men to belong to the early congregations, and the hope that shines forth from the final image of the Job legend comes to life again there. God's blessing is fully appropriated when the People of God follow Job's example and give the daughters "an inheritance along with their brothers." Nevertheless, Jesus' parable of "the compassionate father" shows how closely the terms "father-son-inheritance" belong together even according to New Testament ideas. If it had been about a father and his daughter it would have been almost incomprehensible.

Luke 15: The wealth and inheritance of the merciful father

"Father, give me the share of the property that will belong to me." So says the younger son, and the father "divided his property between" his two sons. The son needed a few days before he "gathered all he had" and went away. The father did not at this time sell his property in order to give him his inheritance. What he gave him was his share of the "fortune" and the "living expense" of the family, that is, of everything gained from the land, all of which the son converted into money.[40] It could be that for a while thereafter it was necessary to live somewhat more sparingly in the house of the father. In any case it seemed so to the older son, and he would later remind his father of it: "this son of yours, who has devoured your property with prostitutes" (15:30). The older son, too, had received his share to be used as he saw fit.

The father had not touched the family inheritance, for it did not belong to him personally. As in the good old times of the past, the father in this parable understands himself as a custodian of the father's inheritance to the sons. The father himself points this out to the elder brother when he says: "Son . . . all that is mine is yours" (15:31). While the younger son has the right to live on the hereditary property, the successor of the father to whom the entire family inheritance will pass will be the older brother.[41] Just that much worse, then, that he does not recognize the one who has come home to be his brother. "This son of yours," he calls him. Can he not, as the one who is nonetheless favored, be generous? In contrast to his repentant brother, he actually avoids addressing the older man as "Father." In refusing to recognize his brother he renounces his father.

The father treats the refugee like a lord He gives him clothing, shoes, and a ring. It would be the older brother who could really feel himself to be a lord, for he has a right to everything, just as did the father. But his father calls him "child," for he stands stubbornly outside like an immature boy. The parable fails to say whether the father later had any success in persuading him. The listener is to think about what happens when the sons of a father who treats both of them lovingly fail to live in harmony in their father's heritage.

The parable would be no parable at all if it simply made "the compassionate father" equivalent to God. A word from the son who returned home draws a distinction between God and the father: "Father, I have sinned against heaven (God) and before you." Parables do not say who God is; they deal with a question that interests people so much that they even name children after it, that is, "who is like God?" (Micha-el). God is like a father whose inherited property is great enough so that all his children can live in it like lords and ladies, even when one son has wasted that part of the living that belongs to him and comes back like a beggar.

The idea of the father as a man who cares for an inherited property continues to have prime importance even in the New Testament, and yet biblical authors do not close their eyes to the fact that pride in the "inheritance of the fathers" could also have its bad effects. In Israel it was not easy to be a man unable to live from the land inherited from his father. What does the Bible have to say about such people? The following section deals with this question, beginning once more with a motif from the story of Saul in 1 Samuel 22.

6. Men without fathers

"Doeg the Edomite . . . was in charge of Saul's servants"
(1 Sam 22:9)

If Doeg had allied himself with Saul out of friendship he would certainly not have become a helper to him in his blind rage. The narrators do not mention the people whose help he must have had to kill eighty-five priests, nor do they give Doeg's paternal name. Doeg is a man without family, without friends, and without honor. And yet the

Bible also speaks of men without fathers' names who deserve admiration. One of them is the Ethiopian Ebed-melech, a minor official at the court of Zedekiah, the last king of Judah.

The fatherless in the king's service

Four officials had obtained from Zedekiah an order for Jeremiah's imprisonment and wish to use the opportunity to kill the prophet. They throw him into a muddy cistern. Jeremiah would have sunk if Ebed-melech had not saved him. The report in Jeremiah 38 lists the four with names and patronymics. Ebed-melech (meaning "servant of the king"), on the other hand, clearly seems to have lost even his proper name. This alien who lacks the backing of a paternal house denounces these four men of Israelite families and is successful in doing so. The author contrasts the underhandedness of the Israelites with the humanity of the dark-skinned foreigner. Prudently Ebed-melech sees to it that the ropes with which he pulls Jeremiah out do not injure him. He does honor to his name, "servant of the king." A king needs to be told when his order of arrest is used to commit a murder. On the basis of what is said about this Ethiopian one can understand why men like him were just as able to attain honorable positions at the court as were men from prestigious paternal houses.

Such a social climber would not, however, act as if he belonged to the families of the land. It is revealing how differently a word of the prophet Isaiah scolds two officials, the palace councilor Shebna and his successor, Eliakim, son of Hilkiah. The prophet accuses the man without name of being presumptuous: "What right do you have here? Who are your relatives here, that you have cut out a tomb here for yourself, cutting a tomb on the height, and carving a habitation for yourself in the rock?" A man without a father should not be able to afford an aristocratic grave for himself like those that fathers of families have in their inherited land. About Eliakim it is first of all said that his service to the king had made him "a throne of honor to his ancestral house." But then that ancestral house becomes his undoing:

> And they will hang on him the whole weight of his ancestral house, the offspring and issue, every small vessel, from the cups to all the flagons. On that day, says the LORD of hosts, the peg that was fastened in a secure place will give way . . . and the load that was on it will perish (Isa 22:16-25).

It was advantageous for kings when officials could not exercise their duties for the benefit of their relatives. For this reason a "fatherless one" had a better chance in the king's service than he could otherwise find in a country in which a man was proud of his family.[42] There were few such social climbers, however. In David's list of officials it is one in six, in Solomon's one in ten. Once it even happened that a "fatherless" foreigner actually became king in Israel. Omri, a man with a non-Israelite name and without a patronymic, was an officer who found himself obliged to pursue the murderer of his own master and in the process became king himself, and such a significant ruler that in Assyria until long after his death Israel was known as the "house of Omri."[43] It is therefore not simply fantasy when, in the Joseph-narrative, the foreign slave becomes the top official. Joseph calls himself "a father to Pharaoh" (Gen 45:8). It is remarkable that it is not Pharaoh but his young minister who is called "father."

"Father": a title of respect for the man willing to serve

As long as Eliakim continued to serve his country and not his tribe the prophet calls him a "father . . . to the house of Judah" (Isa 22:21). A man's reputation is not based on his being a "son of . . . ." Rather it depends on whether he proves himself a "father" for others. Titles of honor, of course, can also be misused when they praise the one who is willing to serve. According to Judg 17:7, a "young man" in Israel was once humorously addressed as "father" only because he provided priestly service for money. The Greek book of Esther says that the villain Haman was known as "father of the king" at the Persian court.[44]

Luke, too, is acquainted with the honorable title of "father." He reports that both Stephen and Paul addressed the Sanhedrin and the people as "brothers and fathers." For Luke the Jews are "brothers" because Christians and Jews have the same family history, but they are also "fathers" because the Christians learn from them their faith in the "God of our ancestors." Nevertheless, as Luke tells it, the brotherly and fatherly service of the discussion of faith was denied to Paul and Stephen, for their message was answered only by cries and shouts.[45]

Such texts demonstrate how much the Bible avoids "father" ideologies. It tests whether a "father" is fatherly. Is a man without a family just a fellow without bonds, or does he fulfill public tasks freely, and even more faithfully, without consideration of a father's house? Do "fathers and brothers" conduct themselves like kinfolk? There was always an immediate cause to ask these questions when Israel's beginnings came to be discussed.

"Fatherless" soldiers

Old Testament traditions remind a family-proud Israel that there were "asocial elements" among the groups out of which it came into being. In the turmoil of the time of beginnings men who had escaped social bonds occasionally joined together around a ringleader and offered themselves as "foreign legionnaires." When David had to flee from Saul he soon had such a throng gathered around himself.[46]

In a long list of thirty-seven names in 2 Sam 23:24-39 a monument was erected to these companions of David. In contrast to the list of officials, only a few have a patronymic. Twenty-three are named according to their place of origin, two according to their mother's name, and two as members of other nations: Zelek the Ammonite and Uriah the Hittite.

Similar things are said about Jephthah and Abimelech, who some time before David attempted to gain power in Israel. They, too, gathered the homeless around themselves, "men who have nothing to lose." Both are sinister figures who exceed even Doeg in their nastiness. Doeg murders the priests of a God whom he does not know; Abimelech forces his way into his father's house and kills his brothers, seventy men, "on one stone." Jephthah kills his only daughter.[47] Must family ties be torn to shreds when a man seeks to gain power?

The biblical narrators are very concerned to show that this was not true of David. The homeless David is joined by his brothers, and he brings his parents to safety. Saul is David's father-in-law, and David honors him as his "father" even when Saul pursues him. Even Saul has to recognize this, and is emotionally stirred. The soldiers whom David had gathered around him, too, were very attached to their families. Once when they returned from a campaign they found their houses destroyed, "wives and sons and daughters taken captive. Then David and the people who were with him raised their voices and wept, until they had no more strength to weep" (1 Sam 30:3-4). Doeg's people are nothing but his extended arm, but there is a different relation between David and his warriors. These men, embittered by the loss of their families, would have stoned David if he had not immediately led them in an action in which they win back the women and children. David shares the troubles of his soldiers. He calls them "brothers" and sees to it that they treat one another like brothers. For the homeless warriors the group around David becomes a new family.[48]

David does not forget these experiences even when he becomes king, and his foreign legionnaires thank him for it. When all Israel had abandoned David during Absalom's rebellion the mercenary leader Ittai the Gittite accompanied him in his flight. David pressed him to stay behind, saying, "Go back, and take your kinfolk with you; and may the LORD show steadfast love and faithfulness to you" (2 Sam 15:20). David is convinced that homeless warriors owe brotherly loyalty only to one another. Why should they follow the homeless David? But Ittai remains true to David, and he and his entire company share David's pain. "So Ittai the Gittite marched on, with all his men and all the little ones who were with him. The whole country wept aloud as all the people passed by" (2 Sam 15:22-23). Nevertheless, David himself demonstrated on one occasion how little a "fatherless man" was worth in Israel.

David's crimes against Uriah the Hittite

A beautiful woman had wakened David's desire. He wanted to know what he could permit himself to do in relation to her, and when he asked it was reported to him that this was "Bathsheba daughter of Eliam, the wife of Uriah the Hittite" (2 Sam 11:3). Both Bathsheba's father and her husband are named in the glorious list of "David's heroes." There Bathsheba's father is named "son of Ahithophel of Gilo."[49]

The Hittite has no patronymic. David is of the opinion that he can allow himself adultery with the wife of a fatherless alien. But Bathsheba becomes pregnant, and the offense threatens to come to light. Because Uriah does not cooperate in covering up the king's deed David sends him to certain death in battle. The fact that he belongs to the "heroes of David," to the group whose "brotherliness" other stories about David movingly recount, makes no difference any more.

However, the alien finds an advocate in the prophet of the God of Israel. Nathan uncovers David's crime and announces to him the wicked results of his deed. The long narrative about the crises of

David's kingdom usually develops entirely out of the interplay of inner-worldly forces, but here (2 Sam 12:1-15) the prophet declares that it is God who allows the results of David's guilt to fall back on him. David broke into the marriage of a man who was an alien to the people and murdered him. Nathan announces to the king what will come of it: a son of David will usurp David's wives, and four of his sons will die. The life and honor of a foreigner are just as valuable to God as the life of four princes and the honor of the king.[50]

The suicide of a grandfather

Nathan's word comes true, and David is forced to flee Jerusalem to escape from his son Absalom. Further, Ahithophel of Gilo, Bathsheba's grandfather, advises Absalom to demonstrate publicly his break with his father by having David's wives brought to himself on the roof of the palace. It is easy to guess how Ahithophel came upon this vicious idea. Because David seduced his (Ahithophel's) granddaughter Bathsheba to adultery, he himself is now to be shamed.

Ahithophel also has a second plan. He wants to pursue David and confront him in man-to-man combat: "I will strike down only the king" (2 Sam 17:2). Absalom does not listen to this, however. And now it becomes clear how much was at stake for Ahithophel in all of this: "When Ahithophel saw that his counsel was not followed, he saddled his donkey and went off home to his own city. He set his house in order, and hanged himself; he died and was buried in the tomb of his father" (2 Sam 17:23). Ahithophel prepares his death like a good family father and is buried in the family grave. He had wanted to restore his family's honor by defeating David or by dying in battle against him. Now his suicide is to demonstrate that he can no longer live in the same land with David.

At this point the narrative speaks of God for the second time: "For the LORD had ordained to defeat the good counsel of Ahithophel, so that the LORD might bring ruin on Absalom" (2 Sam 17:14). There are more important things than Ahithophel's fatherly honor. What would have happened to Israel if Ahithophel had killed David and the fratricide and father-despiser Absalom had become king? The long narrative that began with the crime against Uriah is above all concerned with Israel. What does it mean for Israel that David had established a nation? Can things go well with so much power in the hands of one individual? How do things turn out when he becomes guilty? The narrative describes David in such a way that one sympathizes with this man who suffers just that much more in the crisis of his kingdom because he knows that he is to blame for it. Thus the authors answer the people's concerned questions about the dangers that the establishment of a state brings upon people who up until then had preferred to rely on the brotherly solidarity of strong families and clans. If Israel needed a king, then better not an Absalom who makes his father despicable, but a man like David who is willing to bear the consequences of his guilt.

The resistance of a fatherless man

The prophet Nathan opened David's eyes to the severity of his guilt. Thus the narrators furnish a second answer to concerned questions about the endangerment of Israel by the state, that is, that the king needs the prophet at his side. Nathan is a man without a father's name, committed only to God's instructions, and free to resist the king.

The prophet's resistance does not weaken the king; the opposite is true, namely that the strong one who allows himself to be reminded of God's justice gains new strength thereby. The Davidic tradition contains a famous example of this. David had wanted to build a temple, but Nathan rejected this plan. Although the kings of other peoples pride themselves on building magnificent structures for their gods, the pride of the king in Israel is to be different: "Thus says the LORD: Are you the one to build me a house to live in? . . . the LORD declares to you that the LORD will make you a house" (2 Sam 7:5, 11).

David is not to be the builder for God, but father of a house erected by God, a great dynasty. In the "prophecy of Nathan" it was seen that the longer the "house of David" held sway the less it was a witness of prophetic resistance to the development of royal power and the more it was only the affirmation that God guarantees the continuation of the Davidic dynasty. Later prophets had to learn that guarantees given by God are different from the assurances that a mighty dynasty may give. The following section will enter into the question of which conceptions of fatherhood grew out of Nathan's prophecy with the passage of time.

7. A king like his father David

"Saul was sitting at Gibeah, under the tamarisk tree on the height . . . and all his servants were standing around him" (1 Sam 22:6)

Although Saul's "throne room" is a tree he holds court just as the great kings do in their palaces. He sits, his servants stand, ready to hear him. Israel had learned from older nations how a king presents himself. But in contrast to what was otherwise customary in those days, the Bible never calls the king the "father" of his subjects.

"You are my father and my lord. I have no father beside you." Thus the king of Assyria allowed himself to be addressed by his vassals. In his petition to the Assyrians the king of Judah, too, conforms to this courtly style, saying, "I am your servant and your son. Come up, and rescue me" (2 Kings 16:7).[51]

The Bible calls only one king consistently "father." The kings of Judah are judged on the basis of whether they are like "their father David." Jesus is called "son of David," the throne of his father David is promised to him, and the Jewish people hope for the kingdom "of our father David."[52] For almost four hundred years the dynasty of David ruled in Jerusalem. It is understandable that "son of David" became a word of hope. The people were looking for the king who would free them from foreign domination, and yet biblical traditions also dampened such hopes: It was said already of Solomon that he was "not like his father David," and his son Rehoboam was blamed for the collapse of David's kingdom.[53]

Israel's deliverer must be more than just the son of a father

Biblical authors create a counterweight to inflated expectations of the son of David in that they speak with sober knowledge of human nature about the risks to which the sons of distinguished fathers are exposed. Whoever has easy access to power as the son of a powerful father can just as easily be enticed by power. The story about the crisis of the state (2 Samuel 11–1 Kings 2) tells how David's realm almost fell into ruin already during his lifetime because the king never reined in his power-hungry son. "Now Adonijah . . . exalted himself, saying, 'I will be king'; he prepared for himself chariots and horsemen, and fifty men to run before him. His father had never at any time displeased him by asking, 'Why have you done thus and so?'" (1 Kings 1:5-6). The author of 1 Samuel 8 was already convinced that a hereditary dynasty is basically good for nothing. It is said there that Samuel had to install a king because his sons were bad judges. What can be expected of a "son of David" if even the prophet who gave Israel the kingdom had wayward sons?

Mistrust of the hereditary kingdom can be heard even in the legends of the rise of Saul and David. Although they tell of sons and fathers who understand one another they also emphasize that it is not the father who qualifies his son to serve his people. Jesse brings seven sons to Samuel; whoever has seven sons has been given the fullness of good fortune.[54] David is the eighth, the "superfluous" son whom his father had forgotten, and yet the Spirit who made him Israel's deliverer comes down directly on him.

Young Saul goes out as an obedient son of his father and comes back the anointed one to whom God "gave . . . another heart" (1 Sam 10:9). A strange scene shows what kind of transformation this is. Samuel has named signs by means of which Saul is to understand that he has been chosen as king. One of them is meeting a group of prophets whose ecstasy affects Saul. Passersby comment on the scene: "'What has come over the son of Kish? Is Saul also among the prophets?' A man of the place answered, 'And who is their father?'" (1 Sam 10:11-12). The son of a respected father is found among the prophets, despised people whose fathers are unknown even where they live. For Saul this is nevertheless a sign of his having been chosen to be a prince in Israel.

The traditions of the rise of Saul and David were written down by authors who valued prophetic tradition and were convinced that the Spirit of God alone leads the "deliverer of Israel," so that the question about the identity of the father of the deliverer becomes unimportant. A renowned prophetic saying formulates this thought in an especially impressive manner when it refers to the birth of the son of the young woman in Isa 7:14. From very early times this has been understood by Christians as a reference to the mystery of Christ's birth. It is of primary importance to examine the meaning of this saying within the framework of the historical events about which Isaiah 7 speaks.

Ahaz cares nothing for the traditions of his father's house

In 733 B.C.E. Pekah, king of Israel, allied himself with the Aramean king Rezin against Ahaz, king of Judah. Ahaz appealed for help to the great power Assyria, which gladly grasped the opportunity to seize large portions of Israel. Isaiah 7 testifies to how seriously the prophet Isaiah attempted to restrain Ahaz from turning to the Assyrians for help. Solemnly he tells the king that the two minor kings can do him no harm and establishes this promise in detail. After all, who are Rezin and "the son of Remaliah"? Isaiah refers to Pekah only in relation to his father. Ahaz, the king of the Davidic dynasty that had then lasted more than two hundred years, must certainly have understood what Isaiah wanted to say with this, namely that Pekah was an officer's son who had seized the throne for himself by violent means. With a play on words Isaiah reminds Ahaz that the promise David received through Nathan continues to apply to the son of David even centuries later. God had said to David: "Your house and your kingdom shall be made sure forever before me" (2 Sam 7:16). In Isa 7:9 Isaiah gives new weight to "be made sure":

> If you do not stand firm in faith,
> you shall not stand at all.

Isaiah uses the plural form of "you"; he is not speaking only to Ahaz, but to the entire house of David. From the very beginning he has owed his inner stability to his God. Isaiah exhorts Ahaz not to give up this "firm stand" just because he is afraid of two little kings.

Isaiah had warned the young king against anxiety already in his greeting: "Take heed, be quiet, do not fear" (Isa 7:4). This advice, too, is to remind him of ancient traditions. Israel had often been saved because its deliverers acted without fear. The prophet points out to the king one more element of these traditions: the signs by means of which the calling of the deliverer of Israel had once been confirmed. Samuel, for example, had named signs to young Saul, which then helped Saul to recognize that he had been chosen. Now Isaiah challenges Ahaz: "Ask a sign of the LORD your God."[55] But under the guise of piety Ahaz rejects everything that Isaiah had exhorted: "I will not ask, and I will not put the LORD to the test" (Isa 7:12).

What becomes of promises that a person does not want to accept? Isaiah's answer is the statement about the son of a virgin:

Isaiah 7:14: The father of the Immanuel can be forgotten

After what had happened it is not astonishing that the prophecy begins (in v. 13) with a word of invective: "Hear then, O house of

David! Is it too little for you to weary mortals, that you weary my God also?" When Isaiah challenged Ahaz to ask for a sign he said "your [singular] God." Now he says "my God." He draws a line of separation between God and the house of David. A son of David does not want to know anything about God's promise for the house of David. Is God then still the God of the house of David?

After this scolding, a threat could have been expected: because you have behaved so and so, therefore . . . But with the word "therefore" Isaiah instead introduces his words about the son of the young woman: "Therefore the LORD himself will give you a sign. Look, the young woman is with child and shall bear a son, and shall name him Immanuel." Is that a word of punishment, or a promise? Who is this woman? Who is her child? The immediate context in Isaiah 7 gives an answer to these questions. Ahaz had refused the promises three times. Thereupon the child becomes a threefold sign of the faithfulness of God, who holds fast to the divine promises in spite of all.

Ahaz would not believe, in the first place, that the two hostile little kings would not harm him. Isaiah firmly insists that this word will be fulfilled, and that the child will be a sign of it. Both the enemies of Ahaz will lie prostrate before the child is grown. "For before the child knows how to refuse the evil and choose the good, the land before whose two kings you are in dread will be deserted" (Isa 7:16). The Assyrians did really very soon subjugate Aram and Israel. The rejected promise was fulfilled, though at the price of great disaster. Rich areas belonging to the brother-nation of Israel became Assyrian provinces.

In the second place, Ahaz did not want to get involved with the traditions of deliverance, but Isaiah explains that they will be newly strengthened in spite of Ahaz. The sign is therefore the name of the child. Immanu-El, "God is with us," is a cry of trust meant to encourage a plagued people. "Is the LORD really still with us?" That is what Gideon had once asked (Judg 6:13), but then, encouraged by the signs God gave him, he saved Israel from the hand of crushingly strong enemies. Isaiah, too, could have complained, saying, "Is God still with this people when the king from David's house no longer relies on God?" Yet Isaiah also knows an encouraging sign, the birth of the "Immanuel." In this name can also be heard polemic against the house of the king: God is not with "you" but with "us." The prophet introduces his promise like a sentence of punishment because it is a promise for the people and a sentence of punishment for the house of David.

Third, Ahaz had refused to look for a "firm stand" in the Davidic promise. The prophet makes clear that God nevertheless holds fast to God's pledge, of which the child is in turn the sign. The house of David will continue to exist in a son, and soon the heir to the throne will come into the world. For Ahaz himself this birth will not be a sign of hope, however. Because Ahaz does not wish to be a supporter of the house of David he is irrelevant to the continuation of the same. God designates another mediator of the promise, namely the mother.[56] The father of the child can be forgotten, for his mother will understand the meaning of her child's birth and give him the name that announces this, Immanuel. The child's birth is a sign that, in spite of the terrible consequences that the failure of the king will have, God is "with us," with God's people.

Matthew 1:23: Why Joseph must not be forgotten

The saying about the son of a young woman (or "virgin") was a help for early Christian congregations in their discourse about the birth of Jesus. Matthew takes note, so to speak, of the results of this conversation when he recounts how God's concern for Joseph caused him to send an angel. God is always looking for those who will cooperate in making God's word come true. In contrast to Ahaz, Joseph does not refuse to be a part of it.

"Joseph . . . a righteous man." The words with which Matthew begins the story have great significance in his gospel. Jesus demands from his disciples a "righteousness" that exceeds that of the scribes and Pharisees (Matt 5:22). When Joseph discovered that his betrothed was pregnant, though not by him, he put this "greater righteousness" into practice. The Law gave him the right to separate from Mary. But he was more just than the Law and wished to do this without a judicial proceeding, for then the gossip of the people would not hurt her, but only him. Instead God demands of him that he give up his intention and do the "greater righteousness," the will of God. The angel addresses Joseph as "son of David." Aside from this the New Testament calls only Jesus the son of David. Joseph is to pass on to Mary's child the sonship from David, a fatherly task intended for him. He fulfills it in that he not only renounces his male right to a judicial process but also his paternal right. He accepts Mary together with her child.

The clash over the kingdom rubbed off on the conceptions of fatherhood. In contrast to what is otherwise usual in the Near East, biblical authors never use the word "father" to describe the king as ruler. This reveals some mistrust. A people that had relied on mutual brotherly help wanted to see more than just the One at the top. When the Bible calls a king "father" he is just like every father in Israel: his son will inherit his legacy. But even this conception is valid in only a limited sense. The "father" of kings is David alone because they inherit from him the promise that their kingdom will have permanence. Because the word about "David our father" is of prophetic origin overtones of prophetic criticism can be heard in it from the very beginning. God seeks people to make the divine word real, but God does not necessarily need fathers and paternal houses. The next section will place this thought in a broader context.

8. Prophets are signs of admonition for a people proud of its families

"You conspired against me . . . by inquiring of God for him"
(1 Sam 22:13)

King Saul condemned Ahimelech to death because he consulted the priestly oracle for David.[57] Within the framework of the narrative about Saul's crime against the priests of Nob this is further proof that the king is actually aware of his guilt. Saul knows that David had listened to God when he fled from him. Nevertheless he pursues David and takes brutal revenge on the priest who had received the information about God's will. The narrators are concerned to show that Saul did not have to become guilty. He could have accepted from God his own downfall and the passing of rule to David.

Is it possible to accept one's own downfall? Several centuries after Saul the prophet Jeremiah had to do just that. God demanded of him that he not only announce the downfall of his people but also that he himself become a sign of admonition. In Israel a man was proud that as a father he could pass life on beyond his own death, but Jeremiah was not permitted to have either a wife or children. He had to take upon himself voluntarily what many people had suffered at the fall of Jerusalem when they died without any hope of a continuing life in their children (Jeremiah 16). In a variety of ways prophets have experienced and proclaimed how Israel's concepts of fatherhood, central for its self-understanding, fall apart when the inscrutable God takes a hand in history.[58] This theme is now to be portrayed with the help of a single prophetic figure, that of Elisha. Elisha was once addressed by the king as "father," and himself directs this call to his predecessor, Elijah. What kind of a "paternal image" lies at the origin of these traditions?

The son leaves his father's house

1 Kings 17–19 contains a short document, complete in itself, that attempts to describe Elijah's activity from his first appearance to the calling of his successor. In the first sentence of the little book, which certainly names Elijah as accurately as possible, he is named solely according to the location of his home place, "Elijah the Tishbite, from Tishbe in Gilead." Thus Elijah had no patronymic. His successor, in contrast, is called "Elisha, son of Shafat of Abel-meholah." Abel-meholah, "meadow of dancing," is a place in the fertile pasture land of the Jordan. Elisha appears for the first time in the final narrative of this little book as the son of a rich farmer in that fruitful land. He drives one of the twelve teams with which his father's field was just then being plowed and, as was usual at the time, immediately sowed. Clearly it was important to make use of the favorable weather, and all available workers were used. The son of the farmer, too, participates, for he is, after all, caring for the "inheritance of the fathers" also for himself and his descendants.[59] But suddenly all of this seems to have no worth any longer for Elisha, for Elijah had come by and placed his mantle upon him. Elisha butchers his cattle and cooks their flesh with the wood of the yoke. His team is no longer of any use to him except for furnishing the farewell meal with his relatives.[60]

In the midst of urgent work a farmer's son leaves his father in the lurch in order to follow and serve a man whose style of life is strange and even frightening. Elijah had "passed by," who knows from where and to where. Can it be pleasing to an agricultural baron when his son serves a man who does not even bear the name of his father and who has, therefore, no inherited property to live on? It is easy to imagine that many a father would have forbidden his son to leave in this way. Amos once scolded such fathers: "And I raised up some of your children to be prophets . . . but you . . . commanded the prophets, saying, 'You shall not prophesy'" (Amos 2:11-12).

Amos speaks with the "I" of God. It is God who makes young men to be prophets. Though the word "God" does not once occur in the story of Elisha's call, it does tell about an action of God. Elijah needs only to throw his mantle on him and right away he is ready to leave everything. Elisha's father conducts himself differently from the fathers whom Amos rebukes. Elisha is able to go in peace, taking leave of father and mother with a kiss and from his relatives with a meal. The construction of the narrative indicates that that is by no means a matter of course. God worked a miracle also among Elisha's relatives.

Elisha is "father" of the king and "lord" of his disciples

Elisha leaves his father, and will himself never become a father who lives on his inherited property. The traditions know him as a man without a family and fixed abode. Occasionally he lives in the Carmel mountains. At other times he teaches the elders in "his house" in Samaria or his disciples in a house in Gilgal. Many times he visits a hospitable woman. His style is admittedly more respectable than that of Elijah, of whom one never knew where he was at a given time, and who was obliged to hide from the king. Elisha is respected by the king. He provides water for Israel's army and bread for the besieged city.[61]

On one occasion he took prisoners and led them to the king. The king asks the prophet, "Father, shall I kill them?" (2 Kings 6:21). Elisha counsels sending them home well provided with bread and water so that the enemy will see that Israel is not starving. Occasionally in the Bible a good official is called "father." It is Elisha, however, who really deserves to be called "father" by the king. When he helps in the war it does not mean death for the enemies, but life for Israel. Even when the prophet is dying the king appeals to him for help in the war: "My father, my father! The chariots of Israel and its horsemen!" (2 Kings 13:14). The chariot was at that time the most valuable military weapon and its driver the best-trained combatant. When Elisha died the king lost his fatherly counselor and Israel its powerful helper in war. It is no wonder, then, that the king cries helplessly as he takes his leave of Elisha with this shout.[62]

In other stories, Elisha appears as the helper of a group of prophets. He provides bread for them; miraculously the lost ax that they had borrowed to build a house is returned. Kings of the ancient Near East risked their honor to be "fathers" for widows and orphans, and Elisha proves himself in this area, too. He saves a prophet's widow and her sons from grave privation. Yet the prophets never call him "father." They address him as "master" or "man of God." The prophet's widow refers to her dead husband as "your servant" when speaking to Elisha. Why, considering that Elisha assumes fatherly responsibility for the prophets, is he never called "father" of the prophets?[63]

At the time of Elisha the Aramean wars threw many people's lives out of kilter. Families lost their property, and many no longer knew how they could survive. It was not even possible to bury the dead in peace. Many of the homeless lived within groups of ecstatics.[64] Elisha did not answer the challenge of his time with miracles from above that solved all difficulties. He is concerned that people stand up for one another. When bread is shared it is sufficient for everyone. When Elisha's servant cooks he has the prophets contribute the vegetables that they themselves have gathered, and sees to it that their pathetic contribution does good for everyone. The miracle of the oil helps the widow because everyone is willing to lend her vessels.

All the members of a farm family have to help so that the land will produce enough. Elisha, too, had once—along with eleven others—plowed his father's fields. Inherited property can be lost, and families can collapse. Elisha taught the prophets a kind of solidarity that can help people survive even when there is no hereditary property and no father who cares. For this reason the traditions never call him the "father" of the prophets.

Elisha gains a father

Though the biblical narrators would have liked to present Elisha's relationship with his predecessor, Elijah, as that of a son to his father, they did not really dare to do so. A curious parallel calls attention to this. Just as the king called out to the dying Elisha, so Elisha is said to have called out to Elijah: "Father, father! The chariots of Israel and its horsemen!" (2 Kings 2:12). Yes, Elisha is said to have seen what he described: a wagon of fire in which Elijah rode up to heaven.

In the story of Elijah's ascension various recollections from older stories about Elisha and Elijah are transformed into impressive events. The story of Elisha's call in 1 Kings 11:21, for example, ends with Elisha's "following and serving" Elijah. This causes a chain reaction of events in 2 Kings 2. As Elijah sets out for the place from which he will be taken up to heaven Elisha calmly follows him. Two times prophets stop Elisha and ask him about his "master" Elijah.[65] But Elisha does not behave like someone who is serving his master. Twice he resists Elijah's command. "Stay here!" says Elijah, but Elisha swears "as the LORD lives, and as you yourself live" that he will not leave him. In the end he experiences what he had evoked. It is not death that separates him from Elijah, but the fiery chariot. The living God takes Elijah away alive.

At the same time Elisha had achieved the right to call on Elijah as "father." Despite the command of his "master" he had so long unwaveringly followed Elijah that the latter let him make a request: "Tell me what I may do for you, before I am taken from you" (v. 9). Elijah is not able to grant him what he then requests, however, which is, "a double share of your spirit." According to Deut 21:17 a father gave the firstborn son a share of the inheritance that was twice as large as that of the other heirs. Therefore Elisha wants to be recognized as the firstborn son of Elijah. But the inheritance of the Spirit is given by someone other than Elijah. Elijah does not say who that is, but it is not necessary to ask whom he has in mind: "if you see me as I am being taken from you, it will be granted you; if not, it will not" (v. 10). If God permits Elisha to see the miracle of Elijah's reception, that will be a sign that Elisha inherits Elijah's spirit.

Thus the narrative of Elijah's ascension into heaven presents the call of Elisha a second time and still more impressively as an act of God. Elisha wants to be more than a servant, and at the moment of leavetaking his effort is rewarded. He may call Elijah "father," and is Elijah's son and heir. That is to be credited to his zeal, but especially to God, who permits him to see Elijah's ascension. The gospel of John would describe the believers as "children" who were born not by human will but by the Spirit.[66] The story of Elijah's ascension is like an early anticipation of this. It was not the will of the two prophets that made Elisha an heir of the Spirit that filled Elijah, but the action of God that took Elijah away alive.

The "fatherless" man can become a father

The narrative forms a second "father saying" from an older story into an impressive event. Fatherhood does not mean much in Elijah's life. He had received neither inherited property nor the name of a father, and he had not become the father of a family. Nevertheless as he, weary from his futile efforts, asks God to release him from his prophetic service, he thinks of his ancestors: "It is enough; now, O LORD, take away my life, for I am no better than my ancestors" (1 Kings 19:4). Elijah had gone out alone far into the wilderness. If God fulfills his request and lets him die, no one will know what happened to him. His "ancestors," too, have disappeared without a trace. There is no "inheritance of the fathers," no "grave of the fathers," and no paternal name to remind him of them. Elijah is convinced that there will remain not even a trace of his prophetic activity. Elijah wants to give back to God his entire vain life: "Take away my life!" ("Life" is an expedient translation. The Hebrew word is *nephesh,* whose first meaning is "throat." When there is no breath in the throat a person can do nothing but fight for air. In the throat one experiences how irresistibly, beginning internally, one desires to live. "Take my *nephesh*" means, therefore, "Take me, the human being, who yearns to live!")

Just as Elijah had asked it in the wilderness, so now it comes true in his ascension: God "takes" Elijah away.[67] But God transforms futility into victory, taking Elijah as the "chariot of Israel and its horsemen." In 1 Kings 19 the exhausted prophet had only wished that he could disappear without a trace. Here his wish is wonderfully fulfilled. The prophets, who unlike Elisha do not know that he has been taken away by God, seek Elijah in vain. Elijah leaves his mark engraved on the world, not with a gravestone but with the "son" who continues his work.

Do the Elisha traditions project a particular "father-image"?

Elisha had set aside the inheritance of his fathers. As a man without family he became a "father" for the king and a helper in Israel's wars. The Elisha traditions gainsay the notion that a man can be of use to his people only if he is supported by a strong and united paternal house, yet they do not reject the ideal of family solidarity, which indeed is a solid sustenance for people who have lost their family and homeland. Elisha teaches them that mutual help creates the possibility of life for all, even in a society in which no father has a family inheritance to give.

The story of Elijah's ascension expands the conceptions of fatherhood and inheritance almost beyond the limits of what can be said with these words. Elisha becomes the "son" of Elijah because he experiences that his "father" will be taken away from him. All narratives about Elisha revolve around the question of life. From what does a human being live? Where does the threat of death come from? Among the hill farmers of Israel it seemed reasonable to think through these questions with the help of their conceptions of fatherhood. The man who earns a living for himself and those who belong to him by hard work in mountain fields knows how much he owes the ancestors who cared for the land before him. Elisha, too, receives such an inheritance that someone before him had cultivated. Yet passing on the legacy of the prophetic spirit is something that not even the great prophet Elijah can do by his own mighty and perfect power. Elisha had fought tenaciously for it, and God wonderfully gave it. And so Elijah became a "father."

It was far from the intention of the people who gave form to these traditions to polemicize against a traditionally accepted "father image." It is characteristic that Elisha takes his leave of father and mother, relatives and paternal legacy, with kisses and a meal. Traditional ideas about fatherhood are expanded here in order to speak about the indescribable actions of God.

The traditions about Elijah and Elisha aid the evangelists in understanding the actions of Jesus. New Testament conceptions of the meaning of fatherhood for the disciples of Jesus are also influenced from this direction. Therefore a look into the New Testament will conclude this second survey of biblical conceptions of fatherhood. First, however, a summary will provide a perspective on the Old Testament conceptions of fatherhood that were well known to Jesus and his disciples.

9. In retrospect: fathers need sons

Fathers apply their strength for Israel

In the Bible, Israel's history is often portrayed as events carried forward by fathers and sons. No conclusive overall picture emerges, however. This synopsis will therefore consist of only a few briefly explained memory aids. (The numbers in parentheses refer to sections of the book.)

It will be necessary to distinguish between "father" and "master." In the Bible "father" means "helper" rather than "master." That applies just as much among the People of God (see ch. 1, section 7) as in the political society. While great kings in the Near East had themselves called "father," in the Bible it is the counselors of the king who are called "father," whether they are officials (see section 7 above) or prophets (section 8 above). The disciples, however, do not call a prophet "father," but "master." When he cares for them like a father he does so by teaching them to care mutually for one another (section 8 above).

Another reason why the king was never called "father" was that mutual help was valued above governmental intervention. It was, after all, possible to see to what loss of freedom such measures led in the major centralized kingdoms. It was a matter of pride for a genuine Israelite to give aid to the king from the treasures of his or her house (section 5 above).

The "father's house" has greater political significance than does the father. The people's hope for help was focused less on an individual hero than on a man and his paternal house. What stood behind this fact was the experience that a free people needs many wealthy families who are able to make men available for public duties (section 2 above). It is of no crucial importance whether these men are fathers, sons, or brothers to one another.

Fraternal solidarity is more important than paternal authority. The strength of a father's house did not depend on obedience to a father who made all the decisions for everyone, but rather on mutual loyalty. Father and son took a stand together for their people.[68] Political groups whose men are committed to one another in "fraternal" aid understand themselves as relatives, sons of one progenitor. Saul's followers, for example, are descended, as is Saul himself, from Benjamin. They are prepared to stand with the king, but are nevertheless not ready to carry out orders they do not approve of (section 1 above).

A father is one of many brothers. In Israel's early days its farmers were able to resist the professional armies of the countries that desired to expand their power from the flatland into the mountains only when they helped one another. A father who wanted to preserve his family's land and its freedom needed the help of other people who had the same concern. The ideal of Israel's solidarity as a "society of heirs" in a common land has its roots here (section 5 above).

It was thanks only to solidarity with his "brothers" that a man could be sure of his inheritance. Only because the "fathers" had developed it and cared for it could he now live from it. The graves of the fathers, located on hereditary property, remind him, too, to keep it in order for his descendants. Land did not belong to one person alone. Everyone needed "brothers" to defend it together with him, and everyone was a beneficiary and trustee for coming generations.

A father is one in a chain of fathers. In the Old Testament as in the New, lists of fathers' and sons' names show that God's blessing persists through generations. Mothers seldom appear in them, and daughters never do. In these ranks of men's names are reflected experiences of a people whose life was protected by the heavy work of mountain farmers and the masculine strength of warriors. They show above all that belonging to the people is not based only on natural descent. At a birth it is immediately perceptible that mother and child belong together. Who the father is cannot be so easily established.

The father is the one who passes on rights and is not seen primarily as the begetter. Through the institution of levirate marriage even the man who had died childless could have a son who received his name and inherited property. The son of the father is the one who assumes the rights of the father (section 5 above). Thus the "lists of fathers" represented legal succession rather than natural descent. The identity of tribe, kinship group, or nation remains definite through the ages because new sons are continually assuming old rights. It was known in ancient Israel, too, that Israel had not grown out of twelve sons sired by one man. In Gen 48:16, for example, the expansion of Israel is presented as a judicial act. The aged father Jacob/Israel explains that his name is to live on in Ephraim and Manasseh, the Egyptian sons of Joseph. By birth the two strongest tribes of Israel are foreign. In legal terms they bear the name of "Israel," not that of their "begetter" Joseph.

The names of great fathers become signs of hope. The name Israel, inherited from the tribal father and always the same, is the sign that the people has survived even the loss of its political independence. In times of humiliation it was hoped that other great names of the past, too, could one day again receive new meaning. The hope for a "son of David" (section 7 above) or the confidence that God would not abandon the descendants of "father Abraham" strengthened the conviction that Israel continued to be the same people that had once been blessed in its ancestors. God, it was hoped, would be true to the word once given to the ancestors.[69]

Although Israel understands itself as the people among whom the Law of Moses and the wisdom of Solomon live on, Moses and Solomon, in contrast to Abraham, Jacob, and David, are never called "fathers." Why was such a distinction made?

Fatherhood alone does not guarantee Israel's survival

Fathers protected the continued existence of the people by the fraternal solidarity with which they supported one another through their work in maintaining the inheritance of their ancestors, which preserved a good land for the descendants, through the continual passing on of ancient rights to the younger generation, and finally through a dynasty in which the power was passed on for hundreds of years from father to son. The history of Israel proved that all of this was not sufficient. Land and political freedom were lost, and portions of the people disappeared without a trace. Nevertheless there are other signs beside those dependent on the masculine strength that characterized Israel's identity: the Law, which instructs men, women, and children (see chapter 1, section 6), and the wisdom with which women, too, keep their houses in good order (Proverbs 31). The instructions of Moses and the wise teaching of Solomon are not valid only for the fathers. The fact that Israel survived the loss of its political independence was due to the fact that Israel's faith needs no ideology of fathers and brothers. Therefore biblical authors are able to speak with composure even about the dangers that threaten the father's house both internally and externally.

Conflict about inheritance endangers brotherliness and blots out the names of fathers. It can no longer be determined what forms of inheritance distribution were practiced in individual cases, but it is clear that brotherly solidarity did not always survive when an inheritance was to be distributed. Brothers are more concerned to add the inheritance of a dead man to their property than to take care that his name remain alive in a son (sections 5 and 6 above). But solidarity that is too strong can also become a danger. The person obliged to satisfy too many demands of his father's house has difficulty in being a "father" for his own land. Men who belong to no particular kinship group can many times better serve their people and their king (section 6 above).

Israel owes its continued existence also to the "fatherless." Memories from Israel's early history serve to warn against relying solely on the power of "paternal houses." Israel came into being in a time of turmoil during which many people lost their homeland. Criminals without relationships are capable of taking advantage of such times (sections 1 and 6 above). Yet even David was indebted to a group of homeless people for his ascent. Within a company held together exclusively by mutual assistance the best strength of a father's house, voluntary brotherliness, can thrive. Biblical narrators are also aware that even these bonds can break. David murdered Uriah, his comrade-in-arms (section 6 above).

Paternal love is not a reliable support for a nation. One of the weak points of the paternal house that is described with special frequency is that fathers and sons got into positions of opposition to one another. It is striking from a modern perspective that sons never had to defend themselves against excessively powerful fathers. The harmony between father and son is vulnerable because they are linked by a power that is subject to no rules: namely love (sections 2 and 3 above). Concerning politically significant relations of fathers and sons, too, the story is told in such a way that readers can imagine themselves caught up in the tension-laden reality of the sympathy and antipathy of human hearts.

Fathers mediate between family and people. Biblical conceptions of fatherhood are, therefore, inadequately described when only the role of the fathers is considered in questions about the community of faith and political life. The third part of this book examines how the Bible speaks about the life of fathers in their families. In this context it will be necessary also to give attention to a deficit that, however comprehensible it may be within the texts that speak of the political significance of fathers, attracts attention also in other places, that is, that paternal love is almost never love of a daughter.

Fatherhood appears almost entirely as a bond with a son. All regulations about inheritance are founded on the notion that a family perpetuates itself only in its sons. Only in an emergency and by means of her sons can a daughter ensure the continuation of the family. These legal arrangements contributed substantially to the marginal position of daughters. In Job 42:5 at least one biblical author emphasizes that God's blessing is only fully understood when daughters, too, belong to the father's house in their own right. This discrimination against daughters makes the Bible's conceptions of fatherhood seem questionable in our day. But already within the Bible itself there is a broad stream of traditions that raises even more fundamental questions about the meaning of fathers and sons for the survival of Israel.

When God wishes to give life, God needs no fathers

There were times in Israel's history when the strength that flowed to the people from the houses of its fathers was not sufficient (section 6 above). Israel had experienced that a father can fail so completely that the son must start totally anew. Though David honored his father-in-law like a father, he was forced to erect a new empire over the ruins of Saul's kingdom (sections 1 and 3 above).

Generational conflicts are not necessary. Strife between fathers and sons is not necessarily the accompanying sign of a new beginning. Saul goes out as an obedient son and comes back home as a man who has assumed responsibility for an inheritance different from what he will receive from his father, that is, for the "inheritance of YHWH" (section 2 above). Saul's son Jonathan fought the Philistines in a more contemporary style than did his father. In his friend David he recognized the new king. Yet it never came to a break between father and son because of this (section 3 above).

When bonds between father and son fail to break even though the son embodies a new era, biblical faith recognizes in this the action of God that "turns the hearts of father and sons to one another" (section 3 above). Elisha abandons his family forever but leaves in peace (section 8 above). Gideon tears down his father's altar to Baal and is nevertheless protected by his father against the rest of the relatives (see chapter 1, section 6).

God needs no father to renew the divine blessing. In the conflict with King Ahaz, who rejects the traditions of his father's house, the prophet Isaiah spells out more clearly the conceptions of a new beginning in the son: When the father positions himself to block the will of God, God can make salvation valid through the "son of the young woman." Thus Isaiah expands the prophetic traditions that show how little a father understands of the action of the Spirit (section 7 above). The story of Elijah's ascension examines how the prophetic spirit is bequeathed to others: Elisha acquires the right to be "son" and "heir" of his predecessor by following him until God gives him the spirit of Elijah (section 8 above).

The prophet comes into conflict with his paternal house. That the lives of the prophets have sources of power other than those offered by fathers and paternal houses is affirmed also by the infancy stories of Samuel and Moses. If his father had had his way, Samuel would never have been born. Moses owed his survival to women (section 2 above). The antithesis between paternal house and prophet can even turn into enmity. Gideon, at least, found support from his father in the weakest clan in Manasseh. Jeremiah, however, was threatened with death by his paternal house, and Jesus experienced that his relatives wished to force him to "good conduct" (Jer 11:18-19; Mark 3:20-21).

The guilt of the fathers has its effect on history. Contemporary Bible readers notice how firmly the individual was bound into the society. Biblical authors—fortunately in only a few texts—take up even offensive ideas of tribal responsibility; when fathers have loaded themselves down with guilt, wives and children, too, are executed. More space is given, however, to critical confrontation with these ideas.

Biblical authors make the distinction that while only the guilty man himself may be prosecuted, responsibility for the fathers' guilt does lie on the sons, and experience shows that the sins of fathers do have their entirely spontaneous effect on the sons. Where we say "entirely spontaneous," the Bible speaks of God's activity. The experience that wicked deeds of the fathers have disastrous effects on the sons thus becomes a pattern of thought by means of which historical catastrophes can be understood. When Israel's history is told as "history of the fathers," the fathers are by no means simply being praised. More often biblical voices are revealing the guilt of the fathers so that faith in the saving will of God can be proved when the people distance themselves from their fathers (section 4 above).

The New Testament took up these readymade ideas as an aid in understanding the radical change within which the Church came into existence. Paul, for example, carries forward a theme of the prophetic proclamation when, in 1 Corinthians 10, he understands the history of Israel as a warning addressed to the Christian congregation not to fall into the sins of "our ancestors." Distancing oneself from guilty ancestors opens the way to the salvation God desires to give. Jesus traditions, too, take up this theme. The last section of this second part will deal with them.

10. The disciples of Jesus: a family in which there is no father

The Gospels often sketch their images of Jesus' acts against the background of Elijah and Elisha stories. The scene in Matt 4:21-22 is reminiscent of the call of Elisha. James and John, fishermen on the Sea of Galilee, are at work. Jesus comes by. "Immediately they left the boat and their father, and followed him." Thus Elisha, too, left his work and followed Elijah. Mark follows the old story more closely. Elisha's father had lost only one of many helpers when Elisha went away. These two brothers, too, can in good conscience leave their father. He is rich enough to afford day laborers (Mark 1:20; 1 Kings 19:19-20).

In another scene Jesus challenges a disciple in an incomparably radical manner to break with his father: "Another of his disciples said to him, 'Lord, first let me go and bury my father.' But Jesus said to him, 'Follow me, and let the dead bury their own dead'" (Matt 8:21-22).

The image of a sympathetic Jesus is familiar. He is sympathetic when a mother cries for her dead son; the death of his friend shakes him (Luke 7:13; John 11:34). How did Matthew come to place these hurtfully sharp words in Jesus' mouth?

Matthew 8:18-27: To follow Jesus is to meet "the Lord"

An initial approach can be made by considering the narrative context in which the saying belongs. Having told his disciples to come away with him and to cross the lake, Jesus is delayed a second time by the disciple who asks for some time off. First a scribe had asked Jesus to accept him as a disciple. Jesus had shown him, too, what a strange teacher he is. Students who in those days sought instruction in questions of faith generally lived in the teacher's house,[70] but Jesus explained to this supplicant that he would have no secure place to stay with him, although the need for shelter is so natural that even wild animals, foxes, and birds are aware of it.

The events after the departure of the boat show how it goes with disciples who do not allow themselves to be deterred by the fact that Jesus is a teacher of a different kind. While they struggle with the storm on the lake, Jesus sleeps. They have accepted the fact that Jesus is not the father of a household, and now they learn that he is not even a helmsman who helps with dangers on the journey. While it is true that Jesus lets himself be waked and speaks a word of authority to wind and wave, Matthew no longer calls those who were saved disciples: "*They* were amazed, saying, 'What sort of man is this, that even the winds and the sea obey him?'"

What sort of man? The two dialogues before the departure also provoke this question. What kind of human being is this who does not permit a disciple to show final respect for his father? Who is Jesus? Matthew broaches this question when he places a different form of address in the mouth of each of the questioners. The scribe says "Teacher." In Matthew Jesus is addressed in this way only by people who are not his disciples. The disciples say "Lord."

To his disciples, Elisha was "Lord" and "man of God," for through him they experienced how mightily God can help (section 8 above). It was also a confession of the power of God when early Christian congregations said "Jesus Christ is Lord." They called Jesus "Lord," the address given to God by Jews who no longer pronounced the divine Name YHWH.[71] In Matthew's time there were already Christians who uttered this confession too easily (Matt 7:21; 25:11). The evangelist confronts such people with the experience of the disciple who came requesting time to bury his father, that is, that it is not an easy thing to encounter in Jesus this Lord whose command crassly contradicts human wishes.

Leaving one's father: a prophetic sign

Matthew's congregations were familiar with the Old Testament and knew that God had given the prophets hard commands of this kind. Jeremiah and Ezekiel had been forbidden to mourn their dead. They were to accept vicariously the people's bitter experience of catastrophe. They were to do voluntarily what the coming catastrophe would force their people to do. No one would any longer have the strength to mourn loved ones.[72] Is Jesus demanding such a symbolic act from the disciple who is to stay away from his father's funeral? And if so, as a sign of what?

Just as in the time of the prophets, there was reason in Jesus' time to fear the end of the People of God. In the sharp competition of economic expansion brought on by the inclusion of Palestine in the Roman Empire, people who valued the preservation of the family inheritance more than an irresponsible inflation of their personal income could no longer keep pace. Family agriculture became unprofitable and families broke up. Historical sources speak of the socially uprooted, of monks in the desert, robbers, resistance fighters, despised collaborators, beggars, prostitutes, and sick people with no one to help them. Where was faith still alive when families, the most important groups for faith, were dissolved? (See chapter 1, section 2.)

Jesus responds to this distress when he assists fathers to find the faith "together with their whole household," but also applies himself to cause the "lost sheep of the house of Israel" (Matt 15:24) to be recognized as full members of the people. His group of disciples, above all, is to be a sign of the renewal of Israel when it conducts itself like a family that welcomes former collaborators as well as resistance fighters.[73] The disciples even accept the likes of the brothers James and John, who, though they could have found honorable employment with their wealthy father, nevertheless share with Jesus the life of the homeless. One especially detailed passage about discipleship in Mark addresses this last group of disciples:

> Truly I tell you, there is no one who has left house or brothers or sisters or mother or father or children or fields, for my sake and for the sake of the good news, who will not receive a hundredfold now in this age—houses, brothers and sisters, mothers and children, and fields with persecution—and in the age to come eternal life (Mark 10:29).

It is certainly no mere accident that the enumeration gives the father an inconspicuous place.[74] Daughters, who contributed only in emergencies to the preservation of the family inheritance, were not counted in their fathers' families (see section 5 above). In this quotation the sisters are named even before the father. Just as conspicuous is that the fathers are missing in its second half. Whoever has left a father will find no new father among the disciples of Jesus.

A society without fathers

Jesus brought from Nazareth the concept of family in which sisters, too, were counted. In such small places, where attention is paid to how brothers and sisters grow up together, one also knows what becomes of sisters.[75] "Is not this the carpenter, the son of Mary and brother of James and Joses and Judas and Simon, and are not his sisters here with us?" (Mark 6:3). Jesus' father is not mentioned by the people of Nazareth. In 1 Samuel 22, though it also seems not worth mentioning whether or not the old father, Ahitub, is himself present among the men of the house of Ahitub (see section 2 above), all eighty-five bear his name, for they care for his inheritance, the shrine of Nob and the priestly knowledge. In the family of Jesus there was obviously no paternal inheritance worth mentioning that could have reminded people of Joseph. Therefore Jesus is for the people of Nazareth simply the son of the woman who still lived among them.

Still, it is no small matter even for humble people to leave their family. The saying from Mark 10:29 enumerates in detail how many bonds the disciple of Jesus gives up. For the one who went away the separation may have been more difficult than for those who stayed, for whom this meant one less mouth to be fed from the land. It did, of course, also mean the loss of two strong hands. Thus it could also be explained why the Gospels know only mothers who, together with their sons, belonged to the circle of disciples. If the fathers had gone away from home with their sons, who would then have managed the family property?[76] A father who confessed Jesus would more probably have done as Zacchaeus did, staying home and giving away only "half of [his] possessions" (Luke 19:8). He needed the other half to care for his family.

But the company of disciples was not simply to get along without fathers. There are other words of Jesus that polemicize against fathers.[77] The radical message to the disciple who was not permitted to bury his father cannot be understood as long as one thinks only of the social conditions that explain why no fathers belong to the community of disciples. It has other roots.

Polemic against fathers

In Israel the gravesite of the ancestors located on the family property reminded the living generation to care for the inheritance as their ancestors had done, so that the coming generation, too, could live from it (see section 5 above). At the time of Jesus this ancient sign had increasingly lost its significance because of the many who had lost not only their family property but also the heritage of the patriarchs' faith.

Many people suffered when faith and solidarity disappeared in their families. Shattered families often continued holding fast only to the family custom of honoring their dead. At a burial there was a meeting with those whom they ordinarily never encountered. For such families there was a message of comfort in the harsh symbolic action imposed on the disciple, namely that the shattering of ancient conceptions of family solidarity is something for which they themselves are not primarily responsible. God had laid it upon them, and Jesus commands them to accept it.

The symbolic act that Jesus demands of the disciple would be misunderstood, however, if it were seen as an incitement to break with the faith of the ancestors, the faith of Israel. On the contrary, Jesus takes up a thought from the Old Testament, namely that there can come times and circumstances when it becomes necessary for a new generation to make a new beginning. A story of a new beginning without the fathers can be found already in the history of Israel's beginnings. The entire generation of ancestors who had experienced the Exodus from Egypt had to die in the wilderness, "none of the people who have seen my glory and the signs that I did in Egypt and in the wilderness . . . shall see the land that I swore to give to their ancestors" (Num 14:22-23).

In the Hebrew text it appears that this word of judgment applied only to the men. This cannot be ascribed simply to the fact that biblical authors continually forget the women. From the context of the narrative one learns that Israel had believed that it had to conquer the land by means of masculine strength alone. When it saw that this strength was insufficient, it became discouraged and wanted to give up its freedom and return to Egypt (Num 14:3). To this the judgment responds: God takes away the fathers of a people that believed it could not maintain its existence without the strength of men.

This story was certainly heard with special attentiveness in the epochs when foreign conquerors destroyed Israel's ruling class. What will be the fate of a people without fathers? Who will then safeguard Israel's continuance and its traditions? There was reason also in New Testament times to fear that the traditions inherited from the ancestors could perish and that the end of Israel could come. In this situation the Gospel of Matthew takes up with zeal Old Testament traditions, at the same time warning against making ideology out of the tradition of the ancestors: "Do not presume to say to yourselves, 'We have Abraham as our ancestor'; for I tell you, God is able from these stones to raise up children to Abraham" (Matt 3:9).

The New Testament polemic against fathers does not demand that the new Israel live without fathers. If that were so, why would it be said that Jesus gives salvation "to the father and his house"? It is not fathers who are condemned, but the attitude that would guarantee the life of the People of God through fathers. And yet even this judgment is not simply negative. That becomes clear even in that severe prohibition against burying the father. In the congregation within which the Gospel of Matthew came into being, the impressive image of the burial that Joseph gave his beloved father was certainly also highly regarded (Gen 50:2-3). Those familiar with Old Testament stories about the love of fathers and sons would have to ask what was going on within a son who was not allowed even to weep at his father's grave. The symbolic action demanded of the disciple makes clear that, despite all the joy about a new People of God arising through Jesus, the pain people experience in breaking old relationships is not to be forgotten.

The example from this pericope from Matthew shows, and not for the first time, that even when biblical authors are dealing with the patriarchal order represented by fathers, they keep in sight the individual's experiences with his or her father or a father in the family. The third part of this book turns to the theme of how biblical texts speak of the life of the father in his household.

Notes: Chapter Two

[1] In 1 Sam 22:19 Saul's crime is exaggerated to the point of incredibility: Saul kills every living thing, human beings and cattle, at Nob, a home of priests. This verse was probably added at a later time. The king treats an Israelite community as he should have treated Israel's enemies, but had not (1 Sam 15:3-9).

[2] Cf. 1 Sam 8:11; 20:33; on the story of Saul's throwing the spear at his own son cf. 3 below.

[3] The NRSV says that Doeg "attacked" the priests rather than that he "encircled" them. In either case, how can Doeg alone kill eighty-five men?

[4] As the NRSV notes, the meaning of the Hebrew word rendered "be responsible" is uncertain. It can also be translated "encircle."

[5] Cf. 1 Sam 23:6; 30:7; 2 Sam 19:12; 1 Kings 2:26.

[6] Cf. 1 Sam 14:36; however, this story also reflects a tension between priests and the king; cf. also 3 below.

[7] Cf. Exod 5:22; 14:15; 17:11-12; 32:11-14; Num 11:10-15.

[8] Cf. Judg 6:25-32; 1 Sam 22:3-4. In 1 Sam 17:17-30 David appears as the obedient son of his father.

[9] Cf. 1 Sam 9:5; 10:2.

[10] Cf. ch. 1 above, sections 2 and 4.

[11] Cf. also 2 Samuel 11–2 Kings 2; Genesis 37–50; Genesis 27; Judges 14.

[12] Cf. 2 Sam 14:33; Judg 14:10, 19; 1 Sam 20:31.

[13] Jesus says something very similar in the Fourth Gospel about his closeness to the Father; cf., for example, John 5:20; cf. also ch. 4 below, section 6.

[14] The book of Esther, however, calls attention to the fact that if the Jews had the power they would use it just as heedlessly. The author speaks of the revenge of the Jews on their persecutors with the same words used for the incredibly heedless dealings with human life to which the king of Persia had allowed himself to be seduced by Haman, the enemy of the Jews.

[15] In Josh 7:15 it is said that God's anger against Israel will not abate until Achan and "all that he has" is burned. According to 7:24 his sons and daughters also belong to "all that he has." According to 7:25, on the other hand, Achan alone is stoned by "all Israel."

[16] Cf. 2 Kings 23:16: the bones of the dead defile a sanctuary.

[17] In 1 Samuel 22 a person of alien origin carries out the murder of the priestly clan. In Judg 14:15 it is Philistines who threaten not only Samson's wife, but also the house of her father. According to 2 Sam 14:11 it could, of course, also happen in Israel that a woman had reason to fear that her father's house would be called to account because of her. King David, however, is motivated to guarantee her safety.

[18] Cf., for example, the curses on secret crimes in Deut 27:15-26.

[19] Cf. the legend about the Solomonic judgment in 1 Kings 3:16.

[20] The OT itself disagrees with this story: eleven psalms are ascribed to the Korahites, the rabble-rousers who were killed according to Numbers 16. A medieval chronicle tells of an abbot who nevertheless read Numbers 16 as an instruction on how to act. In the Albigensian wars the population of Beziers had fled into the cathedral. The attackers "knowing that Catholics and heretics were mixed together, said to the abbot, 'What shall we do? We cannot distinguish the good from the bad.' He answered: 'Cut them all down!

The Lord will know his own.'" The abbot cited Num 16:5. (*Caesarii Heisterbucensis Monachi Dialogus Miraculorum* [Cologne, 1861] 1:302.)

[21] That the ancestors' sins continue affecting the present generation is often repeated only impersonally. Cf. Jer 2:5; 3:25; 7:26; 11:10; 14:20, and elsewhere; further Ezek 2:3; 20:24; Lev 26:39-40; Isa 65:7; Ps 106:6 and elsewhere. Amos cites a concrete example of how fathers lead their sons into evil customs (Amos 2:7). During his long life as a prophet Jeremiah had seen that bad customs practiced by fathers, mothers, and children continue to be valued after decades as a good tradition "of the fathers"; cf. Jer 7:18 with Jer 44:15-30. Among other texts, Isa 43:27 speaks of the beginning of Israel's sin as lying with the progenitor Jacob/Israel.

[22] Cf. Ezek 16:44: "Like mother, like daughter."

[23] This statement is often cited as support for the false but widespread idea that the OT proclaims a God of vengeance who carries out collective punishment. In the German *Einheitsübersetzung* an awkward choice of words supports this misunderstanding: "He visits the guilt of the fathers on the sons." Luther translated *pqd* with "visit"; in its original meaning (but not as usually used today) "visit" gives the meaning of *pqd*, "examine critically."

[24] Only this sentence is in the "imperfect," with which Hebrew speaks of events that are not yet "perfect" and capable of being directly experienced. All other "names of God" are formulated as nominal clauses. It is thus that Hebrew speaks of that which is valid for all times. What great significance this saying had is revealed in its being repeated in other contexts in Exod 20:5 and Deut 5:9-10 and alluded to in Lam 5:7.

[25] Ezek 18:2; cf. also Lam 5:7.

[26] This statement became so important for the generation of the exile that other authors repeat it like a dogma: Deut 14:16; 2 Kings 14:6.

[27] To what an extent demanding the death penalty for a murderer was a matter of course in Israel is revealed in judicial proverbs in Gen 9:6 and Exod 21:12.

[28] Kings are called "father of widows and orphans" in the Epilogue of the Code of Hammurabi and in the Ugaritic "Tale of Aqhat" A.v.9. (See James B. Pritchard, ed., *The Ancient Near East.* 2 vols. Princeton: Princeton University Press, 1958. The Code of Hammurabi is at 1:138–167. The Tale of Aqhat is at 1:118–132, with the reference here cited on p. 121. See also idem, *Ancient Near Eastern Texts [ANET]*, 2nd ed. Princeton: Princeton University Press, 1955, pp. 163–177 and 149–155 respectively.) Instances from Egypt are named by H. Brunner, *Altägyptische Erziehung*. Wiesbaden: 1957, 121.

[29] Job called himself "father of the orphan" in his discourse of justification (cf. Job 31:17-19). Prophets accuse profiteers of reducing the number of the independent citizens and forcing Israel to destruction; cf. Isa 5:8; Mic 2:2.

[30] Prov 13:22; 11:29. How alive this concept is in the NT is demonstrated by John 4:12. After more than a millennium stories are still told at the well about the "father" who dug it.

[31] Cf. Gen 25:9-10; Josh 24:30; Judg 8:32; 16:31; 1 Sam 25:1; 2 Sam 2:32; 17:23; 21:14; 1 Kings 2:34.

[32] A (fortunately outmoded) sexual pedagogy once developed from the name "Onan" the term "onanism" for masturbation and used the legend of Onan's death in order to threaten people with the consequences of such "onanism."

[33] 2 Sam 14:7; 1 Sam 24:22.

[34] 2 Sam 17:23; 2 Kings 20:1.

[35] Only images of hope and ideals from a time in which the land no longer belonged to Israel itself describe Israel as a people in which all live "in their inheritance"; cf. Ezek 47:14; Neh 11:20; Josh 24:28. Judges 21:24 speaks sarcastically of Israel as a people less concerned with human life than with living "by tribes and families . . . [in] their own territories."

[36] Ezra 2:61 mentions another way out: the son-in-law takes the name of his father-in-law. If he is a slave (1 Chr 2:34-35) his children do not belong to him in any case, but to his master (Exod 21:4).

[37] Instances of the right of inheritance of daughters and married women in Egypt are collected by Erika Feucht, "Die Stellung der Frau in Alten Ägypten," in J. Martin and R. Zoepfel, eds., *Aufgaben, Rollen und Räume von Mann und Frau* (Freiburg and Munich, 1989) 1:253.

[38] Cf. Gen 25:5-6: Abraham gave Isaac, the heir, "all he had." However, he still had "presents" for the sons he has from his concubines. Abraham is a rich father who, without diminishing the family inheritance, is able to give presents also to the sons who have no right of inheritance.

[39] Among ancient Israelite personal names there are replacement names like "Mescullam" or "Solomon," by which parents express that the newborn makes "whole" again what they have suffered by the death of a child.

[40] The father in the parable is rich enough to divert an entire fortune without prejudicing the family inheritance; cf. Gen 25:5-6 and note 38 above.

[41] This parable, therefore, presupposes a different rule of inheritance from that in Deut 21:15, where not "everything" is apportioned to the firstborn, but only twice as much as his brothers receive. The order of inheritance was certainly not always handled in the same way during all the centuries of ancient Israel's history, nor in early Judaism. The Bible, however, does not give exact information about this.

[42] According to 1 Sam 18:2, Saul would also have liked to bind David to himself as "fatherless."

[43] The two lists of officials are in 2 Sam 8:15-18 and 1 Kings 4:1-6. The biblical historical writers do not approve of Omri because he provided offi-

cial protection in his realm also for the followers of Baal; cf. 1 Kings 16:25. "The house of Omri" was the name given by the Assyrians to Israel even at a time when the dynasty of Omri had long ago been exterminated by the bloody revolt of Jehu; cf. the inscription of Shalmaneser (Pritchard, *The Ancient Near East,* 191–192; *ANET,* 281).

[44] Add Esth 13:6; 16:11.

[45] Cf. Acts 7:2 and 22:1. Stephen tells the Jews their history. Luke has him prove that Jews and Christians have the same "family memories." In his discourse Paul reminds them of this when Luke has him speak to his "brothers and fathers" about the "God of our ancestors"; cf. Acts 22:14.

[46] 1 Sam 22:2; 27:1-12; cf. section 1 above.

[47] For Jephthah see Judges 11 and also section 2 of ch. 3 below; for Abimelech see Judges 9.

[48] Cf. 1 Sam 22:1, 3; 18:2, 27; 24:12, 17; 26:17; 30:4, 23.

[49] 2 Sam 23:34, 39: "Eliam son of Ahithophel the Gilonite . . . Uriah the Hittite." Eliam means "God is uncle."

[50] David himself responded to Nathan's parable about the unmerciful rich man by saying that "quadruple" revenge is just in such a case (2 Sam 12:6). 2 Sam 12:15; 13:23-29; 18:9-18; 1 Kings 2:13-25 tell of the death of his four sons.

[51] For reference to the kings of the ancient Near East as "father" of their vassals, see the article *ʾab* in *TDOT* 1. In the OT the kings are not called "father," but occasionally the officials who surround them are called "father" of the king or of the land; cf. section 6 above. In the same way the king calls the prophet Elisha, the helper in Israel's wars and his counselor, "father"; on this cf. section 8 below.

[52] Cf. 1 Kings 15:3, 11; 2 Kings 14:3, among others; Matt 15:22; Mark 11:10; Luke 1:32.

[53] The judgment on Solomon is in 1 Kings 11:4; on Rehoboam see ch. 3 below.

[54] Cf. 1 Samuel 16. On the concept of the completeness of "seven" sons, cf. Ruth 4:15; Jer 15:9; Job 42:13; 2 Maccabees 7.

[55] Isa 7:11. Gideon, too, requests and is given a sign that he is really a deliverer of Israel; cf. Judg 6:17. The exhortation not to fear the enemy is also a repeated motif in the tradition of the "deliverers of Israel." Gideon had to send home all the soldiers who were afraid (Judg 7:2). On the other hand, Saul was a prisoner of his own fear when, before his last battle, he saw the army of the Philistines (1 Sam 28:15). Just as Saul trembled before the Philistines, so does Ahaz now before the two enemy kings (Isa 7:2).

[56] Isaiah calls her "the young woman." The definite article is applied to a person when it is clear who is meant by the phrase in question. When Isaiah speaks to Ahaz about "the *ʿalmā*" both of them know which woman he

means: the queen. "The *ʿalmā*" was possibly the title of the young queen before the birth of the first child.

[57] The biblical narrators probably no longer knew—or wanted to know—how the "oracle" was administered. They are nevertheless convinced that in the early times, before there were prophets, God had proclaimed the divine will in this way through the priests.

[58] According to Jer 11:18-23 Jeremiah is so hated by his relatives and his paternal house that they want to kill him. This prophetic motif appears also in the Gideon tradition in Judges 6. Saul gets into a group of ecstatic prophets, men of questionable heritage whose fathers are not known (cf. section 7 above). Isaiah proclaims that the promise for the house of David will be fulfilled even without the father, the king, who does not accept it (cf. section 7 above). Nathan belongs to those men whose paternal names are not known, yet as a prophet he dares to confront the king with his crime (see section 6 above).

[59] See section 5 above.

[60] The "people" in 19:21 (Hebrew *ʿam*) are those belonging to someone, here Elisha's "own people," his extended family. "*ʿAm YHWH,*" for example, are the "People of God."

[61] Cf. 1 Kings 18:19-20; 2 Kings 3:15-20; 4:8-10, 25, 38; 6:32.

[62] A third proof that Elisha was considered "father" of a king can be found in 2 Kings 8:9. Hazael, an Aramean officer, calls his lord, the king of Aram, "son" of Elisha. On Hazael's lips this is, of course, wicked irony, for he will seize on a word of Elisha as an occasion to murder his lord. On "father" as an honorary name for officials, cf. section 6 above.

[63] The Hebrew expression "sons of the prophets" simply denotes the prophets as individuals. Elisha takes care of "individual prophets," and they recognize him as "master" and "man of God": cf. 2 Kings 4:1, 40; 6:5.

[64] Cf. 2 Kings 8:1-6; 13:20. Throngs of despised prophets whose fathers no one knows appear also in the traditions from the disorganized period when Saul became king. On 1 Sam 10:9-13, cf. section 7 above.

[65] 2 Kings 2:3, 5, 16.

[66] John 1:13; 3:5.

[67] "Take away" in 2 Kings 2:3, 5, 10 is the same Hebrew word as in 1 Kings 19:4.

[68] In Phil 2:22 Paul mentions the idea of the brotherly cooperation of father and son. Like a "child" with its "father," Timothy fights together with Paul for the gospel of Christ.

[69] On the "father Abraham" motif, cf. Isa 51:2 and Luke 3:8; on the motif of faithfulness to the God of the ancestors, cf. Jer 11:5; Mic 7:20; Luke 1:73, et al.

[70] In John 1:38 Jesus is asked by those who are becoming his disciples, "Rabbi, where are you staying?"

[71] Scribes call Jesus "Teacher": Matt 8:18; 12:38; 22:16, 24, 36. Disciples call him "Lord": 8:21, 25; 16:22; 17:4; 18:21; 21:3; 26:22. Those in search of healing also address Jesus as "Lord": 8:2, 8; 9:28; 15:22; 17:15; 20:30. The early Christian hymn in Philippians 2 transfers the praise of God (Isa 45:23) to Jesus and ends with the confession: "Jesus Christ is Lord" (Phil 2:10-11). In Matthew not only Jesus but also God is called "Lord," cf. Matt 1:22; 2:15; 4:7; 5:33; 22:37; 27:10. In Matt 11:25 Jesus himself addresses God as "Lord."

[72] Jer 16:1-9; Ezek 24:16.

[73] In Matt 9:9 Jesus calls the tax collector Matthew, a man whose occupation was collecting money for the Roman occupying power. According to Matt 10:4, Simon the Cananaean, "the Zealot," belongs to the group of disciples. "Zealots" is what those who offered violent resistance to the Romans called themselves.

[74] In the parallel passages (Matt 19:29; Luke 18:29-30) the sequence is slightly different, but there also the father has an inconspicuous place. It is customary to begin such name lists with "father and mother"; cf. Matt 10:37 and Luke 14:26; Matt 10:35-36 and Luke 12:53.

[75] The precise nature of the relation of Jesus' "siblings" to Jesus was not important enough to the NT authors to make them feel obliged to provide information that would have made it possible to indicate whether they were the children of Mary, or children of another mother among his relatives who, because they had grown up together with Jesus, were called his "brothers and sisters."

[76] Mothers of the disciples belonged to the group of disciples or to the first congregations: Mark 15:40, 47; Acts 12:12; Rom 16:13. Only two fathers of disciples are mentioned by name, and not as "disciples" but as men who worked at their occupations: Zebedee, the father of John and James, and Simon of Cyrene, cf. Mark 15:21.

[77] In Matt 23:9 this polemic is directed against the authority of fathers; cf. ch. 3, section 4 below.

Chapter Three

The Father in His House

In contrast to the first two parts of the book, which dealt with the meaning of fathers among their people, this third part, which explores fathers' private lives, can claim no single Bible verse as a connecting thread. The very nature of the question, however, suggests a "biographical" method as a controlling theme. The investigation will follow the stations of a father's life. What do the biblical texts have to say about a young man's establishing a family? What do they say about the father's responsibility for daughters who become members of a different paternal house when they marry? How do they comment on the father's love for infants and adolescent children in his family? What do they say about the failure and powerlessness of fathers? There are expressive scenes and words about all of these themes scattered throughout the Jacob traditions. It is clear that Israel especially liked to answer the question of how a father should live with his family by citing this figure. Israel saw in Jacob the father to whom it was indebted for its name (see Gen 32:29). Thus each of the sections that follow is based on an individual motif from the Jacob traditions.

1. A new paternal house arises

"I served you fourteen years for your two daughters, and six years for your flock" (Gen 31:41)

Jacob came to Laban as a poor fugitive. Twenty years later he had become the father of a large and prosperous family. How did he manage such an ascent?

Foundations on which a man can build his family

For Jacob, everything had begun with love. For seven years he had served Laban in order to get Laban's daughter Rachel as his wife, but on the wedding night Laban had slipped Leah in on him. How reliable can love be when an amorous young man does not notice in the dark with whom he is celebrating his wedding?

Jacob is obliged to serve another seven years for Rachel and still another six years to attain the prosperity that made him and his family independent. Jacob tallies up his efforts before his father-in-law: "By day the heat consumed me, and the cold by night, and my sleep fled from my eyes" (Gen 31:40). He had worked hard for his family, but he would not have been there with his large family before Laban if Rachel and Leah had not competed with one another to bear him sons. Occasionally they even went over his head to decide with which of his wives he must have sexual relations (Gen 30:14-24). Without his love and hard work Jacob would never have become father of his family. Most important, however, was that he had been lucky. Jacob was a blessed man.

Psalm 127 speaks about God's blessing in a curiously admonishing tone:

> Unless the LORD builds the house,
> those who build it labor in vain.
> Unless the LORD guards the city,
> the guard keeps watch in vain.
> It is in vain that you rise up early
> and go late to rest,
> eating the bread of anxious toil.

The psalm speaks of the concerns of a young married man who needs a house, safety for his family, the possibility of earning a living, and, above all, for so the psalm continues, he needs sons. Three times the verse speaks of effort being "in vain." All work can really be in vain. What good, for example, is a beautiful house if the marriage is broken? Precisely the man who goes about with all his strength and love building a family for himself must consider the question of whether his family will thrive if he, as the father, thinks that the others owe everything to him alone.

Jacob is, of course, aware of the futility that threatens. When he counts up his efforts to build up his family, Laban objects: "The daughters are my daughters, the children are my children, the flocks are my flocks" (Gen 31:43). The father-in-law lays claim to his son-in-law's family. Though this would be outrageous by today's standards, within the context of this story even Jacob himself does not seem sure of his paternal rights. Secretly he had convinced his two wives to go away with him, and they had gone away clandestinely. Now Laban has pursued him, and Jacob is afraid of him.

Only a free man has paternal rights

To whom do the wives and children of a former servant belong? One of the oldest laws in the Bible deals with this question. A freedman, so it says, may take with him into freedom neither the wife his owner has given him nor the children he has with her. Nevertheless, neither may his owner hinder him from staying in the household as a slave in order to continue living with them. The law protects fatherly love, but does not require that a slaveowner give up his or her labor force.[1]

Laban had prepared things cleverly so that he could claim at least Rachel and her child. Originally Jacob had intended to take Rachel as his wife after the end of his years of service, but he had allowed Leah to be substituted, and for the sake of Rachel had been obliged to further service. Laban, however, seemingly out of sympathy for Jacob, gave him Rachel as his wife already in advance, so that he had, after all, received her from the hand of his master. How Jacob then finally manages to free everyone is excitingly told. Nowhere in the Bible is the creation of a new "paternal house"[2] told in such detail, for it is, after all, concerned with the emergence of the "house of Israel." Jacob would never have been able to pass on the name "Israel" if Laban the Aramean had actually kept him with himself.[3]

All this is told as if it were about the private experiences of a young man made strong but also defenseless by love, a faithful man but one who is also capable of being deceived. The attitude of the narrators is apparent: Love has power, but needs protection. How much better it is, then, when not love but the parents' concern brings young people together. It is with obvious pleasure that the narrators of Genesis 24 describe how a marriage happens in the proper manner. The father makes all the necessary preparations: the young people do not become acquainted until afterward: "Then Isaac brought [Rebekah] into his mother Sarah's tent. He took Rebekah, and she became his wife; and he loved her."[4] This was the series of events considered to be correct! Love developed in marriage, in the "tent of the mother," in the security of the parents' house.

An admonitory story about a marriage for love is told in Judges 14. Samson demands that his parents give him the woman who "pleases him." Their marriage is then soon broken in an evil manner. A new marriage needed parental protection for the simple reason that children were married early. On many occasions it was assumed that men would have sons already at age twenty.[5] Psalm 127 congratulates the young father of sons:

> Like arrows in the hand of a warrior are the sons of one's youth.
> Happy is the man who has his quiver full of them.
> He shall not be put to shame when he speaks with his enemies in the gate (Ps 127:4-5).

Sons who stand together are more likely to succeed than a father who stands alone in court. Among a people in which men had grown sons at an early age the ideal of the "brotherly" solidarity of father and son grew out of concrete experiences, for father and son were often equally strong.[6]

Because children were married very young, it was seldom, even in instances less complicated than that of the founding of the "house of Jacob," that marriage coincided with the establishment of an independent household. Normally the parents of the husband took the young couple into their house.[7] There is no biblical text that considers it necessary to say at what point in time the separation from the parental house occurred. Probably the young man simply grew into his own independent life. Tobit himself, for example, negotiated the salary of his son's traveling companion. After the return young Tobias, now already married, pays it out more generously than his father had agreed.[8]

Occasionally, in the event the brothers no longer live in the house of the father,[9] a distinction is made between the man's "brothers" and his "father's house." Genesis 50:8 says why the brothers moved out: they have "children, . . . flocks, . . . and . . . herds." There is no longer enough room for everyone at one place.

When all went well a young married man received paternal rights and independent fatherly responsibility only gradually. At the same time he normally remained a member of his father's kinship group.

Separation from the father's house is a precarious venture

It was anything but a foregone conclusion within the framework of biblical conceptions that a man would leave his father's kinship group and found his own "house." There is blessing for this only when the separation was not undertaken thoughtlessly. Joseph, sold by his brothers, later even becomes a high official in Egypt because he actively seizes the happiness that is offered him even in the midst of his misery. The narrators do not, of course, say that he was "happy," but that "the LORD was with Joseph" (Gen 39:2, 21). Though they derive the action entirely from human deeds, it is really God who guides Joseph's fate. It is significant at what point Joseph discovers this: "Joseph named the firstborn Manasseh, 'For,' he said, 'God has made me forget all my hardship and all my father's house'" (Gen 41:51). It is not when he becomes the chief minister that his life changes, but when he becomes a father. Now he is no longer angry at his brothers, but thankful for the new life that God has given him.

Neither Jacob nor Abraham separated himself from his paternal house on his own initiative. Jacob had to flee from his brother. Abraham obeyed a call from God. Both these two, and Joseph as well, had to take upon themselves work in foreign lands before finally having families of their own. But none of them attributed the achievement to his own strength alone. Programmatically, Gen 12:1-3 places the building up of a new relationship under the promise of God's blessing: "I will make of you a great nation."[10]

Two legends tell of men who, unlike Abraham, Jacob, and Joseph, leave their fathers' family of their own volition. Lot could not stay with Abraham because their herds had become too large. For this reason Abraham gives his nephew the choice of either the North or the South, in either of which he would have lived in hill country as a shepherd and a "kinsman" of his uncle as he had been previously. But Lot chooses the East, the city of Sodom. He barely escapes the destruction of Sodom, and in the process loses his wife and thereby also any chance to have a son in whom his family could have lived on. His daughters seduce him into incest so that, although he does become the father of new "nations," it is only as a man weighted with shame.[11]

The second legend, from Genesis 38, tells that the "house of Judah" also descended from a father who, founding his family on his own initiative alone, came to shame. Judah abandoned his brothers and took a Canaanite wife for himself because he had no father to initiate a marriage for him. Then, to make the measure of impropriety full, he went to reside with her. When he had become the father of three sons and his life was more ordered he chose a wife for his oldest son, as is proper. But this son died without children, and his brother also. Judah thought that the Canaanite daughter-in-law, Tamar, had brought about his sons' deaths, and he denied her his last son, even though this son, according to the Law, was supposed to beget descendants with her for the dead brother.[12] Tamar, disguised as a prostitute, seduced her father-in-law, and he begot twins with her.

The story relates vividly how Judah, who has just condemned his pregnant daughter-in-law to death, suddenly has in his hands proof of his own guilt. A man who, after questionable beginnings, had won respectability and even judicial authority could be tempted to extract himself from the affair. But Judah takes all the blame on himself: "She is more in the right than I" (Gen 38:26). He could have accused Tamar, for she had indeed tricked him. But his guilt is certainly the greater. A rich man certainly did not need to go to a veiled whore. As a father responsible for justice in his home, Judah failed. But as a man who accepts his guilt, he merits respect. Also worthy of admiration, however, are those who passed on the legend. They reminded a people proud of a judicial system watched over by fathers that their male ancestor had disregarded the Law out of fear of an imagined danger.

God's blessing builds a house even for a guilty father

The figure in this legend of Judah as both guilty and yet just was not simply an invented one. David, the most significant of all the sons of Judah, was the same kind of man. He, too, refrained from burdening defenseless people with his guilt. By taking Bathsheba as his wife he saw to it that the child of their adultery received a respectable place in society. When it lay dying he could have been pleased that no child of dubious origin would grow up in his house. Yet he struggled with God for its life, and after it died anyway he comforted Bathsheba. He comforted practically and successfully, for thereby was begotten Solomon, who would consolidate his kingdom. The promise of Nathan began to be fulfilled: God "built a house" for David.[13] The king attempted to lighten the burden for his wife who shared the guilt with him. Unknowingly he was thereby cooperating with God in the building up of his own house.

Without unnecessarily overworking the word "God," the legends about Lot and Judah also tell that God gave offspring to guilty fathers. Both of them would have died without offspring if desperately courageous women had not obtained sons from them by devious means. There is considerable "luck" involved when a woman becomes pregnant after a single sexual encounter. God's blessing brought to fruition what the fathers did with the women. Lot had wanted to give his daughters to the Sodomites; Judah would have permitted his daughter-in-law to die a childless widow. The biblical narrators see the very existence of the peoples of Moab and Ammon—Lot's descendants—and the tribe of Judah as a continuing sign that God does not tolerate the oppression of women by fathers.

Biblical narrators know how much depends on the love, efforts, and courage of the father in the establishment of a family, but they also warn that whoever wants to have a prestigious house for himself alone can easily fall into shame. In these legends women, too, use questionable methods to build the family, and not just Tamar and Lot's daughters, but also Rachel and Leah. All of them want to surpass the others as mothers of sons. But the narrators never point out the dangers this implies. Rachel and Leah are even praised as the women who "built up the house of Israel." Fathers must let themselves be reminded that their strength is not sufficient to build up a house: "I will make of you a great nation," God promises Abraham. "I will build a house for you," God promises David. The "house of Israel," however, was built up by two Aramean women. Why are mothers judged differently than fathers?

Judah and Lot wanted to save their lives and honor at the expense of daughters and a daughter-in-law. Leah and Rachel also struggled for respect, though not for themselves alone. Leah hoped to win the love of her husband by means of her sons. Rachel wanted to be more than just loved. She wanted to be a blessed woman, and to belong to blessed Jacob as mother of his sons. Both of them pursued something that human beings cannot achieve, but only zealously seek, namely, blessing and love. When the Bible speaks in a different way of the mothers' contribution to the building up of a family than it does of the fathers', that also has something to do with the fact that in those days it was considered to be a nonnegotiable gift of God when a woman bore children (and never the result of medical acumen). In contrast, when a wife was infertile a man always had the chance to have children by another woman.[14]

Against this background it becomes even more important to know what biblical authors think of the role that fell to a woman when she married. The following section is dedicated to this question.

2. Fathers give away their daughters

"If you illtreat my daughters . . . or . . . take wives in addition to my daughters . . ." (Gen 31:50)

Laban does not finish his sentence. Jacob is left to imagine for himself what will happen if he does anything bad to Laban's daughters! As long as Jacob lived in Laban's household Laban himself could see to it that no injustice was done to them. But then Jacob took his wives and moved away, and Laban prays, "the LORD watch between you and me, when we are absent one from the other" (Gen 31:49). The divine name occurs only once in the long story, in this sentence. YHWH freed Israel out of bondage; will YHWH not also protect women from oppression? It is significant, though, that Laban does not call for God's help as a guardian of women but as witness between himself and his son-in-law. Ancient Israelite conceptions lie behind this: Judicial conflict was men's business; parties in conflict confronted one another in the presence of persons of the locality, versed in the Law, who made sure that the conflict was settled justly. Thus Laban threatens that YHWH will assume this function as guardian of the right.

He speaks as if his daughters' rights were precious to him. Rachel and Leah themselves think differently of their father. In Jacob's presence they have raised a serious complaint against him: "Rachel and Leah answered him: Is there any portion or inheritance left to us in our father's house? Are we not regarded by him as foreigners? For he has sold us, and he has been using up the money given for us" (Gen 31:14-15). What is the money they refer to?

Why does the father receive the bride price?

Because Jacob had come to Laban as an impoverished refugee the latter had given him his daughters in marriage in consideration of fourteen years of work as a servant. The yield of his work constitutes their "portion or inheritance," say his daughters, though Laban had used it for himself. Their father had sold them off as if they were merchandise, so the two complain bitterly.

The Bible nowhere explains exactly what is to be understood by the bride price. It was certainly not, however, a purchase price. The law for the protection of a seduced woman indicates that it was for the benefit of the daughter, not the father. The seducer had to pay the bride price and marry the woman. "But if her father refuses to give her to him, he shall pay an amount equal to the bride price for virgins" (Exod 22:17). The father is not to be obliged to give his daughter to a good-for-nothing. If the father can find no man for his daughter, the bride price at least secures her life support.[15]

Rachel and Leah are justified in accusing their father. He spent the bride price as if it were money received for merchandise. He even misused the name of God, for he warns Jacob that YHWH will punish oppression though he himself had dishonored his daughters. Fortunately they did not have to depend on their father, for Jacob was a just husband.

There are other women who were not so fortunate; three other stories tell of women for whose honor neither their fathers nor anyone else would stand up.

Judges 19: A father fails to protect his daughter's rights

The book of Judges ends with a legend that tells of evil and violent deeds against a "concubine." *Pilagaš* (concubine) was the designation for a female slave who was a man's life companion, often his only one.[16] Fathers unable to feed their children often had no other choice but to sell them. The Bible does not forbid this, but teachers of the Law, prophets, and sages impressed on the men that slaves, and expressly female slaves, also have rights. The rights of daughters who had been sold were established in detail.[17] The teachers of the Law assume that a father will sell his daughter only to a man he trusts. They are therefore especially concerned that the girl does not get into the hands of anyone else. If her master or his son has taken her as a wife she has the rights of a wife or daughter; her husband could sell her only to her own father. But if she is deprived of the three rights of a wife, that is, "food, clothing, [and] marital rights," she may go away without having to be bought back (Exod 21:10-11).

The "concubine" in Judges 19 was not helped by this legal protection. "A certain Levite, residing in the remote parts of the hill country of Ephraim, took to himself a concubine from Bethlehem in Judah. But his concubine became angry with him,[18] and she went away from him to her father's house at Bethlehem in Judah" (Judg 19:1-2). Just as in these introductory sentences, the saga continues to report what happens only superficially, but always gives just enough information to permit one to imagine oneself in that situation. The distance from "remote parts of the hill country of Ephraim" to Bethlehem could not be traveled in one day. The woman must therefore have had serious reasons for going home. That they were reasons like those named in Exod 21:11 can be imagined when the end of the story is told. Her husband goes to fetch her back, and she dies on the return trip when her husband gives her to wicked street riffraff so that he and his host can have a quiet night.

If she had run away for dishonorable reasons she would hardly have gone home to her father. When the Levite came to take her back he was welcomed into "her father's house." She observed both justice and custom, and the men had to decide what was to become of her. But her father did not consider it necessary to have any discussion with his son-in-law: "the girl's father saw him and came with joy to meet him" (Judg 19:3). Was he happy again to get rid of his daughter, whom he could not afford to feed? The legend does not allow for this excuse, for the father insists that the son-in-law stay with him for five days, eating and drinking.

Whoever hears this story must doubt the efficacy of the laws of justice. The law is based on the supposition that no father will entrust his daughter to a wicked man. In vain this daughter sought her father's protection from her husband. A conflict about the rights of married daughters was settled by men. This woman died an ugly death because she allowed her husband and father to make the decision. Would her rights have been better protected if the public had kept her father and husband under scrutiny? The legend proves just the opposite.

The Levite called Israel together with a terrible sign, the body parts of his wife, whom he had dismembered. There is a decisive statement here at this turning point of the story, where the fate of an individual becomes a concern of all Israel: "Has such a thing ever happened since the day that the Israelites came up from the land of Egypt until this day?" (Judg 19:30). Here the narrators explain why they narrate only externals, but in such a way that urgent questions are posed: "Consider it, take counsel, and speak out" (Judg 19:30). Israel should be capable of judging what is right and wrong. In Egypt, Pharaoh ruled alone. But YHWH brought Israel out of Egypt in order that as a people they should take care that justice be done.

Israel fails terribly. No one grasps what the parts of the body should make everyone understand, namely that a dead person had been defiled. Armed men come together: is that Israel? Their counsel is superficial; the guilt of the husband and the father remains unremarked. Without any concern for the honor of the dead, all Israel, "as one" (Judg 20:8, 11), stands up for the supposedly wounded masculine honor of the Levite, and a war between the tribes breaks out. It is more than obvious who suffered the most from this, for at the end only men survive in the tribe of Benjamin. In order to provide women for them, a friendly city is attacked, whereby only the young women are left alive so that they can bear children for the men who exterminated their families. For these women there are no longer any fathers to whom they could return in case of need.

Because neither the men who represent "Israel" nor the father of the woman paid any attention to what happened to her, thousands died. That is the message of this gloomy legend: If those responsible had only noted the silent accusation of a person who was not even able to cry any more, they might have saved the lives of many.

Deuteronomy 22 and 1 Samuel 13: Rape is like murder

The teachers of the Deuteronomic Law entrusted the protection of married women to their parents alone. After the wedding night the parents were to secure the proof that their daughter had entered marriage as a virgin, and in case of slander by the husband, show it to the "elders of the town," who were to punish the slanderer and provide more security for the woman, also by means of a large sum of money to be deposited with her father (Deut 22:13-21). What is alarming is what would happen if the parents did not secure the proof: the woman was to be stoned at "the entrance of her father's house." Shame affects the parents; death strikes the daughter, and the people carry out the execution. Teachers of the biblical Law did not have the power to abolish evil customs. This law, however, actually endorses a terrible custom, that of taking a man's complaint, even when made long after the wedding, so seriously that it not only demands proof that the woman had been a virgin when she married, but in case this proof was lacking requires her death. Her prenuptial virginity is valued as highly as her life.

The teachers of the Law, however, were consistent enough to rate rape and murder as being on the same level.[19] Rape is no private misfortune. The Law therefore demands that if possible the woman alert the citizens of her city by means of loud screaming. If she does not, she is considered partly responsible and—therein we again perceive the unjustifiably high valuation of virginity—has forfeited her life. Whether and when these laws were applied can hardly be established, but they certainly corresponded to customs once widely practiced.

Second Samuel 13 tells about a woman for whom a cry for help was no help at all. Amnon, a son of David, has raped his half sister, Tamar. She tears her gown, puts ashes on her head, and goes away screaming. Her screams demand the help of the Law. The torn gown and the ashes are signs of mourning the dead. Tamar is as good as dead, for no one will want her any more as a wife, and she will never have children. She is a "desolate" woman, according to the narrator.[20]

Her screams are in vain, and no one calls Amnon to judgment. As the king and father, David would have a double duty to do so. But Amnon had involved him in the matter. He had pretended to be ill so that David visited him and fulfilled his request: Tamar was commanded by her father to go to Amnon because he had claimed that only food from her hand could help him. David visits his son and sends his daughter orders. At first that may seem reasonable. Must a father not be concerned with his sick child? Yet it is an evil omen. David showed paternal concern for the son. To his daughter he does not even pay the ultimate respect of establishing judicially that she was innocent.

Perhaps he is thinking politically. What will become of his kingdom if his eldest son is condemned as the "murderer" of his sister? Would not someone ask why David's adultery had not been judged by any court? The narrators demonstrate what terrible results follow when a father is indifferent to the honor of his daughter. Absalom, Tamar's full brother, takes political advantage of the situation. For Absalom the revenge murder of Amnon is the first step by which he means to get the throne for himself. In the end a civil war shakes the entire realm. None of the responsible people in Jerusalem had asked about the meaning of the cry of the "desolate" woman, and so all the people had to experience what "desolation" is.

Why do biblical authors tell stories of this kind? With total clarity they condemn fathers who disrespect their daughters. Are they protesting conditions of their times? Did fathers normally consume the money of their daughters, as did Laban? Were they indifferent to how their daughters lived with their husbands, like the father of Judges 19? Did they, like David, offer the honor of their daughters for political ends? There are two further narratives we have seen in which the fathers reveal themselves to be no better. It means nothing to Judah that his daughter-in-law is headed for ruin, but he claims rights over her, alleging that she has stained the honor of the family. Lot is willing to turn his daughters over to an evil riffraff in order to preserve his honor as a host.[21]

If fathers had really been like that, would the laws have entrusted them with the task of protecting their daughters from malicious seducers or slanderous husbands? Laws must be adjusted to daily life in order to achieve anything. But it is the exceptional cases that get told as stories. Narratives are intended to shock and motivate. The saga of Jephthah's daughter, too, reveals whom the biblical narrators want to motivate.

Judges 11: Jephthah sacrifices his daughter for the victory

Menaced by powerful foes, Jephthah wants to use a vow to extort victory from God. If he is victorious he will sacrifice whatever first comes to meet him from his house. Is he so ignorant that he does not realize that it is his only child who awaits him most eagerly? For the narrators Jephthah's vow is not only foolhardy, but blasphemous. One cannot, for the sake of God's honor, leave to chance what is to be offered. A sacrificial animal must be carefully selected.

Jephthah wins the battle, and he finds himself in the situation he should have seen coming. He does not take back his vow. Was he afraid of a God who seemingly allows extortion of the divine will? Did he think that a man must stand by his word? The narrators leave these questions open, but they reveal their opinion of Jephthah by the words they place in his mouth. His child must die, and he can think of nothing else but to complain and to accuse his daughter: "You have brought me very low; you have become the cause of great trouble to me" (Judg 11:35).

The daughter, in contrast, is admirable. She supports her father's promise without hesitation. Yet her sacrificial death is not exemplary, for it can only strengthen Jephthah in his tendency to believe more in his vow than in God. The saga portrays the tragic aberration of a child who loves a father who does not trust his God. After all, how can a little girl who has celebrated her father as a hero with dancing know that he is in the wrong?

The girl's female friends make up for what her father has denied her. They weep with her because of her young death. Israel's men make no lament. The weeping of the girls accuses a people among whom not one of those responsible for justice explains to the father, at least out of sympathy for the child, that God does not want such a sacrifice. It is not just by chance that the story begins by saying that the brothers of Jephthah, who is the son of a prostitute, first drove him away and then gave him a chance to become their leader. Israel must share the guilt for the fact that Jephthah's anxiety and pride became greater than his love for his daughter.

The stories about fathers and daughters not only describe the external aspect of outrageous occurrences, but also furnish grounds for a well-founded judgment and prompt specific questions. At first glance much seems normal, especially within the bounds of a patriarchal society. Who else should attend to justice but the men, whose strength the people need? Who else should take care of daughters if not their fathers? The narratives reveal that behind the appearance of justice and political necessity is concealed a contempt for people that is finally capable of destroying all the people. But it is not only the normalities of a patriarchal society that are questioned here. Should not a father who is concerned about his daughter appeal to God? Are father and son-in-law not to feast together? Is it not right to care personally for a son who is ill? Is it not good when a daughter lets her father send her to her ill brother? Is it not right for a girl to celebrate her father as a hero? The normalities of human conduct become questionable; the biblical storytellers teach a kind of questioning that is necessary in every age if human dignity is not to disappear under the cloak of what is considered normal.

The next chapter will turn to simpler texts that contain some ideas about fatherly authority that are still very persuasive today.

3. Paternal authority

"The same night [Jacob] got up and took his two wives, his two maids, and his eleven children, and crossed the ford of the Jabbok" (Gen 32:22)

Finally Jacob returns home as a free man with his family. At the ford of the Jabbok it becomes clear how much he had assumed with this. He gets up before dawn and spends the day helping people and cattle wade through the deep cut of the wild river. Only he himself does not get across before nightfall.

Jacob is the last to cross the Jabbok. He is the first to go out to face Esau, who is approaching with four hundred men. Jacob has good reason to fear Esau. For this reason he lines his family up with care, with Rachel and the youngest child bringing up the rear. Then he goes on alone and throws himself to the ground before Esau.[22] Such scenes make it unnecessary even to ask why women, children, and servants follow the instructions of this father.

With the same words with which the Old Testament narrators tell how much trouble Jacob had at the Jabbok, Matthew tells how willingly Joseph, Jesus' father, accepts the responsibility for his family. The angel commands him: "'Get up, take the child and his mother, and flee to Egypt.' Then Joseph got up, took the child and his mother by night, and went to Egypt" (Matt 2:13-14).

Fathers recognize their responsibility

Paternal authority can come in many different forms. At the time of the Jewish rebellions against Rome, during which the Gospel of Matthew was written, many a father had, like Joseph, secretly brought a mother and child to safety. Shepherds, who move only at the slow pace of their herds, cannot hide, flee, or fight. They must try to get along by courtesy or, if necessary, by obsequiousness, as did Jacob before Esau. It can also be an image of fatherly authority when a man humbles himself so that his family can be safe. Fatherly authority is based on a family experiencing how wisely and strongly a man accepts responsibility for his family's life, dignity, and future.

In the modern Western world, where work and family are almost always separate, a father's commitment to his family seldom becomes apparent. Is that to be regretted? Or should one go into raptures about the times when the life of the family depended on the courage and drive of the father? The Bible does not provide much basis for that kind of enthusiasm. Though one occasionally hears an appeal to the fathers' courage, it is not because the author believes fatherly authority is based on armed conflict.

On the instructions of the Persians, Nehemiah installed a well-ordered administration in Jerusalem, and had to see to the defense of the still-incomplete city wall. He mustered the people by family groups and exhorted the men: "fight for your kin, your sons, your daughters, your wives, and your homes" (Neh 4:14). Trouble with the unstable community forces him to lean on the strengths that already exist in the daily life of the families and family groups. Whoever, like the narrator, tells of men who are prepared to defend the state knows how happy would be the land in which family fathers would not need to be trained warriors.

Israel had once experienced a happy era of this kind. In 1 Kings 4:25 we find a description of how a good period was imagined within the agricultural milieu of the Israelite hill country. The best thing about Solomon's reign is said to have been that grape vines and fig trees were allowed to grow tall enough that everyone had a place to rest peacefully in the shade, content to know that manly courage was not in demand. For Solomon, it was explained, had a professional army, "forty thousand stalls of horses for his chariots, and twelve thousand horsemen" (1 Kings 4:26).

Is there a form of paternal authority also for the everyday routine and for peacetime? A saying reveals what was thought about this in Israel: "A son honors his father, and servants their master" (Mal 1:6). Worthy of note is in what sense son and servant, father and master are similar to one another. The authority of the proper father and the good master do not become visible in their power of command but in their claim to honor.[23] How seriously the distinction is made can be seen from a story in 1 Kings 12.

1 Kings 12: Solomon's son despises his father

After Solomon's death the northern tribes asked Rehoboam, Solomon's son, for relief from the burdens that Solomon had laid upon them. The government officials advised Rehoboam to agree, but Rehoboam allowed his childhood friends to goad him into threatening even harder impositions. The arrogance of these young people is revealed in the obscenity of their speech: "Thus you should say to this people . . . 'My little finger [a slang word for the penis] is thicker than my father's loins [power of begetting]'" (1 Kings 12:10).

One should not speak so contemptuously to representatives of the tribes, and the result was rebellion. Rehoboam fled and one of the old officials died in a hail of stones. The story speaks with highest respect of the old man who puts his life on the line for the son of his old master, even though Rehoboam had ignored his counsel. The story attributes to Rehoboam's foolish arrogance the blame for the division of the kingdom into two hostile states that caused the people to suffer for hundreds of years. It reads like a commentary on the commandment to honor father and mother: "Honor your father and your mother, so that your days may be long in the land that the LORD your God is giving you" (Exod 20:12).[24]

Rehoboam's offense was not that he did not follow his father's example. On the contrary, if he had dealt less harshly with the free tribes than had Solomon, he would have been able to "live long" in the northern kingdom. The promise of life that is linked to the commandment about respect for father and mother is inoperative for him because by parading his virility he has sullied his father's honor.

A son should honor his father. This motif runs through all of ancient Near Eastern literature. An epic from Ugarit, the Tale of Aqhat,[25] enumerates situations in which a father needs a son: "So shall there be a son in his house . . . who takes him by the hand when he's drunk, carries him when he's sated with wine . . . who plasters his roof when it leaks."

When a father can no longer care for his own honor, a real son sees to it that he is spared from being shamed. Over a thousand years later Jesus Ben Sirach says much the same: "My child, help your father in his old age, and do not grieve him as long as he lives; even if his mind fails, be patient with him; because you have all your faculties do not despise him" (Sir 3:12-13).

In the Tale of Aqhat epic the message is that a king needs a good son. According to 1 Kings 12 disaster strikes the land because the son of a king despises his father. But in the commandment about respecting one's parents the Decalogue lays on every adult the responsibility for the welfare of the entire country that God has given to God's people. The story of Noah and his sons explains why it is more than just an annoyance within the family when a son is contemptuous of his father.

Genesis 9:20-27: When a father is despised, brotherliness dies

Noah lies in his tent inebriated and naked, and is found in this condition by his son Ham. One is reminded of the Tale of Aqhat, which says that the son is to protect the honor of his father when he is drunk.[26] That would have been easy for Ham; he would only have had to be quiet about what he had seen. But he tells his two brothers about their father's shame. These two, however, go in and cover Noah while averting their eyes. Succinct as this story is in other respects, the scene requires many words and is almost surrealistic: walking backwards, the two carry the blanket on their shoulders to their father. This picture is certainly no repetition of an image from the everyday life of the family. The mottos at the end of the narrative make it entirely clear that in Noah's sons, principles of public life are spelled out. When Noah hears what has happened he curses the son who left him lying helpless: "lowest of slaves shall he be to his brothers" (Gen 9:25). Brothers have become masters and servant. Whoever instigates contempt for the helpless will find himself subject to the will of the stronger, as well. Companionship in wickedness is not compatible with brotherliness. With this the narrative takes up the theme of the commandment to honor father and mother. The son who honors his father finds life. Noah merits double honor. The sons owe their lives to him, for because of him they escaped the Deluge, and it is scandalous to forget that as soon as the father stumbles. In addition, the story speaks of Noah as the inventor of viticulture, which is so highly valued in the Mediterranean region. It is foolish to despise a father from whom something so valuable can be learned.

Many biblical and nonbiblical texts from antiquity understand paternal authority as above all teaching authority. The story of Noah clearly shows the characteristic form of this motif: the father can teach his sons winegrowing, but his sons ought to use this knowledge differently than he had done. Just as soon as a new cultural asset is discovered it becomes evident that the invention is stronger than its inventor, and Noah is helplessly delivered over to the ridicule of his son. Like the Rehoboam story, this one demonstrates that while there are good reasons to honor the father, it is not a good idea to simply imitate him. The next section takes a critical look at the topic of the father's teaching authority.

4. Fathers teach their sons

"When Jacob ended his charge to his sons, he drew up his feet into the bed, breathed his last, and was gathered to his people" (Gen 49:33)

Acting as though he were in control of the time of his death, Jacob turns his deathbed into a lecture podium and dispenses a long farewell speech to his sons. It begins solemnly: "Assemble and hear, O sons of Jacob; listen to Israel your father" (Gen 49:2). This scene does not describe Jacob's death as it could have happened. It represents an idea of the relation of a father to his sons that was highly significant throughout antiquity.

Fathers and sons constitute the chain of bearers of tradition

An Egyptian teacher of the third millennium B.C.E. was convinced that it pays for the son to listen to his father: "If he has grown old, he acquires great honor, and he speaks thus to his children by renewing the teaching of the father . . . so that they in turn may tell it to their children."[27] A biblical prophet of thousands of years later does not speak much differently: "Tell your children of it, and let your children tell their children, and their children another generation" (Joel 1:3).

The more rapid the sequence of new and unimagined problems humanity must face, the more alien the thought becomes that fathers deserve respect because they pass on wisdom. It occurs constantly in the Bible: fathers instruct their sons about history, the order of the world, festival customs, laws, practical expedients, and the entire style of life.[28] Sometimes it involves nothing more than the thoughtless repetition of formulas of speech. Deuteronomic preachers, on the one hand, encourage everyone to learn the Law in the assembly of Israel: "men, women, and children, as well as the aliens residing in your towns."[29] But when they speak of learning in the family, they think only of the father instructing the son.[30] Probably they had become accustomed by the schooling process to speak in this way, for in schools for priests and officials the teachers were called "fathers" and the students "sons."[31] With their established patterns of school language, the teachers of Deuteronomy unintentionally contributed to solidifying the opinion that the traditions of God's people are best entrusted to fatherly teaching authorities, an opinion that persists down to the present day. But the ancient topic of the teaching authority of fathers does not go uncontested in the Bible.

The issue of a father's authority to teach

In Prov 17:6 the thought that the aged merit honor as the bearers of tradition is modified in a "typically biblical" manner: Just as father and son are to be fond of one another in a "brotherly" way, so young and old redound mutually to one another's honor.

> Grandchildren are the crown of the aged,
> and the glory of children is their parents (Prov 17:6).

The criticism becomes clearer in other places. While the book of Job bitterly opposes the teaching of the elders because they do not really help in time of trouble (Job 12:12), Ps 119:100 soberly emphasizes the superiority of a young man: "I understand more than the aged, for I keep your precepts." The psalmist does not reject the traditions, for this entire psalm speaks the traditional language, but the author declares that what matters is the truth that has been experienced and practiced in life, which is often more likely to disclose itself to the young than to the old, who often limit themselves to what has already been pondered and repeated.

This little rivulet of debate within the broad stream of voices who merely parroted the teaching about fathers gave early Christian teachers courage to perceive in the message of Jesus the renewal of Israel's faith. Matthew's Gospel maintains, on the one hand, that "not one letter, not one stroke of a letter, will pass from the law until all is accomplished" and warns, on the other hand, that one should not be content with what "was said to those of ancient times" (Matt 5:18, 21). In Matthew we also find the most distinct biblical rejection of the teaching authority of fathers: "and call no one [of you][32] your father on earth." This sentence is framed by two similar exhortations: there are to be no rabbis or "masters" among the disciples, for teaching authority belongs to Christ alone: "you are all students" (Matt 23:8). The key expression "students" [Greek: "brothers"] may well have given the occasion for inserting the "father" sentence among the statements that Christ alone is teacher. Christians were convinced that women, too, were "brothers," that is, fellow inhabitants and heirs in the household of God.[33] However, the expression also contributed to the eventual exclusion of women when questions of doctrine were up for discussion. That "brothers" also included "sisters" was ignored.

The Bible has an overwhelming majority of references showing that traditions are entrusted to fathers and sons. Nevertheless, the exclusion of women from "brotherly" learning and teaching within the People of God cannot be justified by citing the Bible, for in those places where formulas were not simply repeated, but where there was serious thought given to the common life of the people of God, the topic of the "teaching of the fathers" is not to be found. In this new era, when daughters have the same chances to learn as do sons, what was begun here might finally be realized.

There is another topic from the literature of antiquity that cannot be allowed to stand unchallenged: fathers are often reminded of their right, even their duty, to discipline their sons.

Should fathers discipline their sons?

Biblical wisdom teachers adopted this topic, together with many others, from Egyptian examples. In hieroglyphic writing, words for "education" were always accompanied by the determinative "man striking" symbol. An Egyptian exhorts:

> A son does not die from a thrashing at his father's hand . . .
> But whoever loves his son so much that he perishes
> destroys himself.[34]

A biblical saying has much the same message:

> Those who spare the rod hate their children,
> but those who love them are diligent to discipline them
> (Prov 13:24).

Many sayings urge the children to take to heart the punishment of the parents, as well as encouraging parents to make use of the rod.[35] In the Jerusalem Bible translation one of them sounds as if some parents had chosen a punishment much more severe than the rod:

> All the while there is hope, chastise your son,
> but do not set out to destroy him altogether (Prov 19:18).

Was it necessary to warn fathers not to kill their children in anger? Is the saying actually opposing a "paternal right" over the life of a child?[36] A literal translation of Prov 19:18 echoes the ancient Egyptian saying:

> Discipline your son, that is hopeful;
> Do not kill him; do not destroy your own longing for life!

An "ill-mannered" son will hasten to an early death, and the father is then guilty not just of his son's death but also for the fact that there is no one to continue his life work.

The story of the great crisis of state in David's realm describes how much misery is caused by inappropriate paternal love. It brings death to the son and civil war to the entire nation. David should not have granted amnesty to his fratricidal son Absalom or permitted him to return home: "So he came to the king and prostrated himself with his face to the ground before the king; and the king kissed Absalom" (2 Sam 14:33). The narrators have good reason to refer repeatedly in this scene to David as the king, for only a king has the right to disregard the law and kiss the murderer. Yet David was guilty of having forgotten that he was the king. He brings back the son who will provoke rebellion and civil war. The story urgently emphasizes how important it is to educate with firmness a son who will bear political responsibility.

In contrast to what is said in the adage, there never appears in the biblical narratives a father who disciplines his son. On the contrary, fathers suffer under their sons and fail to defend themselves (see section 8 below). Do the teachers of wisdom talk so much about the rod because fathers seldom applied it? Concerns for the public welfare can be heard in their exhortations. In free Israel all free men belonged to the politically responsible. Thus this would certainly apply even more to the young men who had been educated in the schools for public servants. If their training failed, many would be put at risk. But should the rod be used to educate people who would later bear responsibility for others?

The "strong hand" of mothers

The messenger of God gives the mother Hagar a different kind of counsel: "Come, lift up the boy and hold him fast with your hand, for I will make a great nation of him" (Gen 21:18). Every leader of human beings should have experienced being led by a strong hand. According to the story in Genesis 21 that can also be a mother's hand. Hagar has to assume the father's duties for her son because Abraham had sent her away, and the divine messenger encourages her. The final sentence of the legend confirms that she succeeded in doing so. Hagar does what fathers usually do: "His mother got a wife for him from the land of Egypt" (Gen 21:21).

A heading in the book of Proverbs tells of a mother who trains her son in political responsibility: "The words of King Lemuel. An oracle that his mother taught him" (Prov 31:1). The word here translated as "taught" ordinarily connotes "to discipline with the rod." The mother "disciplines" with her words. If necessary a young man who had gone astray could also sometimes be corrected with a switch. Yet the education of a person who may bear royal responsibility for others must be done differently. Lemuel's mother does not try to convince her son how superior to him she is. She speaks to him from the heart:

> "No, my son! No, son of my womb!
> No, son of my vows!"

Her correction grows out of a love that shows high respect for the son, something that gives him self-esteem.

Fathers, do not provoke your children to anger!

The sayings about the "corporal punishment" of the child had more effect in the history of upbringing than did the "correction" that Lemuel received from his mother. Proof of this is provided already by a late biblical writing. At the time of Jesus Ben Sirach the "undisciplined" son could no longer plunge his land into misfortune, for the Jews had long since lost their political freedom. Sirach nevertheless persists in the opinion that a father must discipline his son:

> Bow down his neck in his youth,
> and beat his sides while he is young . . .
> Discipline your son, and make his yoke heavy,
> so that you may not be offended by his shamelessness
> (Sir 30:12).

The older aphoristic wisdom advises that students and growing children be disciplined. Sirach, however, thinks a father must assert himself against the child with blows. How miserable the authority that has to prove itself this way!

Fortunately, there are later biblical voices with a different message. The letters to the Ephesians and to the Colossians also bear the marks of having originated in a politically unfree society. The commandment about parents, which originally urged adult sons to protect their parents' honor, becomes a commandment of obedience for children. The promise that belongs with it has lost its political meaning, and now promises the obedient child a reward: "Children, obey your parents in the Lord, for this is right" (Eph 6:1; cf. Col 3:20). "Honor your father and your mother." This is the first commandment with a promise: "so that your days may be long in the land that the LORD your God is giving you" (Exod 20:12).

The Christian mission had much success with the lower social classes, slaves, and women, who valued the fact that in the community of Christians everyone was regarded as a "brother," but the congregations attached even greater worth to appearing before the public as a respectable group. For this reason the admonitions in the letters to the Ephesians and Colossians urge not only the children but also women and slaves to respect the authority of the father of the house as was expected in those days.[37]

But the conviction, inherited from the first People of God, that fathers, too, should be "brothers," continued to have its effect. "Bow down his neck!" Jesus Ben Sirach exhorts. And yet the family rules in these letters contradict him: "Fathers, do not provoke your children, or they may lose heart" (Col 3:21). "And, fathers, do not provoke your children to anger" (Eph 6:4). Such admonitions would not have been recorded if they had not been necessary. There must have been some fathers who intimidated their children and provoked them to rage. But when the leader of the congregation cautioned the fathers in this way the children, who had themselves just previously been addressed, must certainly have paid close attention. When they understood that their fathers were being publicly reminded before the congregation of their limits, that was at least a help to them in maintaining their self-respect and courage.

The idea that paternal teaching authority carried with it the right to discipline is derived from proverbial wisdom. That means it belongs to the "province of pedagogy," not the everyday life of the family. A great theme of the Bible, the love between father and son, appears in the "Wisdom literature" only as a warning against failed paternal love. Narrators who were concerned with the meaning of paternal love for the history of Israel speak much more subtly (see ch. 2 above, sections 2 and 3). In the section that follows this theme will be taken up once more in order to show how biblical texts speak of paternal love as a power at work inside the family.

5. How fathers love their sons

"His life is bound up in the boy's life" (Gen 44:30)

So says Judah, Jacob's son, about his father and his youngest brother. Without suspecting it he thereby brings a serious conflict to a positive end. The brothers had once sold their hated brother Joseph, favored by his father, as a slave. As a high official in Egypt, Joseph has a chance to test his brothers. With patient cunning he is able to maneuver them once more into the same situation. Once more the father could lose his only beloved son, and this time the brothers could even consider themselves innocent, for Joseph has arranged things so that Benjamin seems to be a thief, and is justly arrested. Nevertheless, Judah lays his life on the line for his father's self-willed favoritism. He wants to remain in his brother's place as a slave in Egypt because "his [the father's] life is bound up in the boy's life."

May a father love one son more than all the others? Do the authors of the story believe Judah is right? In what follows, other biblical texts will first be examined in terms of what they have to say about fatherly love. Against this background it will then become clear how intensively the story of Joseph pursues the question of the nature of fatherly love.

Fathers and little children

How does a father love his little child? The Bible says little about it. That is not because fathers were indifferent to small children.[38] On the contrary, the two Old Testament texts that tell about a father and his little child describe how much a baby can mean to its father. The first text is an episode in the long story about the crisis of state in David's realm. David's adultery with Bathsheba could have remained an infidelity without consequences if David had not sired a child. With the husband's murder David thought he could hush everything up; he takes Bathsheba as his wife and the child is born in his house. When the prophet announces to him the death of the child David could have been happy that no son of dubious ancestry would grow up in his house. Yet he fights for the life of the child, praying and fasting so excessively for days on end that no one dares to tell him when the child dies.

The second text is a saga of Abraham. Abraham's son by his maid is a happy child who "makes everyone laugh,"[39] which Sarah cannot stand. Is this foreigner's child going to usurp the place of her son, whose very name (Isaac means "he laughs") shows that he is the one who is to laugh in the house of Abraham? Sarah demands that Abraham reject Ishmael. But Ishmael is more important to Abraham than avoiding marital conflict: "The matter was very distressing to Abraham on account of his son" (Gen 21:11).

The continuation of the story, of course, portrays another image of this father. A command from God moves Abraham to give in and send Hagar away with Ishmael. The narrators, however, do not excuse Abraham on this account. Though it is true that he obeyed God, he should not have done so in this manner. The Law of Israel demanded that when a man sent away a slave—especially a female slave—he must provide for her and make sure she was able to start a new life in freedom. Abraham does not give Hagar even enough to enable her to survive. Hagar is at a loss for help, and Ishmael would have perished if a messenger of God had not urged her to take her child "fast with your hand."[40]

There are fathers who, though they take pleasure in their children, do not give them what is necessary to live. The narrators' low opinion of Abraham's attitude shows up in the contrast they draw with God's attitude: "God heard the voice of the boy" (Gen 21:17). God does not remain indifferent when a child cries in hunger.

This legend is not, of course, told only to criticize fathers. It is a tale of the future destiny of nations. Ishmael is the progenitor of stalwart desert tribes who often made life difficult for Israel. Israel was to keep in mind that enmities do not always arise only out of the wickedness of others.[41] The story of David, too, has to do with a political question. David himself wants to bear the results of his own guilt. If David can help it, the child of adultery will not suffer from the fault of the father.[42] Such a king merits Israel's trust.

The Bible says so little about the father's affection for a little child because it is one of the daily and natural features of private family life, about which biblical authors speak only when such things have to do with their principal topic, that is, the basis on which the People of God live out their fellowship with one another. When they do speak of fathers and children, however, they show how highly such a little child is valued: a king fights for a little child's right to live, and a mother who has been left in misery by the father is encouraged by God to lead her child into life.

The father and the only son

How can it work: living as the people chosen by God? This principal question asked by biblical authors does not deter them from attention to the individual. The Bible was formed within a culture that considered many sons a cause for happiness: "Happy is the man who has his quiver full of them" (Ps 127:5). It is therefore remarkable how many stories deal with a father and a single son. Saul and his father worry about one another; Jonathan stands at his father's side like a brother, and Saul is attached to Jonathan. The father cannot free himself even from a son who has gone wrong. Samson's father goes to his son's wedding even though, to his parents' distress, the latter enters into a bad marriage. David kisses the fratricide Absalom.[43] A father's distress and love focus on one son even when he has many.

The "one" son is not always the firstborn. In the Joseph story the father favors, each in his turn, the two youngest. Abraham's true son, Isaac, is also the younger and, like Joseph and Benjamin, the son of the only wife loved by his father. The narrators concede to fatherly love the same right that also characterizes the love between man and woman, namely the right to choose. This they observed from life. Love is never doled out wholesale; it is always the "only" child who is loved.[44] The teachers of Deuteronomy are connoisseurs of human nature who know that though love does not allow itself to be regulated, it should not disturb the peace of the family. Therefore they order that at the distribution of the inheritance the father must be justly generous also to the unloved son (Deut 21:15-17).

The very image of his father

Certainly it is only rarely that a father's love comes into conflict with his concern for the inheritance. One of the greatest of human joys is to be able to give the fruit of one's work to well-loved progeny. That is true today and was so thousands of years ago when Egyptian teachers of wisdom declared how good it is when fathers have sons who "receive what they have created."[45] Jesus Ben Sirach praises the son who cares for his father's inheritance: "When the father dies he will not seem to be dead, for he has left behind him one like himself" (Sir 30:4). Sirach uses a word that has become highly significant through its use in the creation story in Genesis 1:

> So God created humankind in his image,
> in the image of God he created them;
> male and female he created them (Gen 1:27).

God, so these authors dare to say, deposits in human beings the same hope that a father places in his son and heir. God hopes that God's work, the whole creation, will be preserved by them. But God passes on this inheritance differently than did the fathers in Israel. In ancient Israel a "father" in the full sense of the word was only the man who could bequeath an inheritance to a son. Women could inherit only if necessary, and only as representatives of their sons. God, on the other hand, entrusted to men and women the preservation of the divine work. God created a double image of God's own self, a masculine and a feminine.[46]

In Genesis 1 one of the greatest inner strengths known in ancient Israel becomes a sign of how profoundly God is committed to human beings. The hope that the inheritance would continue to be well cared for deeply concerns fathers in the agricultural people of Israel. Death cannot totally destroy the life of a father who has a good son who will continue his work. To a man who has no son, in contrast, the assurance of God's blessing gives only reason to lament: "O Lord GOD, what will you give me, for I continue childless, and the heir of my house is Eliezer of Damascus?" (Gen 15:2). Abram has no son; when he dies, everything will belong to a stranger. What is a blessing good for if a human being receives it only for his or her own short life span?

Pitiable is the man who has sons but loses his inheritance. According to 1 Chr 3:16-17 King Jehoiakim had sons, yet Jeremiah mourns him as "childless" because none of his sons was able to continue the royal succession (Jer 22:30). Only the man whose son continues the life of his father when death takes him away has real participation in life.

Against the background of all that biblical texts say about the bonds that bind the father to the son, the curiously different tone in which the Joseph story speaks becomes apparent. The happiness with a son and heir pales before the stronger feeling of paternal love.

The son set free

At first glance the main theme of the story of Joseph seems to be one of fraternal conflict and reconciliation. The inner unity of the story, however, is established by the theme of paternal love. At the beginning the image of Joseph's exaltation takes root in the father's memory, where it remains until Jacob sees it before him as concrete reality. Though Jacob is irritated at the naïve young showoff who relates dreams in which he sees himself as the honored center of the family, the narrators nonetheless add: "but his father kept the matter in mind" (Gen 37:11). They speak with foresight of the time when the family will in fact bow down before Joseph, the administrator of Egypt. There are fathers who resemble Jacob in this; they pay attention to their child with the alertness of love, and when it is grown they recall that one could already see in the child what was to become of it.[47] When Jacob is forced to believe that Joseph is dead, it is also fatherly love that makes every other kind of paternal satisfaction seem worthless to him: "All his sons and all his daughters sought to comfort him; but he refused to be comforted, and said, 'No, I shall go down to Sheol to my son, mourning'" (Gen 37:35). Only in this scene do the narrators mention the women of the family. Their appearance has significance: Jacob could see how powerfully his own life was continuing in the families of his sons and daughters-in-law. But he finds no comfort in this. Comfort does not deny the pain, but shows that life goes on and continues to be worthwhile. But Jacob no longer has eyes for this. Curiously, when Jacob finally sees his beloved son again, he once more speaks of death: "Israel said to Joseph, 'I can die now, having seen for myself that you are still alive'" (Gen 46:30).

The Song of Solomon compares love and death: "love is as strong as death" (Song 8:6). Both exercise the same power. Love demands the whole person including body as well as soul, as death also does. To someone in love, the life of the beloved is just as important as is his or her own life. What later poetry says hyperbolically about love between man and woman is said here, simply and understandably, about the love of fathers. Jacob could have been disappointed in how different Joseph had become. Joseph himself makes that unmistakably clear to him when he says, "all shepherds are abhorrent to the Egyptians" (Gen 46:34). As the father of a family of shepherds Jacob will spend the end of his life with his unloved sons in Goshen, the land of the "abominable" shepherds. The story emphasizes how "Egyptian" Joseph has become when it reports how skillfully Joseph has dedicated himself to specifically Egyptian tasks (Gen 47:13-14). There is no reason, however, to lament this alienation. On the contrary, because Jacob stays in Goshen there is no danger that his kinship group will take on an Egyptian lifestyle and fail to become "Israel." And because Joseph remains in Egypt the family of Jacob does not die out, for as administrator of Egypt Joseph provides bread for them.

By giving this twist to events the narrators criticize the manner in which Jacob had previously "bound up" his life with that of his son. Jacob's paternal love needed to mature. He refused to let Benjamin go away. When he had found Joseph he no longer wanted anything but to see his son alive. That was enough for him, but also the only thing capable of giving a meaning to his life that even death could not affect.

With the help of an implausible plot twist the Joseph story portrays how Jacob learned the mature paternal love that allowed his son to have his own, alien life. Joseph becomes administrator of Egypt and Jacob remains a shepherd. In reality, in those days only unusual circumstances could alienate a son from the life of his father. Daughters, on the other hand, left their father's house, and in a daughter a father could not love what he hoped for himself, neither the strengthening of his domestic power nor the hope for descendants. Jesus Ben Sirach laments that a daughter brings her father nothing but cares.[48] Any man who loved his daughter would have to do so for herself alone. Hardly ever does anyone speak of the love of fathers for their daughters, however. Is that because the love that "brings in nothing" is rare? With this issue in mind, the following section is again dedicated to the theme of "fathers and daughters."

6. How fathers love their daughters

"Afterwards [Leah] bore a daughter, and named her Dinah"
(Gen 30:21)

Leah had greeted each of her sons at birth with an aphorism. With each of these sayings she spoke of her hope finally to win Jacob's love. For Dinah she coins no aphorism; for the sake of a daughter

Jacob will certainly not give her the affection that her sons had not earned her.

Only two biblical texts tell of fathers who love a daughter. A third does so at least comparatively. Why does this theme find hardly any interest among biblical writers? Are they of the opinion that love for a daughter, as opposed to love between father and son, belongs only in the private, interior space of the family, and is therefore not relevant to the questions that move them, questions about the foundations of the life of the entire People of God? At first glance the first of these three texts seems to confirm this. It is therefore just that much more surprising when it then becomes clear that the welfare of all Israel depends on whether a father loves his daughter.

A poor man loves his lamb like a daughter (2 Sam 12:3)

A poor man owned a single ewe lamb. It grew and matured in his house along with his children. It ate of his bread and drank from his cup. It lay in his lap and was like a daughter to him.

It hardly seems of general interest how profoundly a poor man had hung his heart on a lamb. As king of his people, however, David is convinced that it is his concern. When Nathan tells him that a rich man had taken the lamb and slaughtered it, David immediately takes the side of the poor man. He is outraged: "the man who has done this deserves to die!" A king has to defend the private welfare of the poor. But with a few short words the prophet turns David's judgment back on himself: "You are the man!" The people must be protected from a king who breaks into the private life of others and destroys it, as David did in his adultery with Bathsheba and his murder of Uriah.

The parable of the poor man's lamb has a key function in the long narrative about the crisis of state in David's kingdom. The next episode demonstrates how explosive the comparison of the lamb with the daughter was. If David had prized his daughter Tamar as much as the poor man did his lamb, he would have recognized the danger that threatened her from her brother Amnon, and then many disasters would have been averted for the entire people (see section 2 above).

Job's daughters have the right of domicile with their father

The second text was discussed from another perspective in an earlier section of this book. Job regains an incredible measure of his original happiness at the end of his story. But Job himself contributes something to it. He takes pains to ensure that he will never again lose the delight that he finds with his daughters. Just like their brothers, they can remain within their father's inheritance based on their own rights. The book of Job alludes to many older traditions, generally very critically. The fact that his daughters' exceptional right of inheritance belongs to the image of Job's new happiness constitutes an answer to the questions provoked by the gloomy stories about the disdain for daughters. When God makes the divine presence felt and human beings allow themselves to be moved by this to conduct themselves justly, then alienation no longer threatens a father's love for his daughters.[49]

The comparison of the lamb with the daughter and the statement about the right of inheritance of Job's daughters are succinctly formulated and easy to understand. But today the time has come to bring both texts into the light and to highlight them. Fatherly love of daughters has meaning beyond the realm of merely private happiness. More and more people are coming to recognize how much is at stake for all humanity, and so also for the Church, in the question of whether women will find the courage to apply themselves in public with all their strengths. A father who gives his daughter loving recognition awakens courage of this kind. It is therefore good that, in a detailed story from the New Testament, a father who loves his daughter occupies center stage.

Jairus loves his daughter

As governor of the synagogue Jairus is, so to speak, professionally obliged to maintain a dignified demeanor, especially when confronted by a miracle-worker with a popular following. Nevertheless, with a gesture that certainly must have seemed just as exaggerated in those days as it would today, he throws himself at the feet of Jesus, in full view of many people of his city, and pleads on behalf of his sick daughter. The father seeks help for his child: what does he care about his public reputation? Jesus is immediately prepared to go with Jairus to his house, but on the way he allows himself to be detained until it is "too late." People come and inform Jairus: "Your daughter is dead. Why trouble the teacher any further?" (Mark 5:35). These people may be forgiven for their unbelief. How could they imagine that Jesus could still help? But it is hard to understand the tone they use with

Jairus. They show concern for the teacher, but they have nothing but reproach for the father who has lost a child. Or are they perhaps of the opinion that no one needs to mourn the loss of a daughter?

It seems curious that Jesus lets things go that far. The crowd obeys him, as is demonstrated when he sends it away. Why did he not do so right away? Had he not noticed how urgently Jairus needed help? Mark forms the story in such a way that one has to ask who Jesus really is. He is the helper who immediately follows a father who pleads for his child. But those hard-hearted people are also correct when they describe Jesus as a teacher. He allows himself to be detained because he wants to teach Jairus what faith means. At first it may seem incomprehensible that Jesus takes time for this while the father is anxious about his child. At the end of the story, however, it will be seen that this was just the way by which Jairus won life for his child.

Jesus does not use a know-it-all attitude of superiority to teach Jairus. He gives him a chance to discover for himself the power of faith. In the crowd that detains him, a woman who has been hemorrhaging for years manages to touch Jesus without being noticed. Her hope comes true; she discovers that she has been healed. In a far more literal sense than is understood today she is given her life back. Hemorrhages were considered a sign of life flowing away, of a body at the mercy of death. But Jewish piety honored the living God by not allowing anyone who bore such a sign of death in his or her body to come into the divine presence. Blood, as they expressed it, makes one "unclean," that is, incapable of calling on the living God.[50]

Jairus would have noticed nothing of this miracle. But Jesus does not let the woman slip away. He moves her to confess "the whole truth" before all the people. This request also seems strange. Did Jesus not see how difficult it must have been for her to tell the story of her healing before all the people? As "unclean," she would have been obliged to stay away from her people. For uncleanness is "contagious": whoever touched her could not again participate in the worship service without first completing the requirements for purification. But how could people who unavoidably touch others in a crowd know that they would have to purify themselves before coming into the presence of God? The woman was reckoning with the fact that God's honor would be offended. If she had met someone who knew about her ailment, many things could have happened. People who believe that they are defending God's honor can be terrible. Jesus demanded a public confession from the woman so that all could know that she was clean. Above all, she herself is to know that she has done nothing wrong. Jesus expressly confirms it to her, saying, "Daughter, your faith has made you well" (Mark 5:34). She had trusted that it was better to endanger God's honor than to continue excluded from the People of God. And that, says Jesus, is the faith that had rescued her from the power of "unclean" death.

Mark's decision to insert this incident here was well considered. Jairus, the man who would soon hear that his daughter had died, is her witness, and the evangelist shows that Jesus had not forgotten him and his anxiety for his daughter. An indication of this is given by the "fatherly" form of address to the woman who had been healed, inappropriate from the mouth of the young Jesus, and one he never otherwise used: "Daughter!" In addition, Mark tells that the hard-hearted messengers of death came while Jesus was still speaking with the woman. But Jesus notices them and is immediately ready to help Jairus, saying, "Do not fear, only believe" (Mark 5:36). The double exhortation makes clear that the time in which Jesus had spoken to the woman was not lost time. "Only believe!" Jairus had seen in the woman what faith is. She had trusted that God is less concerned with divine honor than that she, rescued from the power of death, might belong to the People of God. "Do not fear!" Jairus need not fear that he cannot produce that kind of faith, for just as the woman presented herself to God, so he himself had already done: he disregarded his own reputation when he pleaded with Jesus for his daughter and threw himself to the ground before him.

Mark turns the miracle story into a story about the kind of faith taught by Jesus. The miracle itself happens quite unspectacularly. Jesus awakens the child just as do parents waking a child who had perhaps overslept: "Talitha cum!" ("Little girl, get up!"). The miracle of the raising appears like a bit of everyday family life. Jesus helps all the participants out of their overwhelming astonishment by saying that they should "give her something to eat" (Mark 5:42).

The resurrection is meant to seem at first to the girl like an everyday occurrence. It does not do any child good to be the focus of appalled amazement. But the parents, too, should not become mere astonished witnesses of a great miracle. They are parents first and foremost, and they should take care of their child. Finally, the three disciples whom Jesus had taken along are also witnesses of the miracle.

They, too, are to see that the love of parents who take care to see that a child can live, even if only by giving it something to eat, is more closely related to faith than is astonishment at an exceptional event.

At the end Mark adds another bit of information. The daughter is twelve years old. She is at an age to be married. Soon she will leave her father's house and give her life force to another family. Jairus had not won her back for himself. A father's love, like any love, is distinguished by loving the other just as well as oneself, and for just that reason being prepared to give one's life to the other. The story of Jairus shows that such a love is a fertile ground for the faith that Jesus taught: the faith that gives life.

Despite all this, the Bible's most famous father story, Genesis 22, describes how Abraham, "father of faith," is prepared to kill his only beloved son. What kind of faith is this? In the next section we will seek access to this story.

7. Abraham binds his son (Genesis 22)

A father receives a dreadful command from God. He is to sacrifice his son, and immediately he gets up to do what is demanded of him. Not until the last moment, when he has already raised the knife, does a messenger from God stop him. What kind of conception of God does this story convey? What kind of faith is this, that brings a man to this point?

A provocative story

The narrative in Genesis 22 resists all efforts to nullify its provocative nature. "Abraham built an altar there and laid the wood in order. He bound his son Isaac, and laid him on the altar, on top of the wood" (Gen 22:9).

How obedient may a child be to his father and a man to his God? The narrator has thought himself into even the powerfully concrete details of this question. He does not say how Isaac reacted to the realization that he was to be the sacrifice. Perhaps he continued obedient even then.

Every child will seek to avoid the killing blow, however, and Abraham had to bind his son in order to at least spare him unnecessary pain. If we take these words seriously, and the complicated narrative style leaves no alternative, Abraham is at this moment a terrible father. With violent actions he forces his child to submit to an appalling command of God that the son himself has not received. Without embellishing anything, the narrator says what Abraham is prepared to do: "Abraham . . . took the knife to kill his son" (Gen 22:10).

At the end, it is true that God does not want the sacrifice of Isaac. A ram is found to be the sacrificial animal, and Abraham, "since you have not withheld your son, your only son, from me" receives a great blessing. But does a good end justify every affliction endured? The biblical editors who inserted this story into the context of the Abraham tradition did not ask anything very different. The following discussion approaches the story first by asking: Why do the redactors assign it the position it occupies?

The literary context of the narrative

A title sentence calls attention to the well-considered location of this story: "After these things God tested Abraham." The last event before this took place in Beer-sheba. Abraham had made a pact with the Philistines there and then lived as a foreigner among them for a long time. At the end of the narrative about the sacrifice Abraham returns to Beer-sheba and continues to dwell there. The story that follows even assumes that he lives there alone, without his wife. Sarah died at Hebron, and "Abraham went in to mourn for Sarah and to weep for her" (Gen 23:2).

Thus Abraham receives God's cruel command while he is living as a stranger among a foreign people. The redactors who placed the narrative here cause the readers to consider, in the person of Abraham, the primeval figure of faith, a question that Israel, scattered among the nations, had to face. It is an urgent question even today: Does faith undergo change in a faithless environment? It is equally significant that the story ends in Beer-sheba. Beer-sheba is a border town of the land that God gave to Israel, the last outpost before the wilderness.[51] After enduring such an extreme experience of God, Abraham was living only on the outer periphery of his divine inheritance.

With the plural expression "these things" the title also refers to the many experiences of God that Abraham had already lived through. In the story itself there is a reminder of the decisive beginning event:

God had commanded the young Abraham: "Go . . . to the land that I will show you" (Gen 12:1). The old man is told: "go to the land of Moriah" (Gen 22:1).[52] Does it not in fact happen that after a long life with God the decision for God can be more difficult than ever before? Israel, too, experienced this when, at the end of its long life in the "promised land," it confronted questions of faith that were ever more difficult. In spite of all, however, the redactors do not evade the oppressive question about God. They do not, for example, imagine that Abraham, infected with heathen horrors, had only imagined that he heard that dreadful command from God. They say plainly that it was God who was testing Abraham.

With the word "test" the title offers another instruction for reading. The word is significant primarily in the wilderness traditions. One location of the wandering in the wilderness is called Massa, "put to the test." Ten times, so says Num 14:22, God consented to be tested by this willful people, and remained with them in spite of all. At a time when the remainder of Israel was threatened with destruction the preachers of Deuteronomy taught their people to understand the "test" in the wilderness differently. They urged them not to think only about the miracles in the wilderness, but about the "whole way" on which God had in those days brought Israel through a life-threatening country, through "an arid wasteland . . . to humble you and to test you" (Deut 8:2, 15-16). Those who allow themselves to be led by God can come to places where no human being can live. The story in Genesis 22 shows how it is possible to believe that the "testing God" who leads people in this way is YHWH, the God of Israel.

The title in Genesis 22, therefore, instructs one to think through, in the figure of Abraham, the great man of faith, the historical experiences of a people threatened by destruction. How can faith meet the test when God leads people through the "wilderness"? How is it possible even then to hold fast to the faith of Abraham and to trust the word of God?

The historical placement of the story

In distinction to the biblical redactors, modern commentators have often attempted to mitigate the harshness of the story. Important above all, they say, is the prevention of the sacrifice of the son; Genesis 22 is said to be a didactic story meant to underline the abolition of the sacrifice of the firstborn in favor of animal sacrifice.[53] However, there are good arguments to show that in the epoch when the remnant of Israel feared for its existence the story was not only being interpreted by redactors but was actually being formulated. God's dreadful command is not simply cleverly invented in order to be refuted. The story evokes horror at the father who "binds" his son in order to "slaughter" him, but also at a God who brings him to it. This is the expression of actual experiences of terrible trouble.

Genesis 22 does not work as a didactic story about the laws concerning the firstborn simply because firstborn sacrifices were offerings of food. Animal fat was burned. The meat was consumed in a festive meal that portrayed the communion of God and humanity and gratitude that God's blessing had responded to human efforts.[54] From Abraham, however, a "whole offering" is demanded, and as a whole offering, in which everything is burned, he finally brings the ram. In addition, the "substitution" of the offering of the firstborn was done by the offering of animals, not by the older practice of sacrificing children. Historical sources first report child sacrifice—observed with horror—as the aberration of nations that believed their cruel deity had destined them for disaster.[55]

Child sacrifices also came as a prelude to the destruction of Jerusalem. Jeremiah 19:5 emphasizes so strongly that YHWH "did not command or decree" them that one has to conclude that the people of Jerusalem must indeed have been very convinced that God demanded something of that kind. Ezekiel could not imagine that people would think up such sacrifices by themselves, and dares a terrible explanation, namely that God had given laws that were "not good" in order that Israel should become "defiled," that is, deliver themselves over to death and depart from the living God.[56]

It is at this place in history that Genesis 22 belongs. The story's point of departure is an encounter with God as unbelievable as that described by Ezekiel. When God consents to be experienced in such a way as Abraham experienced God, how can one then live with such a God? How can the believer obey the God who puts him or her to the test? How does God then give divine blessings? One sign that it is the "how" questions that matter is the often-admired narrative skill of the text. It is not art for art's sake. The story lets one experience, concretely and in detail, how faith functions when put to the test.

A story about a father's difficult journey of faith

Abraham's journey begins with God's call: "Abraham!" and with the response of the believer who offers himself for service: "Here I am." But God does not want him as merely an individual who vouches for himself alone. From the father he demands "the only son, the beloved." At the end of this intensifying progression stands the name "Isaac." It is hard for a father to give up the hopes that the son personifies, and still harder to give up the only beloved child. A father will do both of these things if they lead to the son's finding the purpose of his life. But Abraham is asked to give up not only his hope and love but the son himself. There are extreme historical situations that make such demands, in which parents know that they are risking their child's life when they raise it in the faith. May they then protect its life at any price? Jews have suffered through such situations in our century also.[57]

In spite of its incomprehensible harshness, the divine command still leaves room for hope. God wants to name the place of decision; will God give it a bad name? The narrators thus refer to the end, when Abraham will find a good name; "The LORD sees," or "The LORD will provide" (Gen 22:14). It is not said at the beginning whether Abraham understands that God is giving him hope along the way. The story is only about his unquestioning obedience.

The preparations for the journey show how concretely difficult decisions of faith are converted into the small change of daily activity. The donkey is saddled, two servants and the son stand ready, and Abraham splits the wood. Why does this not happen until now, and why does he not make use of the help of the young men? Why does he want to take along wood from home? The story is set up to provoke these questions. They force one to recognize that Abraham wants to bear all the effort of carrying out the divine command himself and to be ready to obey instantly when the time comes.

Three days Abraham journeys without looking to the right or the left. Although the wood constantly reminds him where he is going, he catches sight of his destination very abruptly. Isn't this usually the case when someone is forced to give up well-loved ideas about God? Suddenly the decision is there.

But before the story comes to its climax and turning point it shows precisely how Abraham had understood the divine command.

Abraham leaves the servants behind and tells them what he and his son are intending to do: "we will worship, and then we will come back to you." Abraham had understood that God had given him hope along the way. He is convinced that father and son will not have two different roles to play. Both will "worship," that is, dedicate themselves unreservedly to God, and both will return. This hope had determined Abraham's attitude from the beginning. He had taken the young servants along as accompanying security, and now he himself carries the knife and the fire, that is, the things that can kill, because he wants to protect the life of his child.

God had commanded him to take his "only" son. On the climb to the mountain of offering this word is repeated: "So the two of them walked on together" (Gen 22:6). In Hebrew "together" and "only" are two forms of the same word. Thus the language holds ready an expression for a basic human experience. Everyone wishes to be "only" for someone else, and whoever has a human being who is "only" for himself or herself seeks to be "together" with her or him. The conversation between father and son insistently portrays the fact that they belong together: "'Father!' 'Here I am, my son'" (Gen 22:7). Abraham answers just as he had answered God. He puts off the future, whether hoped-for or dreaded. He wants to put himself at the disposal of the child who is present, just as he had done with God. But Isaac wants to know from his father what is going to happen. Wood and fire are ready, but where is the sacrificial lamb? Abraham answers honestly, but only to the point that the child can understand. "God himself will provide the lamb for a burnt offering, my son" (Gen 22:8).

In the end Abraham will name the place of offering "YHWH provides," or "YHWH will see."[58] On the ascent he still does not know what God sees, but he goes on, trusting that God will not lead him to a place that merits a deadly name. And the son goes with him in the confidence that his father's faith is not invalid.

A story about the saving name

At the turning point of the story, however, the father becomes an enemy who "binds" the son and intends to kill him. Still the narrator continues to create sympathy for Abraham. He describes the sacrificial act in steps that grow continually shorter, as if Abraham were waiting to be allowed to stop at every movement. He puts off the killing as long as he can, altering the sequence. Normally an animal is killed first, then laid on the pile of wood.

The calling out of a name holds him back from the last step, a different call than at the beginning, a double call, and urgent: "Abraham! Abraham!"[59] Abraham had, without ever looking up, held strictly to God's command. Does the double call reveal that God is disappointed? Not until after the divine messenger has expressly freed him from that terrible command does he look up and see the ram, caught in the thorn bush. Could he not have seen it earlier, and interpreted this unusual event then as he now does? His act of violence against the child was unnecessary.

From the beginning the author of the story had made everything lead up to the name Abraham gives the place: "The LORD sees." With this name Abraham admits his failure. It is not enough that the believer only repeat: "Here I am." The trust that God would not lead him to any evil place should have given Abraham the courage to look around to find help. Abraham did not have it, and God had to see for him.

The angel of God replies to Abraham's confession with a great statement of blessing. The saying is a late composition, a combination of sayings from all the traditions of the ancestors.[60] All the blessing of all fathers and mothers comes upon Abraham because he had "not withheld his son" from God. The closing verse of the story shows that Abraham actually lost his son. He returns alone, without Isaac: "So Abraham returned to his young men, and they arose and went together to Beer-sheba; and Abraham lived at Beer-sheba" (Gen 22:19). Isaac's life was saved, but from now on Abraham lives alone in the last outpost of the wilderness. He did not receive the great blessing for himself, but for his descendants.[61]

Human beings always have to think themselves anew into the story of Genesis 22 because instead of furnishing ready answers the story merely shows how they are to be sought. The most important of the signs used by the narrator has not yet been mentioned: the divine name YHWH does not appear in the story until the double calling of Abraham's name: "But the angel of YHWH called to him from heaven, and said, 'Abraham, Abraham!'" "The incomprehensible God" consents to be experienced through putting people to the test. God consents to be known as YHWH, whom Israel knows by name, in saving Abraham from committing the terrible deed. Yet the God who is near remains the distant God. YHWH addresses Abraham by means of a "messenger," and from heaven.

Genesis 22 shows how it can be possible, better, that it is already almost impossible, to live in faith in God's word in a time when God's will to bless can become unrecognizable. By allowing one to share the experience of what causes the breakup of the most important "mutual bond" known to ancient Israel, namely, that of the unity of father and son, this story describes the fractures Israel's faith overcame at such times. This story portrays the breaches that Israel's faith would have to get over during such times in that it allows one to share the experience of the breaking up of the most important "mutuality" known in ancient Israel, the solidarity of father and son. It breaks down because of the terrible experience of God and because Abraham's trust did not go beyond slavish obedience, doing what he was told to do without looking up. Though Abraham failed, he nonetheless received a blessing for his descendants because when he was put to the test by the incomprehensible God he remained open to YHWH's call.

8. Fathers without power

"Then Jacob said to Simeon and Levi,
'You have brought trouble on me'" (Gen 34:30)

Jacob brings a serious complaint against his sons. They had brought a life-threatening disaster upon him.[62] But they respond without emotion, "Should our sister be treated like a whore?" (Gen 34:31). They have the last word. Why does Jacob put up with their biting reply?

Genesis 34: Jacob is silent

Three times in this story Jacob is silent even though a word is expected from him as the father. The first time his silence is still comprehensible. Though the young man Shechem had seduced Jacob's daughter, Dinah, he had fallen in love with her and asked his father to negotiate with Jacob for her hand. Jacob says nothing until his sons arrive, for in this delicate matter he wants legal assistance at his side. But the sons demand that the men of Shechem's city first be circumcised, and Jacob is silent about this, too. Does he really know his sons so poorly that he does not suspect what they are up to? The marriage contract is drawn up according to law and custom.[63] When Dinah is in Shechem's house her brothers attack the city, take Dinah away, plunder the town, kill the men, and lead the women and children away as captives. They have an easy time doing it because the men were still ill with fever after their circumcision. To say that Dinah had been treated like a whore was an impudent lie. It is Jacob's sons who are the criminals, not Shechem. Like pimps they had taken advantage of Shechem's love to enrich themselves. But Jacob has to put up with their insolence because he shares their guilt. If only he had corrected them as sharply ahead of time as he now complains about them!

The name "Shechem" shows that the issue was, after all, more than a mere private affair. Shechem was the most important city of the west Jordanian hill country, and older than Israel. Through the words of the progenitors the narrators warn that doing evil to the fellow residents of the land through disregard of valid agreements and a sacred custom will endanger Israel's existence.

There are also other biblical narratives that reproach a people proud of their traditions with the shameful things in their midst. Fathers fail to defend themselves against their malicious sons. Jacob is not the only such father; Isaac, Eli, and David are also included. Biblical authors may have been moved to speak sympathetically for such fathers more by an impressive historical event than merely by the abstract thought of the meaning of fathers for a tradition-bound people. No sooner had David established a state and given Israel something of a secure place among their neighboring peoples than his realm was severely shaken. Absalom had stirred Israel up against his father, and David abandoned his capital city without a fight.

2 Samuel 15: David flees

The long narrative in 2 Samuel 11–20 gives an unvarnished account of how David himself is to blame for this disastrous development. Because he has adultery and murder on his conscience he is not capable of judging his sons, who are guilty of similar offenses, and thus paves the way for the revolt of power-hungry Absalom. Nevertheless, the narrator draws a stirring picture of David's flight: "But David went up the ascent of the Mount of Olives, weeping as he went, with his head covered and walking barefoot" (2 Sam 15:30).

The father leaves his house and the king his city. No one is to see his shamed face. Defenseless, with bare feet, he seeks exile. He had sent back the priests who wanted to escort him with the Ark of the Covenant, as was usual in important campaigns. He does not want to wage a holy war against his son Absalom and against Israel.

He is, of course, unable to restrain either his friends, who have remained close to him since his days as a partisan, or the foreign legionnaires who are loyal only to him personally and not to Israel. These warriors take up the fight as Absalom attacks. David pleads with them: "Deal gently for my sake with the young man Absalom" (2 Sam 18:5). But he loses his son, and the narrator speaks of it in a way to make one sympathize with a man who is aware of his guilt, who still loves his son, but cannot mourn because he must again assume responsibility for Israel (see 2 Sam 19:1-15). However much the narrators sympathize with the unhappy father, they are not interested in the drama of the family but in the fate of Israel. This is the first time in Israel's history that so much power is placed in the hands of one person. What does it mean that so much power is possessed by a father who is not able to rein in his own power-hungry sons?

Another question appears here for the first time: how long may a king continue to reign when he is plagued by old age? The story deals with this, too. David, weak with age, allows court intrigues to oblige him to install as his successor a son who does not actually have the right of succession. Thus by seeming chance Solomon, the man who will solve the problems left by his father, takes the throne (1 Kings 2:13-46).

Perhaps memories of the great king David have contributed to the fact that the figures of powerless fathers, too, lived on in the legends of Israel. The progenitor Jacob is portrayed in the saga about the crime against Shechem as a father whose consciousness of his own guilt leaves him defenseless, and old Isaac is a father who waits too long before he passes on the succession to a son, and blesses the right one only by chance.

Genesis 27: Isaac trembles

Isaac was already blind and weak with age when he decided to pass on his blessing to the firstborn. He can find the strength to do this only when he has been fortified with a meat dish. But that becomes his undoing. Before Esau can hunt and prepare the game for him, Esau's mother and brother have already deceived the old man with a cleverly prepared meal of goat's meat. Thus the younger son, Jacob, Israel's progenitor, wins the paternal blessing. The narrator makes no secret of what he thinks of the deceit. He encourages sympathy for the father who has been deceived: "Then Isaac trembled violently" (Gen 27:33).

Such scenes reveal why the stories of the Old Testament still make a vivid impression after thousands of years. The narrators cite no examples worthy of emulation and provide no ready judgments. They speak with sympathy about weak and guilty people, portraying accurately and soberly the effects of weakness and guilt. The saga of Jacob's deception of his father does not just tell of a bad experience that may happen to a father in his family. The people in Israel for whom the traditions of Jacob were first told were also meant to tremble. Because of this deceit Jacob had to flee, and became a servant of Laban the Aramean. Had the story been only a little different, Jacob might never have become the progenitor of a free people (see section 2 above).

1 Samuel 2:29:
Can a father do more than reprimand his wicked sons?

Another father who fails to fight against the evil actions of his sons is the "very old" Eli. The authors of this narrative clearly attached little value to the narrative skill that, avoiding ready judgments, tempts one to feel oneself into the situation of human beings. What more can a very old man do than to reprehend the atrocities of his adult sons with unambiguous words? Nevertheless, a "man of God" criticizes not the sons, but the father: "Why . . . honor your sons more than me by fattening yourselves on the choicest parts of every offering of my people Israel?" (1 Sam 2:29). Eli himself was a pious priest. It is only his sons who take the best of the believers' sacrificial offerings for themselves. Why does their father deserve this severe indictment?

It sounds pious when someone says that a father ought to honor God more than his children. But how does one honor God? Even the story to which this episode about the criticism of the man of God belongs has no glib answer. Eli and his sons are only secondary figures. They guard the Ark of the Covenant, the central shrine of Israel, at which God is present. In their fights with the Philistines, Israel brought the Ark to the battle so that God would help, and Eli's sons accompanied it. But the Philistines captured the Ark. The story describes how this event upset Eli. A messenger comes to the old priest and says:

> "Israel has fled before the Philistines, and there has also been a great slaughter among the troops; your two sons also . . . are dead, and the ark of God has been captured." When he mentioned the ark of God, Eli fell over backward from his seat . . . and his neck was broken and he died (1 Sam 4:17-18).

He dies a nasty death. The story says expressly that it was not the worry about Israel or about his sons that killed him. The pious priest is shaken by the fate of the Ark, which is in the hands of a people who do not honor it. But then it is shown that God needs neither priests nor the people of Israel in order to uphold the divine honor. Of its own power the Ark demonstrates its terrible superiority in the land of the Philistines. Priests must protect God's honor, not for the sake of God but for the sake of their fellow human beings. Eli's sons have sinned because bad priests obstruct Israel's way to God.

The episode of the "man of God" is not really a part of this story. It does not carry the action forward, but only comments on it. Teachers of the Law inserted it. They use the example of Eli to show that even a father who is weak with old age becomes guilty when he does not protect Israel from the wicked deeds of his sons, for the Law of Israel would put in his hand the means to do this. A law from Deuteronomy shows what these commentators are thinking.

Deuteronomy 21:18-21: The rebellious son must die

With laborious exactitude the law describes a criminal offense and its legal consequences:

> If someone has a stubborn and rebellious son who will not obey his father and mother, who does not heed them when they discipline him, then his father and his mother shall take hold of him and bring him out to the elders of his town at the gate of that place. They shall say to the elders of his town, "This son of ours is stubborn and rebellious. He will not obey us. He is a glutton and a drunkard." Then all the men of the town shall stone him to death.

In our day this law shocks us. It requires of parents that they drag an alcoholic son before a court that can actually condemn him to death. Does not precisely a young person who is addicted need the love of his parents? When one attempts to understand this law in terms of its historical situation, however, it does have something to say that merits consideration. Deuteronomy was formed at a time when the existence of the last remnant of Israel was threatened. Stories about wicked sons who brought disaster on Israel acquired a ring of truth at that time. The example of dangerous public wickedness chosen by the teachers of the Law will not seem meaningful to many people today. Drunkenness is considered to be rather erroneous behavior on the part of an individual who ruins his own life. In the days when Israel feared for its existence the matter was thought of differently. A person who at a time of extreme necessity consumes everything only to achieve a brief rush deprives his fellow men and women of what they need for survival, and is no better than a murderer.

When the life of everyone is at stake, all who have legal responsibility should participate in the decision. For this reason the Law specifies a public process. The execution, too, is to be carried out by all those who possess legal responsibility, with the exception of the parents. It is to be plain to all that what is at stake is not a settlement of accounts between the parents and the son, but the survival of Israel.

Did parents in those days actually bring themselves to drag a wicked son before the court? Biblical narratives tend rather to suggest that Israel's fathers were more like David, Eli, Jacob, and Isaac, who did not denounce the evil deeds of their sons even when they brought everyone into danger. In modern commentary on this law one can, of course, read another supposition, namely that Deuteronomy thereby "limited" the "unlimited power of the *paterfamilias* in that patriarchal society."[64] Deuteronomy 21:18-21 prescribes that the parents appeal to the local court. Was this anything new? Did the fathers themselves previously have the power of life and death over the members of their families? Was it Deuteronomy that first took it away from them?

Even as "judges," fathers were in need of help

The only biblical text in which a father pronounces a death penalty is the story in Genesis 38. Judah hears that his widowed daughter-in-law is pregnant, and orders: "Bring her out, and let her be burned" (Gen 38:24). Though the saga only outlines the judicial proceeding, it nevertheless makes clear that Judah did not possess "unlimited" judicial power. There are others who act with Judah and "bring her out." These unnamed persons are not merely Judah's assistants in enforcement. They allow Tamar to send them to Judah, before whom they lay out Tamar's articles of evidence. They do not serve Father Judah, but justice. Guardians of justice are a "brotherly" company also in this saga.

The reason the Deuteronomic teachers of the Law want the mother also to participate in the legal action against an obstinate and willful son is not the necessity of limiting the power of the father. Rather, they combined two different older concepts. In order to protect the life of the accused as carefully as possible they specify that the parents shall contact the court only after having first vainly attempted to bring their son to his senses by a graduated series of warnings and corporal punishments. Thus teachers of the Law are in continuity with Wisdom teachings, which warn the father not to neglect corporal punishment (see section 4 above). At the same time they think of the Ten Commandments, which protect the father and mother against sons who disrespect the parents' right to life and honor, and warn sons not to strike, curse, abuse, drive away, or rob their helpless parents.[65] The vehemence with which they speak reveals how necessary such warnings were. An adage warns: "The eye that mocks a father and scorns to obey a mother will be pecked out by the ravens of the valley and eaten by the vultures" (Prov 30:17). This is a gruesomely correct image of a disgraceful death: Birds of carrion begin with the eyes, where they can most easily get at the interior of the body. This is no "pedagogically" exaggerated picture, but a real warning, for a death threat against the son who deals wickedly with his parents is contained also in the collections of the Law: "Whoever strikes father or mother shall be put to death. . . . Whoever curses father or mother shall be put to death" (Exod 21:15, 17).

These are not, of course, practicable penal laws. Whoever wants to hurt his or her parents by cursing them can easily evade legal prosecution if the curse remains secret. Abuse of helpless old parents certainly does often remain hidden from public view. With the law against obstinate sons, the teachers of the Law who created Deuteronomy intended to encourage parents to seek help against wicked sons.

It can happen that fathers are powerless against their sons. The laws themselves, as well as the stories that deal with them, reveal one more reason why biblical authors come to speak of the experiences of individuals. Private life is not interesting for its own sake. Every individual, however, weak or strong, should ask what consequences his or her personal decisions will have for others, and perhaps even for the entire people. The next section will briefly summarize the meaning of this point of view insofar as the Bible speaks of fathers.

9. In retrospect: fatherhood and fatherliness

Why the Bible speaks so often about fathers

In ancient Israel there were occasions for remembering the history of the people as a living continuity of generations sustained by fathers and sons. There were three particular areas in which the past was experienced as a power that continued active in the present: For the farmers of the hill country where productive farmland had to be won from a stubborn soil by the hard work of men and continually cared for, fields and orchards were a concrete image of how the past becomes the present, and sustains life now. The ancestors had laid them out, the father maintains them in good order to pass them on to his son. They are "the heritage of the fathers" (see ch. 2, section 5 above).

In the midst of this little people, often under attack, who were forced by necessity alone to accept the state, which in those days meant the kingdom, every generation found itself newly obliged by fathers to see to it that the sons became capable of taking over public responsibility. The past lived on in basic principles of justice and education.

In a traditional society in which knowledge and ability grew slowly, with fathers passing on necessary knowledge and practical skills to their sons, one noted how much the present was indebted to the past (see sections 3 and 8 above). Certainly sterile scholastic knowledge was also passed on unquestioningly (section 4 above), but with the reference to teacher and student as "father" and "son" there remained at least a sign that both belonged to a society that gains strength for the future from the past.

Thus fathers and sons experienced the meaning of the past whenever they shared responsibility for the inheritance of justice, political life, and the transmission of knowledge and skills. It is no wonder that this way of seeing things dominates in the Bible also. Although biblical authors know that women could do justice to these "tasks of the father" (section 4 above), they were not able to conceive of the history of Israel as a coherent whole carried forward by mothers and daughters. Women, after all, had to apply their strengths to the immediate present, in providing food and clothing and caring for the babies. And the Old Testament is a product of its times. Israel had lost its political freedom, and tried that much harder to preserve its identity in the memories of the past. Traditions were collected and edited. During such times women retire even more into their private space (see ch. 1, section 3 above).

Because the Bible originated as a witness of the history of the People of God it speaks incomparably more often about fathers and sons than about mothers and daughters, but that makes it all the more striking when the Bible does emphasize that the People of God do not live by the strength of men alone. (See, *inter alia,* ch. 1, section 3; ch. 2, section 2; and sections 1 and 8 of this chapter.)

To what extent is the priority of fathers self-evident for biblical authors?

"Patriarchalism" has today become hardly more than a dirty word, and for this reason bad images of fathers are considered an authentic image of the patriarchal society and accepted as such in the Bible for no other reason than that they are bad. It must be emphasized, on the other hand, that the Bible never simply states how things once were. In order to establish what was "normal" and accepted as such by biblical authors it is necessary to observe with what intention something was said. That can most easily be determined when the function of a statement can be examined in the context of a story. It is also necessary to weigh statements from different texts and to examine historical sources from the Bible's milieu. Some of the results obtained in this way need to be listed, in the first place those that disagree with modern understandings of biblical patriarchalism.

There is in the biblical traditions no support for the opinion that the father was the supreme judge in the family. It was not the father who alone watched over the rights and the correct conduct of the daughters-in-law and daughters, but a man with his "brothers." And even more certainly the Bible does not anywhere promise the fathers the right to dispose over the life and death of their children, even though that was the case in the society within which it came into being. (See ch. 2, sections 3 and 4; and sections 3 and 7 of this chapter.)

The fact that women and children could lose their freedom because they shared legal liability for the debts of a father, and that fathers could sell their sons and daughters into slavery, represents no proof of the terrible power of the father. Fathers who had been brought so low by economic necessity were no mighty lords in relation to their families, but pathetic people. Biblical storytellers, prophets, and teachers of the Law advocate the freeing of slaves, and when that is not possible, the human dignity of slaves, and expressly of female slaves, criticizing the rich who take advantage of the predicament of poor parents. (See sections 1, 2, and 5 above.)

There is another outrage that also undermines the idea that the fathers were more important in public life: after the killing of their male relatives, women and children were abducted as booty, the spoils of war's brutality. Biblical sagas relate with revulsion that this happened not only among Israel's enemies, but also among the people God honors as the "father of widows and orphans." (See sections 2 and 8 above.) Teachers of the Law demand that a captured woman at least be treated as a person who mourns "father and mother," advocating the same rights for her as those possessed by a daughter of Israel who has been sold (Deut 21:10-14).

On the other hand, biblical texts assume as self-evident that only a free man who has been married has full rights as a father (section 1 above), that fathers supervise the marriage negotiations for their children (sections 2 and 8 above), that young married couples belong in the house of the husband's parents (section 1 above), and that the "bride price," which is meant as an economic guarantee for the wife, be administered by her father (section 2 above). Above all, legal problems were to be resolved by men. Of course one should rather call that a "fratriarchal" or "brotherhood" system than a "patriarchal" one. (See sections 1, 2, and 8 above; also ch. 1, section 7; ch. 2, section 8.) Should we, just because these regulations are unfamiliar to us today, blame biblical authors for accepting them?

How biblical texts encourage an examination of long-held ideas about the preeminence of fathers

Some biblical voices simply repeat without criticism concepts that need to be contested. They comment approvingly on the fact that wives and children have to die with the guilty father (ch. 2, section 4), and that prenuptial virginity is as important as the life of a woman (section 2 above). The oft-repeated *topos* that sons are called to enter the ranks of those who learn and teach also needs to be contradicted insofar as it excludes daughters (section 4 above).

A challenge to these positions finds supporting voices in the Bible. Christians often proceed on the conviction that the New Testament corrects the Old. That this correction does not occur automatically can be noted when the New Testament speaks about "brothers" and falls back into older ideas antedating the congregation that includes men, women, and children (see ch. 1, section 6; and section 4 of this chapter). The Bible is no book of progressive instruction that takes the student by the hand and leads him or her from truth to truth. It encourages one to recognize and question reality. Teachers of the Law and of Wisdom do not prescribe what is to be done, but call attention to ways in which the right can be sought. The intention of narratives is to shock and to shake up, so that what seems self-evident may be called into question.

Therefore, while biblical writers consider it necessary that fathers allow themselves to be bound into the generations of the fathers and solidarity with brothers, they also question to what extent Israel can rely on the familial attachment of fathers, sons, and brothers (see ch. 2, sections 3 and 7). With conspicuous frequency their father-images are darkly clouded. They tell about fathers who, out of love for their sons, consciousness of their own guilt, or the weakness of old age, fail to check the evil carryings-on of their sons (section 8 above). An unlucky father drags his beloved son along into destruction (see ch. 2, section 3). The sons of a weak father fortunately protect him from shame (section 3 above). Nothing like the "Oedipus problem," which since Freud has had a determining influence on the modern image of fathers, appears.[66] Fathers are happy to have their sons as "brotherly" helpers at their sides (see ch. 2, section 9; and section 1 of this chapter). Elderly parents are advised that adult sons will lend them support or, if need be, the public will help them against a son. That the aged David did not choose his successor in time does not mean, as far as the narrators are concerned, that he did not permit his son to assume power. But while he was still a strong man he should have ceded the throne to Absalom rather than fight against his son (see ch. 2, section 2; and section 8 of this chapter).

The father of a wealthy family was seen to possess the highest measure of responsibility. Biblical authors warn that responsibility increases with the scope of freedom. They examine less rigorously the conduct of mothers, whose area of activity is limited to the interior of the family, than that of fathers and grown sons (see section 1 above). A word of juvenile arrogance (section 3 above) or a false step (ch. 2, section 6) can have evil effects on a person who is politically responsible. Therefore fathers need an opposite number. It is not always good that sons agree with their fathers (see ch. 2, section 3; and sections 2 and 7 of this chapter), and it can happen that a son upholds the honor of his father, and servants the honor of their master, even when they act differently than he does (section 3 above). Biblical narrators are not interested in setting up fathers as examples. Even Abraham's trust in God's word did not keep him from transgressions. He sends his son Ishmael away without provisions (section 4 above), and in his blindly obedient faith he does not think to look around for deliverance for Isaac; yet he is a good father who does not treat his child any differently than his God (section 7 above). On the other hand, fathers do not serve only as deterrent teaching examples. Jephthah sacrifices his daughter for one victory, but it can also be asked if the son of the prostitute whom his brothers drove away from his father's house was solely responsible when his thirst for power became stronger than his paternal love (section 2 above).

Regarding the wicked behavior of fathers, too, the stories are told in such a way that one can imagine oneself in their situation, though without excusing them. The stories expose fathers who, in the interest of enhancing their own reputation, act inhumanely against those who have been entrusted to them (see section 6 above). They reveal how easily destructive wickedness can masquerade as good paternal behavior and as respect for a right entrusted to fathers (section 2 above). They do not do this with ready judgments, but awaken sympathy and indignation by means of stirring scenes. Those who engage themselves with these stories should experience how easily a person who claims preeminence for himself and, as did fathers in those days, considers himself to be in the right passes indifferently over the rights of his fellow men and women. If the father in Judges 19 had loved his daughter, if David had concerned himself as much for Tamar, who had been raped, as for his sick son, then these fathers would have worked justice for their daughters and the entire people would have been saved from disaster (sections 2 and 6 above).

Why fatherhood and fatherliness are not always easy to reconcile

It is perhaps in their shocking stories of paternal failure that biblical authors most clearly reveal that they are concerned neither to show what fatherhood was in those days nor what it basically should be. Instead God, who does not will that some people should oppress others, moves the authors to speak often and accurately about what fathers do with their responsibility. They force those in positions of responsibility to pay attention to the value of the right to life and dignity of every person, even the lowliest.

The biblical authors' seriousness on this point shows, among other ways, in how the "guilt of the fathers" continues to be visited on the "fathers and sons," down through history. It is often emphasized that this is so, though biblical teachers of Wisdom also insist that human judicial skill must be fair to each individual, and prophets announce that each person, father and son, is judged for himself (see ch. 2, section 4). David struggles with God for the life of the child he has sired in adultery because he is determined, insofar as possible, to bear his guilt by himself, demonstrating thereby that he is a king whom the people can trust (see ch. 2, section 6).

For biblical authors the father's love, whose only object is the beloved son, is the basic experience that reveals the incomparable value of the individual (section 5 above). In the same way it can be shown what motherhood and fatherhood are: just as the mother applies herself with her body and her life for the child who would otherwise perish, so fatherhood is revealed in a man's readiness to ensure life and a future for his children (section 1 above; see also ch. 2, section 6).

When the Bible speaks about paternal love it is almost entirely as love for a son. The principal reason for this may be that it was more necessary to pay attention to this. The love of parents accepts the child as it is. But in the son fathers also had to see a person who would one day be responsible for others (sections 4 and 8 above). Parents are available as father or mother for each individual child, but fatherhood included responsibility for an entire "house," in which many would live and continue to live. In those days people idealized a time when people could be seated without anxiety, "each under his own vine and fig tree" because the responsibility for the "house of Israel" was in good hands (section 3 above). Nowadays people yearn for a time in which the care of small children and the family's day-to-day life does not drain mothers' energy, so that they might share with fathers the heavy responsibility for the "house" of this earth. Today, therefore, it is just as necessary to consider with care how fatherly love for daughters is to be reconciled with "fatherhood."

It could also be that the Bible speaks so seldom about the love for daughters because they leave the father's house. Fathers were not able to love in their daughters the joy that comes when one can entrust one's lifework to a beloved person. A father could turn to his daughter in love only with that love—so difficult to learn—that loves the daughter as herself, while making possible for her and permitting her an independent life (sections 5 and 6 above). The Old Testament tells how Jacob demonstrated this precious kind of fatherly love when he rediscovered his beloved son as an Egyptian. But the murderer Cain is also such a father who made possible for his son Enoch a new beginning unencumbered by his father's name and manner of life (see ch. 2, section 4). Jesus teaches Jairus, the head of the synagogue, that the love with which the father, unconcerned about his own honor, commits himself to his daughter is fertile ground for life-giving faith (section 6 above).

At the time of Jesus the old ideas about the public responsibility of fathers had long been undermined, for political freedom had been lost. Education of the sons and preservation of paternal authority had now come to be valued above all as support for inner-family order, and the commandment about parents as an exhortation to childlike obedience (section 4 above). The parables show how carefully Jesus observed this retreat of fathers into private life. He tells of minor events in the inner space of the family, about a man who does not want to disturb the sleep of his children who are sleeping in the same room with him, and about a child who asks his father for an egg (Luke 11:7, 12).

Above all, however, with his message of the fatherhood of God, Jesus gives an unprecedented new dignity to the ideas about the fatherliness that proves itself in commitment to the beloved. In the Sermon on the Mount he declares that the "Father in heaven" knows the concern of housewives with the daily needs of eating, drinking, and being clothed. The disciples, on the other hand, are to turn, unburdened by this concern, to the great public "fatherly tasks" of "righteousness and the kingdom of God" (Matt 6:33).

The fourth chapter of this book concerns itself with the question of how the biblical message of God's fatherhood reveals itself in light of the ideas of human fatherhood and fatherliness that were elaborated in the first three chapters.

Notes: Chapter 3

[1] Cf. Exod 21:2-6, the first commandment in the oldest OT law collection. Menservants and maidservants who had grown up in the house were particularly valued; cf. Gen 14:14.

[2] Moses, too, had received from his master a daughter for a wife; see ch. 1, section 5 above. But his father-in-law became his friend. On his own initiative he again returned to his son-in-law his wife and sons after Moses had led Israel to freedom (Exod 18:2, 5).

[3] According to 1 Chr 3:24 sons of an unfree son-in-law were considered to be sons of a free father-in-law.

[4] Gen 24:67. Cf. also Deut 22:16; Gen 38:6 and elsewhere. The father "gives" the son a wife.

[5] In Num 14:29 and 32:11 it is assumed that twenty-year-olds would already have sons at the Exodus from Egypt. According to 2 Chr 25:5 twenty-year-olds were mustered for military service, and according to 1 Chr 23:24 Levites began their service as priests at twenty.

[6] Cf. ch. 1, section 7, and ch. 2, section 2 above. How important it is to have brothers at one's side in legal disputes can also be seen in Gen 31:23, 37. Laban has brought along his own "kinsfolk" and, strangely enough, Jacob also suddenly has "kinsfolk" with him. Are the narrators thinking of his servants as legal assistants?

[7] Daughters-in-law are reckoned to the family as a matter of course (Gen 7:7; Luke 12:53) but sons-in-law never. According to Sir 7:23 the young married man belongs under the supervision of his father.

[8] Tob 12:1; cf. also ch. 1, section 4 above.

[9] Gen 50:18; Judg 16:31; 1 Sam 22:1.

[10] The authors are thinking of the "great nation" Israel; *ʿam,* after all, means both "people" or "nation" and "kinsfolk."

[11] Cf. Gen 13:5-13; 19:1-38. On the judgment of biblical narrators on the action of Lot's daughters see ch. 1, section 5 above.

[12] On the legal institution of levirate marriage see above, ch. 2, section 5.

[13] On Nathan's promise in 2 Samuel 7 see ch. 2, section 6, above.

[14] Gen 29:31–30:24 tells of the competition of Jacob's two wives at having sons, which was not always conducted by impeccable means. The infertility of a woman is in biblical traditions a recurrent occasion for violent disputes among married couples, but also with God, who refuses the blessing of children; on this see Annemarie Ohler, *Mutterschaft in der Bibel* (Würzburg, 1992) 131ff., 227. The infertility of men is mentioned only once, in Deut 7:14; Israel's law provided curative measures for it (cf. ch. 2, section 5, above).

[15] This could also explain why the narrators in Genesis 38 consider it possible for Judah to hold judgment over his widowed daughter-in-law Tamar even though she was once more living with her parents. She lives from the "bride price" that Judah had to pay, and is for this reason a member of his house, just as she was earlier.

[16] The inscription on a grave from the eighth century B.C.E., discovered near Jerusalem, leads to this conclusion: "This is the grave of . . . yahu, governor of the palace. There is here neither silver nor gold, but only his bones and with him the bones of his maid. Cursed be whoever opens this!" (Otto Kaiser, ed., *Texte aus der Umwelt des Alten Testaments.* II, 4 [Gütersloh: Gerd Mohn, 1988] 559). With this inscription a high-ranking official protected himself against grave robbers. His "maid" is, as he publicly announces, to remain "with him" even in death.

[17] Exod 21:7-11; cf. also Deut 15:12-14; Jer 34:8-22; Job 31:13; Nehemiah 5.

[18] The above translation follows the ancient Greek tradition. Hebrew manuscripts give another reason: she "prostituted herself against him." The Greek text is probably the original. The Hebrew text tradition builds the expression "prostituted herself" into an unusual grammatical construction that would fit well with "become furious."

[19] According to Deut 22:26 rape is "like . . . someone who attacks and murders a neighbor."

[20] 2 Sam 13:20.

[21] Cf. section 1 above, and ch. 1, section 5.

[22] Cf. Gen 33:1-3. Esau had been so badly cheated by Jacob that Jacob had to flee from him; cf. Genesis 27.

[23] That a proper servant carries out the master's command only when it does not besmirch the master's honor is presented by, among others, the saga

in 1 Samuel 22 with the example of Saul's servants; cf. also ch. 2, section 1, above. Cf. further the story of the servant of the king, Ebed-melech, in Jer 38:7-13 and also in ch. 2, section 6, above.

[24] The biblical commandments for parents and the corresponding proverbs always consider the mother equal in rank at the side of the father. Cf. on this Ohler, *Mutterschaft in der Bibel,* 147ff.

[25] Ugarit is a Syrian city that perished in the fifteenth century B.C.E. The Tale of Aqhat, Tablet 1, lines 25–35, is quoted here according to James B. Pritchard, *The Ancient Near East,* 2 vols. (Princeton: Princeton University Press, 1958) 1:119.

[26] That this motif, whatever its form, was always well known in biblical times is attested by Isa 51:17-18: Jerusalem is helplessly drunk on the wine of God's anger, but no son or daughter is there to protect the city and take it by the hand.

[27] The Instruction of the Vizier Ptah-Hotep, 497ff.; cf. H. Brunner, *Altägyptische Weisheit* (Zürich and Munich, 1988) 131.

[28] Fathers instruct sons about the world order: cf. Deut 32:7 and also the Babylonian creation epic Enuma Elish VII, 147; about the history of their people, cf. Judg 6:13; Jer 29:19; Ps 78:2-4, among others; about festival customs, cf. Exod 12:26-27, among others; about laws, Gen 18:19; Deut 6:7, 20 and others; about practical skills. Just as Gen 9:20 speaks of Noah as the first vinegrower, so Gen 4:20-21 knows of an "ancestor" of the tent dwellers and cattle breeders and of an "ancestor" of the zither and flute players. In 1 Chr 4:14 a "father of the valley of the artisans" is mentioned. In Jer 35:6-7 the special lifestyle of a community is explained in terms of the orders of an "ancestor."

[29] Deut 31:12; cf. more on this in ch. 1, section 6 above.

[30] Cf. Deut 4:9; 6:7, 20; 11:19; 32:46; cf. also Exod 10:2; 12:26, 13:8, 14 among others. (NRSV translates "sons" as "children" throughout.)

[31] Cf. Prov 4:1; 1 Sam 3:6.

[32] Matt 23:9. According to classical Greek grammar this sentence is incomplete; a word like "a(n)" is missing. In the preceding and following sentences, however, parallel statements use a correct grammatical construction in the passive voice: "Nor are you to be called instructors . . ." The differing form of the sentence about fathers could be explained as a gloss that had been inserted into the passage, disrupting its normal grammar.

[33] In Gal 3:28 Paul emphasizes that in Christ the differences in rank of man and woman fall away, as also between slave and free, Jews and Gentiles. That does not hinder him from speaking in the same context of the vocation of Christians to be "sons of God." Because only sons had the right of inheritance, women, too, were seen as "brothers" called to sonship.

[34] According to H. Brunner, *Altägyptische Erziehung* (Wiesbaden, 1957) 56 and 186.

[35] Parents were urged to discipline their children (Prov 19:18; 29:17), to use the rod (Prov 22:15; 23:13-14; 29:15). Children were exhorted to accept discipline willingly (Prov 13:1; 15:5; 23:12).

[36] Neither the story of the death of the daughter of Jephthah nor that about the curse of Saul, which affects his son, presupposes the existence of such a paternal right; cf. on this section 2 above, and ch. 2, section 3. The same is true for Genesis 22; cf. section 7 below.

[37] The accusation of Tacitus (*Histories* V, 5) that Jews placed little value on parents, children, and siblings is slander (cf. ch. 1, section 2 above) but reveals to what means one could resort in the society of that time to stir up enmity against an unpopular group. When, on the other hand, Christians were accused of prompting children to disobey parents and teachers (Origen, *Contra Celsum* III, 55) this, too, was a reflection of the results of Christian mission. The "house rules" exhort the Christians, if possible, to give no fuel to such reproaches.

[38] To what extent love for a small child was taken for granted can be seen in Wis 14:15. The author explains to himself the Egyptian cult of the dead by understanding that in this way fathers console themselves for the death of a child.

[39] This is a more precise translation of the expression in Gen 21:9, which the NRSV gives as "playing."

[40] On this, see also section 4 above. The laws about the liberation of male and female slaves are found in Deut 15:13-17.

[41] The version of the Abraham saga recorded in Genesis 21 probably goes back to the troubled time when the existence of the small nations in Canaan was threatened. This is shown by, among other things, the reference to the deuteronomic law (cf. previous note) that originated at that time. At such times mothers must take courage to assume paternal tasks, as did Hagar (cf. section 4 above).

[42] 2 Sam 12:15-23; cf. also ch. 2, section 6, above.

[43] The brothers of Samson and those of Jonathan are mentioned respectively in Judg 16:31 and 1 Sam 14:49. The participation of Samson's father at his son's wedding is related in Judg 14:10; David's reconciliation with Absalom is in 2 Sam 14:33.

[44] In Prov 4:1-27 a teacher of wisdom describes the instruction he had received from his father as words of love when he discloses that he had received them when he was "a son with my father, tender, and my mother's favorite" (4:3).

[45] Cf. the Teaching of Merikare 276, in Brunner, *Altägyptische Weisheit,* 152.

[46] For Gen 1:27 see also n. 1 to the Introduction and ch. 4, section 7, below.

[47] Luke will sketch an image of the mother of Jesus after this example: Luke 2:19, 51.

[48] Sir 7:24-25; 22:4-5; 42:9-14.

[49] On Job's daughters, cf. ch. 2, section 5, above. For stories of the mistreatment of daughters, cf. section 2 of this chapter.

[50] See also above, ch. 1, section 4, n. 8.

[51] Israel extends "from Dan to Beer-sheba": Judg 20:1; 1 Sam 3:20; 2 Sam 3:10; 24:2; 1 Kings 4:25. Beyond Beer-sheba one leaves Israel's land; cf. Gen 46:1-2; 1 Kings 19:3.

[52] The reminiscence of Gen 12:1 is even clearer in the Hebrew because one can understand "Moriah" as "place of seeing."

[53] Cf. J. Scharbert, *Genesis 12–50,* NEB (Würzburg: Echter, 1986) 168, and on the laws in Exod 22:28; 34:20; 13:11-12.

[54] Cf. Deut 15:22-23; Num 18:17-19. The "whole offering" is never spoken of in connection with the offering of the firstborn. For instance, the offerings of firstfruits by Cain and Abel are called "gift offerings." God's gift to humankind is thereby celebrated. In Exod 13:11-16 the offering by which the firstborn son is redeemed is called a sacrifice, the term for solemn offerings normally associated with meals based on meat.

[55] Cf. Otto Kaiser, ed., *Texte aus der Umwelt des AT,* II, 4. (Gütersloh, 1988) 806–807. The Bible knows of kings who offered their sons for the sake of their troubled country (2 Kings 3:27; 16:3; 21:6). There is nowhere any evidence of a "normal" family custom of child sacrifice.

[56] Ezek 20:25-36; cf. also Jer 7:31; 32:25; Ezek 23:27; Deut 18:20.

[57] Emil Fackenheim, *Quest for Past and Future* (London, 1968) 19 views the experiences of Jewish parents in the Nazi period against the background of Genesis 22. Already in medieval times Jews understood pogroms as repetitions of the offering of Isaac.

[58] Gen 22:14. With the "seeing" in v. 4 the story prepares for this place name; cf. n. 52 above.

[59] In Exod 3:4 the double cry is a warning of deadly danger: "Moses, Moses! . . . Come no closer!" Luke, too, understands the double call of the name as an insistent warning; cf. Luke 10:41 and 22:31. Cf. further the double call in Ps 22:1.

[60] With Gen 22:17-18, cf. Gen 12:2-3; 15:5; 16:10; 18:18; 24:60; 26:4-5; 28:14; 32:12.

[61] At the beginning of the story the name "Moriah" already alerts to this. "Moriah" occurs additionally once in 2 Chr 3:1 and is there the name of the hill on which the Jerusalem Temple is built. God permits Abraham to discover the place at which God wants to give the people blessing if they at least confess that "YHWH sees."

[62] Jacob uses a word that ordinarily refers to the shattering of all Israel; cf. Josh 6:18; 1 Sam 14:29; 1 Kings 18:17.

[63] Cf. the law that protects seduced maidens in Exod 22:16-17.

[64] Cf. Georg Braulik, *Deuteronomium* (Würzburg, 1992) 2:157.

[65] Cf. Lev 20:9; Deut 27:16; Prov 19:26; 20:20; 28:24.

[66] Paul Ricoeur, *Die Vatergestalt. Vom Phantasiebild zum Symbol. In Hermeneutik und Psychoanalyse* (Munich, 1974) 315–393, uses this hypothesis as the key to biblical "father texts."

Chapter Four

Our Father in Heaven

The Old Testament employs many images to say how God wants to be "related" to human beings—like a father, but also like a mother, a friend or blood brother, a spouse or bridegroom, a rich relative. Out of this treasury of images, with few exceptions the New Testament adopts only the language about God as Father; above all, Jesus' impressive message about his Father continues exercising its effect.[1] The language of Christian faith and prayer extracts from the Bible's imagery of the fatherhood of God almost exclusively the idea that God is Father. That, however, is not enough. The Bible's images prompt one to ask in what way God wants to be Father.

We can also learn from feminist biblical criticism how important these questions are for a living faith. Such criticism brings a "hermeneutics of suspicion" to the question whether religious language takes sufficiently into account the experiences of women, and protests the precedence of the discourse about the fatherhood of God. It really is worth noting that the Bible speaks of the motherliness of God only in a comparative manner—God is *like* a mother—while in the New Testament God is so often called Father. Such questions arouse sensitivity for the fact that there is no word that perfectly expresses the reality of God, not even one as well-attested and well-loved as the word "father." The reality of God is not to be confused with the human associations that also resonate in this word.

Another especially weighty reason for understanding the "father" words as figurative expressions derives from the fact that the idea of

God's fatherhood remains problematic in the Bible. The biblical narratives tell about fathers who suffer because of the wicked deeds of their sons (see ch. 3, section 8 above), who are dependent on the help of their sons (ch. 2, section 2 above) or the solidarity of their brothers (ch. 1, section 3 above). Their hope of living is based on their belonging to a line of fathers and sons (ch. 2, section 5 above). All of this, one would think, is unsuitable material for imaging the fatherhood of God. Nevertheless, these aspects of human fatherhood are not excised when biblical texts speak of God as a father. Biblical "father language" calls attention to the fact that the confession of the "Father almighty" with which the Apostles' Creed begins leads, as do all statements of faith, to a question into which believers must enter ever more deeply, but can never solve; that is: How can God be for us simultaneously both Father and almighty? In the following section it will be shown that this question is immediately provoked by the earliest texts that speak of God as Father.

1. Jeremiah's message of the fatherhood of God

Jeremiah is the first in the Bible to speak about God as Father. It was the terrible events of his time that gave him occasion to do so. He experienced the decline of Judah. The Babylonians destroyed Jerusalem and the Temple. The rest of Israel lost all the things that helped them to see themselves as the People of God. Would not the thought that God is Father be a source of comfort in such trouble? Do not children remain children of a father no matter what? Jeremiah saw something different in the fathers of his people. Fathers do not always remain fathers. Those who were deported lost the hereditary property from which their families had lived. The men of Judah could no longer devote themselves to the pursuit of justice for those who belonged to them. How could they still be distinguishable as fathers?

Jeremiah declares that things are no different for God. God, too, no longer has an inheritance, but in contrast to the men of Judah, God has left home freely and willingly.

Jeremiah 12:7-8: God surrenders paternal rights

I have forsaken my house,
  I have abandoned my heritage;

> I have given the beloved of my heart
> into the hands of her enemies (v. 7).

The prophet gives the terrible events of his time an equally terrible interpretation: God will hear no more of paternal rights and duties. God "disowns" this family. Among the duties of a father is providing legal protection for the helpless. Psalm 68:5 praises God as such a Father:

> Father of orphans and protector of widows
> is God in his holy habitation.

With the destruction of the Temple God had given up even those paternal duties. God's people were "fatherless" in two respects, for the men could no longer be fathers and God no longer offered any fatherly protection.[2] Jeremiah does not, however, accuse God in the name of the abandoned people. He proclaims that God is accusing the people:

> My heritage has become to me like a lion in the forest (v. 8). Can a "heritage" be like a lion? The incoherent image corresponds to the incoherent behavior of the people. They had lived in God's city as if in a lawless wilderness and in the Temple as in a "den of robbers" (Jer 7:11). God leaves a "house" that is, after all, nothing but a jungle. Jerusalem is not just a powerless victim. The destruction of the city only makes a reality of what has long been true internally.

The word "father" does not appear in this statement. Instead, Jeremiah applies concepts that paraphrase the legal relation between father and son: house and inheritance. God's inheritance belongs to the Babylonians; God's house is destroyed and the circumstances of justice are broken. But the saying reveals, even in the form of its language, that God does not get free from "the beloved of my heart": God carries on an internal dialogue for lack of anyone to whom to complain, yet the emptiness is so painful that God cannot be silent.

Jeremiah did not need to invent this image of fatherly pain. The tradition of David tells of a father who goes weeping out of Jerusalem, leaving his city and his house to his rebellious son. Jacob hangs on to his son with his "throat"; he needs him the way the throat needs air to breathe (Gen 44:30).[3] "Beloved one of my throat" would also be a more literal translation of "beloved of my heart." Jeremiah understands the decline of Judah as a revelation of God's power, but not of divine paternal power, for God gives up fatherly rights and responsibilities. But he also understands the catastrophe as a sign of how powerless God is, though not in relation to the Babylonians, for it is God who has yielded up the city to them. God is powerless because unable to reveal himself as father to "the beloved of my heart."

In three of Jeremiah's other sayings "fatherhood" is a reflection of God's deep, internal longing. In distinction to this saying, the prophet there expressly refers to God as "father."

Jeremiah 3:4, 19: God yearns to be called "My Father"

In Jeremiah 3 the intimately familiar salutation "My father" appears two times.[4] In the first, God quotes Israel's conversation with bitter irony. The rains had not come, and the people want to touch God's heart. Should they present themselves to God as children who can count on their father's compliance? or as a wife who reminds her husband of the loveliness of her youth?[5] Best would be both at once! And, to make the insult complete, they promptly turn away from God and do not speak with God but about God, and who knows with whom. They express their impatience: "My Father, you are the friend of my youth—will he be angry forever, will he be indignant to the end?" (Jer 3:4).

The second time it is God who links the images of father and husband, addressing Israel the wife:

> I thought
>   how I would set you among my children,
> and give you a pleasant land,
>   the most beautiful heritage of all the nations.
> And I thought you would call me, My Father,
>   and would not turn from following me.
> Instead, as a faithless wife leaves her husband,
>   so you have been faithless to me, O house of Israel (Jer 3:19-20).

The prophet dares to look into God's thoughts; hidden in God lives the longing to be called "My Father." With double boldness Jeremiah portrays how vulnerable God is. The abuse of the name of father hurts God deeply. Only one question: why does God yearn to hear precisely this expression? Jeremiah was familiar with Hosea's message. It is also a word from Hosea that reveals what God hopes for:

God wants to hear the term of endearment "my husband" from Israel the wife.[6] In contrast, Jeremiah declares that God has upset well-worn customs and given the most beautiful legacy to a woman who is legally incapable of inheriting anything, all so that she will call God "My Father." Jeremiah portrays the internal driving force of Israel's history in its land, the end of which he experienced, namely, God's search for a son. The prophet imagines God as one of the fathers of Israel. When there was no son to carry on the heavy work on the land, the land became run down and the memory of the one who had once cared for it was lost. God does not want to be forgotten either, and it was for this reason that God dealt with womanly Israel as with a son.

Jeremiah's thoughts go still further. The relation between father and son was, after all, not determined only by questions of inheritance. Biblical narratives describe how father and son are close in their thoughts even when they are far apart from one another. Adolescent sons were legal assistants for their fathers. Among the traditions of Israel's first king, the unhappy Saul, are bright pictures of Jonathan, who held to his father to the death. It was such a son that God had sought, a mature son who does not say "father" only when he wants this or that. God had given Israel the land so that it could take care of itself and so that "My Father" would not be anything else but an address of love. Jeremiah does not alter the image of marriage because the love of woman is less important to him than the love for a son. The trouble of his era drives him to imagine God's longing differently. God hopes for the strong son in whom the memory of God's name can live on in a wicked time, but God is disappointed, for Israel is a faithless woman.

With his message of God's fatherhood Jeremiah seeks a basis for his hope that can survive the destruction of Jerusalem. In Israel only a man who was able to pass on an inheritance and install a son in his rights was considered a father in the full sense. When the prophet attempted to interpret the events of his time by means of this father image he saw that God could not be Father, for the inheritance was being lost, and there was no son through whom God's name could live on. Yet biblical traditions also tell about a bond between the father and the son that, because it lies hidden in the heart, can actually be stronger than the individual. Here the prophet finds some cause for hope. Though Israel is incapable of loving as a son does, in

God lives the longing to be called "My Father," and the history of Israel shows how much God is moved by it. Jeremiah dares to imagine that in God, too, the power that binds to the longed-for "son" is stronger than God's very self. God can put aside the rights and duties of the father, but longs for this "beloved" as if God, too, had a "throat" that is unable to do anything but gasp for air. Must this lively love, which is, after all, God's love, not necessarily triumph? Two statements from Jeremiah 31 describe how that can happen.

Jeremiah 31:9, 20: God wants to be a motherly father

The fatherly words in Jeremiah 31 are an early testimony to how fervently the return of the deportees was hoped for. For the prophet it is a complicated hope. Two and three times he builds up, so to speak, a stage within the stage so that hope can have space to move. He imagines that God pictures how the homecoming will be. God wants to be with God's own in the same way as once at the Exodus from Egypt. And yet there is no song of victory:

> With weeping they shall come,
> and with consolations I will lead them back,
> I will let them walk by brooks of water,
> in a straight path in which they shall not stumble;
> for I have become a father to Israel,
> and Ephraim is my firstborn (Jer 31:9).

God is a father who spares no effort to make sure those who belong to God come home in safety. Israel's traditions know such fathers. Jacob, for instance, had proved himself in this way at the Penuel ford (cf. ch. 3, section 3 above). But Jeremiah cannot imagine that those who return home would simply rejoice, for the memory of those who had perished without hope must be especially painful to them during their move to freedom. God does not insist that all tears be wiped away as soon as God is revealed as Father. God understands the art of comforting. Comfort takes grief seriously; if not, the distressed would feel themselves mocked, as if they were just too stupid to assess everything correctly. A comforter shows how to find new life even in sorrow. The God who comforts does not bring forth great miracles as at the Exodus. God shows the people "brooks of water" and secure paths. In the daily life of the family, comfort is often a skill of the mother,[7] but Jeremiah sticks with the father image. His reason for doing so is not that a woman would not have been trusted to find secure ways. Israel was familiar with the fatherly mother who in the desert takes her child "firmly by the hand" (cf. ch. 3, section 4 above). Jeremiah speaks about the father because he links the moving image of God's concerned attentiveness with concepts from the realm of the Law. As the name of the father lives on in the firstborn, so the people of YHWH come to life again when their strongest tribe, Ephraim, comes home.[8] But Jeremiah understands this legal bond of God with Israel as an expression of inner sympathy. After all, mothers also invest in the lives of their children, often more passionately than fathers.

In Jer 31:18-22 the maternal features in the image of God's turning to the people are even more conspicuous because words such as father, house, and inheritance are not to be found. Here, too, the prophet understands events of world politics as part of an internal history. Although the exiles' opportunity to go home is a result of the collapse of a despotic political regime, the prophet has a more radical change in mind, namely, that the exiles come to remember their God once again. Israel's renewal must begin with Israel itself; the "firstborn son" needs to be aware of his rights as a son. And yet Jeremiah presents it in such a way that everything appears to depend on God, for Ephraim remembers only that God was not successful at raising the son: "You disciplined me, and I took the discipline; I was like a calf untrained" (v. 18). The people are like an unruly and dangerous good-for-nothing. Of their own strength they do not succeed even in returning to their God. Ephraim pleads: "Bring me back, let me come back" (v. 18). But God answers immediately with overflowing emotion:

> Is Ephraim my dear son?
>   Is he the child I delight in?
> As often as I speak against him,
>   I still remember him.
> Therefore I am deeply moved for him;
>   I will surely have mercy on him (Jer 31:20).

Does Jeremiah have before his eyes the image of a mother who is obliged to think about her problem child? The last word of the statement, "to have mercy" *(rḥm)* belongs to the same word root as "mother's womb"*(raḥemah).* In her womb a woman has a physical organ through which she shares her life with the child. But does not also a father give his children living space in which, when they live with him, they can grow toward independence? In 2 Kings 4:18 is told incidentally, and thus that much more credibly, how in those days a child took part in the life of the father. A little boy wants to be with his father, who is working with the reapers in the field. In Ps 103:13 YHWH is praised "as a father [who] has compassion *(rḥm)* for his children."

Whether Jeremiah is consistent in his use of the father image is not as important as the recurrent image substitution. Instead of a dangerous good-for-nothing, God apparently cannot help but see a joyous, likable child. Jeremiah interchanges the images in order to make understandable why God's powerful love nevertheless depends on the voluntary initiative of the person. God chooses family images in which the inscrutable God appears easily understandable. In Luke 15 Jesus tells of the father of a family who waits so intensely for his son finally to remember him in the midst of his chaotic life that he spies the returning son from afar and runs out to meet him. This is how Jeremiah sees the God of Israel. God is happy finally to be able to show the people all the sympathy that is stirred up within God by their miserable situation. The difference is only that in the words of the prophet an even smaller sign is sufficient: the son does not need to return home, but only to ask for the courage to do so.

The words about the homecoming of Ephraim belong to the many unfulfilled promises of the Bible. The deportees of the northern kingdom were, after all, lost without a trace, just as were the other small, subjugated peoples of the Middle East. All that remained of Israel were those who survived the demise of the southern kingdom of Judah. Yet Jeremiah's visual images of the motherly and fatherly God continue to be preserved, for they testify to the driving force that kept the history of God's people in motion despite this breach, namely, God's longing for the true son.

After Jeremiah the message about God the Father did not again receive great emphasis until Jesus. The following section asks why no other biblical voice between Jeremiah and Jesus speaks with comparable insistence about the fatherhood of God.

2. The biblical message about God the Father within the framework of the history of religion

The kinship group of YHWH

Israel is one of the peoples that did not appear in Canaan until the beginning of the Iron Age. In contrast to the older city-states and the great kingdoms on the Euphrates and the Nile, these new people called themselves "kinship groups." In the Old Testament, Moab is called the "kinship group" or the "people" of the god Chemosh (*ʿam* has both meanings), and early Old Testament voices speak of Israel as the "kinship group," the "son," or "sons" of its Father.[9] But Jeremiah is the first to speak of God as the "father" of Israel.

ʿAm YHWH, "People of God," is an expression of faith. The song of Deborah (Judges 5), the oldest detailed hymn in the Old Testament, tells about this faith. A group of farmers, severely tormented by their enemies, had already chosen "other gods," but then joined together and moved as "people of YHWH" against the enemy cities. One locality that stays out of the pact is cursed because "they did not come to the help of YHWH . . . against the mighty." The *ʿam* of YHWH comes into being when people recognize that they belong together and "come to aid" God. The song impressively describes how powerfully God helps them. YHWH comes in a powerful rainstorm and "the stars fought from heaven." Why the God of Israel was not called "father" is easy to understand here. That would be too little. The father is only one among many in the kinship group, and often his sons become stronger than he.[10] However, when Israel trusts that "YHWH is among the heroes" (v. 23 variant) it receives help that no father can give. Parallels to the first sentence of the Christian creed, the confession of the "Father almighty, creator of heaven and earth" can be found more easily in the religions of many ancient civilized peoples than in the Bible.

The universal fatherhood of God

In contrast with the Iron Age peoples, in the state religions of the Near East and Egypt, which were already ancient at that time, great gods were called on as father and often at the same time as mother: "father of heaven and earth";[11] "father of the regions of the world"; "father and mother of that which he has made"; "father of the gods";

"father of humanity."[12] Hymns named the creator of the universe divine father and praised the fatherly and motherly compassion by means of which he maintains everything alive. A Sumerian hymn praises "Father Nana" (the moon god):

> Mother's womb that gives birth to all,
> gracious Father, who bears in his hand the life of all the land.[13]

Even the warlike creator god Marduk is called a merciful father: "Sweet is your favor, and your mercy like that of a father."[14] However our ears may hear it today, the "Father almighty" with which the Christian creed begins also includes the powerful goodness of God through which all things that exist are inwardly related to one another. Pagan piety did not specify whether the gods encountered the world in a fatherly or a motherly fashion. In the Acts of the Apostles, Luke has Paul speaking in the same way. Everything that lives is secure as in a mother's womb: "In him we live and move and have our being" (Acts 17:28).

Only a single biblical text speaks of God as Father of the universe: "For this reason I bow my knees before the Father, from whom every family in heaven and on earth takes its name" (Eph 3:14-15). In many cultures the names of fathers establish relationships that persist through the years. Like family fathers, "founding fathers" also wish to make their names "eternal." In Eph 3:14 this right of fathers is contested. Whoever honors God as Father recognizes that in all the tribes named after fathers it is only the one Father of the world who is remembered.[15]

Ephesians 3:14 is the only biblical statement that deviates from the approach initiated by Jeremiah, the first in the Bible to speak of God as "Father." For him "father" was not a concept of origins, but a word of hope that gave new vitality to the faith in Israel as the "kindred of YHWH." Later biblical voices proceeded farther along on this way. What they seek in God is not the father of the world, not the name-giver of all the paternal tribes, but "Our Father," the father of the tiny society to which they themselves belong.

God, our Father

Jesus does not speak of God as the father of the world. In the Sermon on the Mount he says that it is "your Father" who "makes his sun rise on the evil and on the good." The Lord of all the world is father to the little group that Jesus had gathered around him. Like other Jewish teachers of his time Jesus instructs his disciples to say "Our Father" in addressing God. The naturalness with which early Christian congregations spoke of God as their Father is evident in Paul's letters. In his greetings the apostle normally says "our Father."[16]

That Jeremiah did not adopt the concept of the universal fatherhood of God is comprehensible. In Jeremiah's time the people lost everything by means of which they could recognize themselves as a nation, and the remnant of Israel had to ask themselves if the ancient article of faith about the "kindred of YHWH" was still valid. As it was handed down, this faith demanded that the people and God come to one another's aid, as is proper among relatives. But how should the people who were victims of nothing so much as the politics of the great powers come to the help of their God? It would have been senseless to take a defensive stand as the farmers of Israel had once done. Jeremiah discovered a more fitting image in the daily life of the family, namely that parents are helpless victims of their sorrow when they cannot comfort their suffering child because it refuses to come to them. Israel needs only to come to YHWH's aid as can every child. "With weeping they shall come": so begin the fatherly words in Jer 31:9.

Jesus and the early Christian congregations, too, responded with the words "God, our Father" to experiences of their time in which it seemed as if God's people were dissolving into splinter groups. The little company of Jesus' disciples understood themselves as a beginning place of justice and peace out of which the People of God would go forth renewed. In his time Jeremiah had counseled the deportees to seek the new beginning of the people of God in the everyday life of their families.[17]

At the time of the New Testament natural family ties had been destroyed much more fundamentally. Although it did happen that a "father and his whole household" came to faith (see ch. 1, section 2 above), in the company of Jesus' disciples people came together who had fallen out of every family situation. Thus Jesus speaks of the disciples as an incomplete family that receives a father only in the Father of Jesus (see ch. 2, section 10 above).

Family romanticism, which seeks salvation in the healthy family, was far from Jeremiah's intention. In his pictorial imagery about God's fatherhood he does not transfigure secular family life; rather, he takes a critical look at an everyday religion in which one entrusted oneself personally to a God to whom one says "my Father."

God, my Father

Personal names are the oldest layer in the Old Testament in which God is called "Father." The most familiar is Abraham, which means "the father is exalted." Many other people in Israel's early days bear names of this kind. With this the young Israel continued a custom of name-giving that had already existed in Egypt, Mesopotamia, and the city-states of Canaan. Just as in Israel, so the pagan relationship names praised the strength and friendliness of a god or a goddess.

Semitic personal names from the Israel of the late Bronze Age and the early Iron Age are witnesses to popular piety that entrusted itself to a deity as if to a relative.[18]

Abraham/Abram	the father is exalted	
Ahiram	the brother is exalted	king of Byblos, 11th c. B.C.E.
Amram	the uncle is exalted	father of Moses
Ammiel	God is uncle	father of Bathsheba
Joab	YHWH is father	David's general
Abishai	the father has come	brother of Joab
Ahijah	YHWH is brother	Solomon's minister
Abinadab	the father is magnanimous	Non-Israelite (2 Samuel 6)
Ahimelech	the brother is king	priest in Saul's time
Abiathar	the father has abundance	son of Ahimelech
Abimelech	the father is king	King of Tyre, 14th c. B.C.E.
Abimelech		Prince of Shechem (Judges 9)
Ahinoam	the brother is charming	wife of David
Abigail	the father rejoices	wife of David

and many more.

By means of such a name parents placed their child under the protection of a god or goddess to whom the person would be obligated for life. In the second millennium B.C.E. a man who was obviously already a father of a family dictates to his slave a letter to his personal tutelary god: "Say to the god, my father, the following: 'Why were you idle in relation to me? I wish to see your face and to kiss your feet! Behold also my family: Look at them, both great and small!'"[19]

In Ugarit there were names like "the Lord is mother" or "Astar (the god) is mother."[20] Perhaps someone was thereby entrusting a child whose mother had died to the god who was for him or her the most loved. But in early Israel one was able, according to the witness of these names, to imagine God only as a masculine relative such as father, brother, or uncle. For this reason alone it is good that the piety that speaks out of these names was not directly operative in the Bible.

The custom of naming children after relatives was lost after the time of David. Children came to be given names of prayer, such as Jeremiah, "YHWH has exalted." Nevertheless, these names speak of the same simple hope for a friendly God who is concerned for the individual, who "gives, recognizes, loves, helps, saves . . . ." The vow that Jacob made when he had to leave his home and family also testifies to this piety that expects practical help from God in everyday concerns. "If God . . . will give me bread to eat and clothing to wear, so that I come again to my father's house in peace . . ." (Gen 28:20-21). After his happy homecoming Jacob promises to prove his thankfulness by building a shrine. Though the editors of the Jacob tradition do not reject this piety, they contrast the comforting encounter with God of the runaway Jacob with his frightening experience as he returns home. During an entire night Jacob struggles with a man who does not identify himself and in the morning dismisses him as one both blessed and wounded (Genesis 32). With the same care Jeremiah takes pains to speak of the God who is acquainted with the everyday joys of fathers as being also the God who is incomprehensible. To the deportees he writes that it is the "Lord of the armies" who can imagine how fathers will again pluck up their courage (see ch. 1, section 3 above). But in his statements about God as a father he is concerned with the mystery of Israel's story, which since ancient times has been moved by God's longing to be called "My Father" (Jer 3:4).

The traditions about Jacob are much more uninhibited and natural than Jeremiah in satisfying the desire for comprehensible signs of God's nearness. According to Gen 28:18 Jacob anointed the stone at which God had appeared to him and named it "the house of God." In Israel, as also among related peoples, stones and wooden stakes were simple signs, affordable to everyone, of the helping presence of God. But Jeremiah rejects a piety that believes that when God is appealed to as "My Father," God is as easily accessible as a stone:

> [Those] who say to a tree, "You are my father,"
> and to a stone, "You gave me birth" (Jer 2:27).

When Israel cares about God only as long as God seems to be a compliant father or a mother who can be extorted, it wounds God most deeply in God's hidden longing.

Matthew 6:32: Your Father knows that you have need of all of these things

Even the best practices of piety can go bad and make God into nothing more than a thing of utility. At the time of Jesus it was not stone and wood that were wrongly used, but a form of prayer. In the Psalms, in order to unite all the people in praise of God, people of prayer witness publicly that God has helped them.[21] At the time of Jesus there must have been those who wanted in this way to demonstrate that they were good members of the family of God who knew precisely what "our Father" does. In his answer to this, Jesus refrains one time from calling God "your [plural] Father": "pray to your [sing]. Father who is in secret; and your [sing]. Father who sees in secret will reward you" (Matt 6:6). God is not Father just for the company of disciples. For the individual, too, God is "your" [sing.] Father. The best of ancient family piety lives on in this word of Jesus, that is, the personal bond of the individual with the God well known to him or her.

A second element of that everyday religion appears in the Sermon on the Mount: the trust that God will make people's simple needs God's own concern. In this context Jeremiah, with his solemn title for God, "Lord of hosts," had recalled that the God who is nearby is also the Incomprehensible One. Jesus names God "Father," yet he, too, proclaims the incomprehensible God: "Therefore do not worry, saying, 'What will we eat?' or 'What will we drink?' or 'What will we wear?' . . . your heavenly Father knows that you need all these things. But strive first for the kingdom of God and his righteousness" (Matt 6:31-32). Jesus stands everything on its head. The concerns of housewives are taken on by the heavenly Father, who in turn lays on human beings the care for God's kingdom and God's righteousness. Influential voices of the Old Testament teach that the Law reveals the ways of justice. On the other hand, an important part of Jesus' message says: Do the will of the Father. The next section addresses the question of what these words have in common and what differentiates them.

3. The will of the Father: the Law of God

Matthew 21:28-29: A parable about the will of the Father

When a father sends his sons into the vineyard one of them says "yes," but does not go, while the other says "no," and his father accepts it. This father does not seem to possess much authority. But then the second son is sorry, and he goes after all. The parable closes with a question that at first seems easy to answer: "Which of the two did the will of his father?"

But what motivated the second son to do the father's will after all? Was he sorry that the vineyard was becoming run-down? Did he want to spare his father annoyance? Did he regret having disappointed his father? The parable says nothing about it. One must also take into consideration that the one who said yes is the elder son, who will one day possess everything that his father now has, while the second son has only the right to live with his brother (see ch. 2, section 5 above). He is therefore doing work that benefits his brother more than himself.

The parable gives easily understood access to a difficult word of promise. According to Jer 31:33-34, in the new covenant God will write the Law on people's hearts. How is that to happen? The parable explains this in two ways. The father's will finds an echo in the son's heart, and the listeners will have to weigh in their hearts what kind of echo that is. Is it in his love as a son, his responsibility for the inheritance, or in the magnanimity with which he does work for which his brother would have been at least as responsible as he?

The Old Testament does not speak of the "will of the Father" but of the Law of God. At Sinai God did not encounter the people of

Israel as Father, but as teacher of just rules for life. Nevertheless, Jesus was not the first to speak of God as a Father in the context of the Law of God. Four Old Testament texts preceded him in this.

Deuteronomy 1:31: The father brings the son to the place of the renewal of the Law.

In view of the imminent end of Israel, deuteronomic teachers of the Law renewed the Law of Sinai. It is characteristic that Deuteronomy presents itself as Moses' farewell discourse delivered before he, like so many of the deportees, had to die outside the Land. The book begins with a sermon that describes the journey from Sinai to this place of Law renewal as a way "through all that great and terrible wilderness" (Deut 1:19). The preacher adds: "that you saw." In this direct address is still reflected the shock at the fall of Judah that was still fresh in their minds. The sermon is directed to people for whom the world has become a life-threatening "wilderness."

Soon thereafter the preacher's image of the journey through the wilderness seems to become an idyll: God carries Israel through the wilderness as a father does a child. Yet the author warns that the peaceful picture means to portray a God who fights. God, so he says, fought "on your side" in Egypt. God did the same in the wilderness "that you saw." All of this seems too idyllic. In the "wilderness" that the addressees of the sermon are experiencing God had certainly not fought for them, but left them to be destroyed. Nevertheless, the preacher continues: "and in the wilderness . . . you saw how the LORD your God carried you, just as one carries a child, all the way that you traveled until you reached this place" (Deut 1:31).

The preacher alternates between you (plural) and you (singular) and does so at telling places: "Your [sing.] God" is reminiscent of the simple mundane piety in which the individual saw God as a fatherly protector. God's battle need not be anything spectacular. It can also consist in this, that people survive a "wilderness" and then, as the People of God, receive the Law anew.

With the image of the father who carries the son the author interprets a second element of his narrative of the wilderness. At the beginning he had said that Moses "could not bear" the people (1:12) with "the heavy burden of your disputes." In response, the people chose men who helped Moses (1:16). In good times no one should bear the burden alone. It was too much even for Moses. In terrible times, however, when the people are not able to put their lives in order, they can be confident that God will carry them like a child.

Jeremiah had proclaimed that it was already sufficient when Israel approaches God like a child who runs crying to its father (see section 1 above). The people described by the deuteronomic preacher do not trust the Father for anything. In the wilderness they had lost all hope. On another occasion, when they had wanted to force a good ending, they had failed miserably. The people for whom the sermon was intended certainly were also acquainted with both possible outcomes. Israel is actually incapable of the cooperation that a child contributes when it seeks help from its parents. A little child can do nothing, and God must carry it, but God brings it to the place of the renewal of the Law. When need be, God acts like the father of a little child, but only in order once again to become the lawgiver who guides a mature people to choose representatives to bear their burden. The preacher is moved by the question of how God is to create a people of God's own choosing when the people are incapable of doing their part. A curious poem transcribed in Deuteronomy 32 and transmitted as a song of Moses deals with the same question:

Deuteronomy 32:6, 11: Israel's creator behaves like a father bird

A part of the song in Deut 32:7-17 tells how Israel, although chosen and richly endowed, does not care at all about God. This story is doubly framed. The beginning part of the inmost frame speaks of God as the Father:

> Is not he your father, who created you,
> who made you and established you? (Deut 32:6).

The final part of the frame (Deut 32:18) speaks of God as of a mother who bore Israel with birth pains.[22] In the outer frame the poet laments how futile it is for God to be both Father and Mother to this people. God's children "have dealt falsely with him" and in turn "he spurned his sons and daughters" (Deut 32:5, 19).

In the advanced civilizations of antiquity the creator deity that maintained all living things was addressed as father and mother. All is concealed within its goodness, and nothing that is can exist without it. The poet may also have taken the thought of a fatherly-motherly God from the everyday religion that is attested in many personal names (see section 2 above), for creation motifs appear here also. Ili-bani, "My God is my begetter," was the name of a man in Mesopotamia. Guden of Lagash (ca. 3000 B.C.E.) prayed to a goddess of his city:

> I have no mother, for you are my mother;
> I have no father, for you are my father.[23]

But what Deuteronomy 32 says about the children of the fatherly-motherly God would have been just as unthinkable in the popular religion as in the high religions of the ancient world, that is, that God is in distress because God's sons and daughters have forsaken and revile their God.

The poet has his own reasons for taking up the primeval images of God as creator, mother, and father that were so beloved in the world of that time. The history of Israel proves to him that Israel has no inner security in itself, and that only its origin in God gives it stability. By full application of her strength, God the parturient had brought her people into the world, and as Israel's creator God is not the commanding sovereign. With toil God had "made" and "erected" the people. God had expended much effort to create this people. Should this all be in vain?

It is this question that moves the poet to call attention to God not only as creator but simultaneously as Father. He wants to prepare the father-image that will appear in the midst of historical narrative to show how Israel's origin continues to have an effect on its history. It is a remarkable image of God as a father bird. The eagle pushes its fledglings out of the nest so that they learn to fly, but always maintains a readiness to catch a tired young one.[24] God is the working creator, the birth-giving mother. As a father bird concerned about his offspring God continues the effort to assure that Israel learn to fly like an eagle. Israel is pushed out into the uncertainties of history like a fledgling out of the nest. But God, who pushes it, is moved by the same hope as the fathers in Israel who needed sons who would stand at their sides like brothers. God hopes for a strong, independent people. The language and images of the songs of Moses are unique in the Bible, yet the message of his fatherly words is none other than that proclaimed by the preacher in Deuteronomy 1: God is father in order to assist Israel to a life of responsibility for itself.

The poetry in Isa 63:15–64:12 also relies on the thought of God as father in order to consider the question whether Israel is even capable of living according to God's Law. It is an extensive song of lament that the poet places in the people's mouth. In distinction to the Song of Moses, it refers in its "father words" to well-known concepts and even verbatim to older biblical texts.

Isaiah 63:16 and 64:8: Israel's ultimate hope lies in its Father and Creator

> For you are our father,
>   though Abraham does not know us
>   and Israel does not acknowledge us;
> you, O LORD, are our father;
>   our Redeemer from of old is your name.
> . . .
> Yet, O LORD, you are our Father;
>   we are the clay, and you are our potter;
>   we are all the work of your hand.

The motive of the complaint is the desecration of the Temple. It cannot be determined which concrete event is meant, for more than anything else Israel is lamenting its internal condition. Because of its inner guilt it no longer has any strength to live: "We all fade like a leaf, and our iniquities, like the wind, take us away" (64:6).

Twice the song calls God "our Father." With the first, twofold cry for the father the poet modifies two expressions of Jeremiah. The words of God in Jer 31:20 reveal how greatly Israel's misery disturbs God. Here the people direct the same words to God: "Where are your zeal and your might? The yearning of your heart and your compassion?" (63:15). The answer is given by the people themselves. It is, at any rate, also passed on to them by the tradition. It cites the word of God in Jer 31:9: "I have become a father to Israel" (cf. Isa 63:16). Out of the comforting promise of Jeremiah has come an accusing question. When will God finally fulfill the promise?

Soon thereafter the writer repeats the cry of "Father!" but first he alludes to other well-known words of the prophets. Israel had once passed on the blame for the loss of its political freedom to its fathers, who had obstructed for it every chance to live a correct life. Similarly, many people prefer to blame their failed lives on their parents rather than take the responsibility themselves. The prophets had forbidden the people to speak in this way (see ch. 2, section 4 above). In Isaiah

63–64 the poet imagines that the people had grasped this warning. Between their calls to God as Father they speak of their human fathers: "For you are our father, though Abraham does not know us and Israel (Jacob) does not acknowledge us; You, O LORD, are our father."

The renewed cry of "Father!" is no simple repetition. After the recollection of the fathers of the past it has a new meaning. Those fathers are dead, and blaming them is useless. But Israel, too, which tumbles in the wind like wilted leaves, is too weak to bear its own guilt. The only thing left to do is to roll the blame onto the living Father who encourages them, onto God. Out of the complaint has come a cry of trust.

Toward the end of the song the people once again call God "our" Father, this time also in an expression of trust: "Yet, O Lord, you are our Father; we are the clay, and you are our potter; we are all the work of your hand" (64:8). Israel does not want to be anything else but material in God's hand: is not such trust all too simple? Has the poet forgotten that God wants to create a mature people of God's own choosing?

There are fathers who see their children as "raw material" in need of being molded into the correct shape. It becomes clear how far this understanding of God is from the poet's intention when, in the midst of hearing these verses, one also hears the older text that is reformulated here. This time it is the words of Deutero-Isaiah, prophet of the Exile:

> Does the clay say to the one who fashions it, "What are you making"?
> or "Your work has no handles"?
> Woe to anyone who says to a father, "What are you begetting?"
> or to a woman, "With what are you in labor?" (Isa 45:9-10).

"Woe!" was called out at lamentations of death. People who question why they were conceived can already be mourned as dead, so says the prophet. With this saying Deutero-Isaiah reacts to things he had experienced with his fellow-sufferers in Babylon. He had announced to the deportees that God would create for himself a new people, but they considered this nonsense. If God wants to take Israel's life, why the gruesome long way around through destruction and abduction? To this the prophet replies with the lament for the dead. That is, if the remnant of Israel fails to take on the new beginning as it was given, and complains of God-the-Potter's clumsiness, then Israel really is dead.

In Isa 64:8 the cry of woe becomes a statement of trust. God is a potter for whom "faded leaves" are clay that can be formed. In this resides the last hope for the guilt-ridden people. To entrust themselves to this creator as to a father is the only thinkable support that Israel still has.

The serious games that the scripturally learned poet plays with traditional texts are not easy to understand. Yet the intertwined pathways of the search for God are, in a difficult world, still more passable than the slippery roads of a simplistic conception of the fatherhood of God on which faith too easily slips and slides. An example of inappropriate simplification appears already in the saying about fatherhood in the book of Malachi:

Malachi 2:10: Have we not all one father?

"Have we not all one father? Has not one God created us? Why then are we faithless to one another, profaning the covenant of our ancestors?" (Mal 2:10). As do older voices, Malachi says that God is Father and creator for Israel and "for all of us," and yet by this he means only half of Israel, the men. How can he do this?

In Malachi's time the Jews who had returned from the exile lived a poor existence in Jerusalem. Many feared that the little group would lose its identity because many men had foreign wives who raised their children in their own language and customs (see ch. 1, section 4 above). A detailed report about this closes with praise for the men willing to get a divorce: "All these had married foreign women, and they sent them away with their children" (Ezra 10:44).

Fathers separate themselves from their children. It is not clear whether they gave their wives at least enough to live on. The Abraham legend in Genesis 21 (see ch. 3, section 5 above) shows how easily a man could excuse himself from this responsibility, but it also tells that God notices when the child rejected by the father cries. In the light of that older biblical text, Mal 2:10 should be contested. The concept of God's fatherhood is abused when it is used to advance a sense of "brotherhood" from which women and children are excluded solely because they are foreigners.[25]

The concern about Israel's survival is comprehensible, but can one appeal to God the Father in order to promote a brotherly fidelity that consists in being untrue to one's wife? Malachi 2:10 confirms with what matter-of-factness the renewed Israel assumed that each man who called on God as Father was obligated to protect his inheritance and the people from harm, but the verse also confirms how easily a good intention spoils when it becomes all too self-evident.

Once again: The parable about "the will of the father"

It was not simply by chance that the parable with which this section began spoke about work in a vineyard. "God's vineyard" has been from time immemorial a description of Israel. Jesus' saying about "the will of the father" renews the thought that God as "Father" wants to help his people to a life of responsibility for themselves. In the life of human beings not all those who live from the inheritance of the same father get along well with one another, but when there is no "brotherly" solidarity among a group of heirs the inheritance perishes. In Mal 2:10 this concept of the People of God is trivialized and misused. Jesus' parable gives it a new radiance. For the father's sake the younger son does the work that will benefit the older son more than him.

The special message of Jesus is reflected in this, namely, that it is the one disadvantaged by law who does the will of the father. In this way, too, Jesus fills with new power ancient concepts of the People of God. According to the witness of Old Testament texts even the legally disadvantaged—women and children—should participate in the learning of the Law and in the worship service (see ch. 1, section 6 above). Jesus carries this line of thought strongly forward. He brought to the center of attention people who, because they were not considered to be exactly the strongest supporters of the "heritage of God," had been left on the periphery. It would seem to be more reasonable that the strong, those who "bear the burden of the people," should occupy the center, but Jesus warns against taking self-evident matters of this sort all too much for granted. How he does that in his message about fatherhood will be one of the themes of the following section.

4. The Lord's Prayer: Testimony to Jesus' message about the Father

The prayers of children to the incomprehensible God

That Jesus lived with the Old Testament as his Scripture is also noticeable in his message about God the Father. Jeremiah had proclaimed how greatly God yearns that Israel would, with honest heart, call him Father. The prophet had promised that the "Father of Israel" would immediately turn to this "child I delight in" as soon as it simply asks for the will to repent (see section 1 above). Jesus teaches his disciples what they can do in order that God's longing and promise be fulfilled. They are to call God "Father" and speak with God as little children probably most often address their parents, that is, in direct requests that are clearly stated.

The requests in the Lord's Prayer are nevertheless not childish wishes, but grave problems that make it almost impossible to believe in God's fatherly love. If the realm of righteousness and peace belongs to God, why do injustice and war rule? If God wills people to be free, why not carry out the divine will against all the powers that hopelessly enslave them? How can it be that people who allow God to lead them could come into temptation? Jesus transforms insoluble questions of faith into the requests of children.

Luke follows the Lord's Prayer with two parables that illustrate this difficult teaching in a simple way. The first tells of a father who, for the sake of a friend, disturbs the nocturnal sleep of his children. God is like a man who is willing to sacrifice the sleep of his own children for the sake of a friend. The second passage dares to make an even bolder comparison: "Is there anyone among you who, if your child asks for a fish, will give a snake instead of a fish? Or if the child asks for an egg, will give a scorpion? If you then, who are evil, know how to give good gifts to your children, how much more will the heavenly Father give the Holy Spirit to those who ask him!" (Luke 11:11; see Matt 7:11).

Are wicked men good fathers? Starting with the example of the murderer and city-founder Cain, Old Testament narrators have given thought to this question (see ch. 2, section 4 above). Jesus chooses a much less complicated example. Even the simple things of everyday life are signs that God's fatherly goodness can be depended upon even when God seems "like one of you." Jesus' message about the Father is difficult because it does not leave out painful issues of faith. It is as simple as a child because Jesus speaks of the "Father in heaven" as the God who is close, who can be found by anyone who lives humanely.

The childlike requests of responsible people

One of the petitions of the Lord's Prayer resembles a child's plea also in respect to its content. Only well-cared-for children can afford not to think further than the bread that they need at the moment. Adults have to make provision also for those who cannot plan for themselves. But Jesus is particularly concerned that people who are prepared for responsibility also learn precisely this petition. The variation on this theme from the Sermon on the Mount also emphasizes this. Believers should leave to the heavenly Father the concern about eating and drinking and "all those things" and instead take upon themselves what only God is able to do, the responsibility for God's reign. Jesus carries to extremes the underlying thought of Old Testament "instructions for fathers," that is, God's hope of having strong sons. Does he not go too far? The history of Christianity furnishes terrible examples of what men who think they must act for God are prepared to do. The petition for bread helps resist this danger.

This petition stands at the pivotal point of the Lord's Prayer. On the one hand, it begins a new section. After the great petitions that are concerned with "your name, your kingdom," and "your will," those who pray look at their own lives. They think about "our bread," the forgiveness of "our sins," and ask that God not lead "us" into temptation. In the last petition it becomes clear who is saying "we" and "our." These are people who allow God to lead them on the way of life. It can happen to them that it is God who "leads them into temptation." It can happen to them as it happened to Abraham, who understood only one thing, which was to obey God, and who would have treated his son unhumanly if God had not saved him from the worst possible outcome (see ch. 3, section 7 above). The extreme claims that life with God places on one can turn into the temptation to undervalue simple shared humanity (see ch. 1, section 4 above). Therefore the petition for bread teaches the disciples to move into the ranks of normal people. They confess that they can fail in the same difficulties as do other people.[26]

On the one hand, then, the petition for bread belongs to the second part, where the Lord's Prayer speaks of human pitifulness. But it also belongs to the first part. There can be no deliverance from evil except through the petitions that follow, for here, as in the introductory petitions, the concern is for a good gift of God. Jesus places the childlike wish for bread on the same level with the great petitions that, transcending all human limits, ask for the sanctification of the name of God and the coming of God's reign.

Here it is once more revealed where Jesus begins when he renews the thought of God's fatherhood: with the little people and the weak.

For this purpose he stands an old biblical motif on its head. The preacher in Deuteronomy had said that God carries the people like a child so that they can come to the place where they can learn responsibility for themselves (see section 3 above). Jesus teaches those who bear responsibility for the reign of God that this far-too-difficult task can succeed only when they carry it out like children. The main thing for children is the joy of living. They have no understanding of money, power, and public prestige. When the effort expended by someone for the reign of God brings him or her more than what children need in order to have joy in living, he or she can no longer really join in the prayer for daily bread.

The father who is ready to forgive

In the Lord's Prayer the concept of a fatherly God seems almost to disappear behind thoughts about the inscrutable God. There is only one sentence that does not look pleadingly to the future in which God will be revealed in power, but to a present that everyone can enter who wills to do so: "forgive us . . . as we also have forgiven our debtors" (Matt 6:12). Matthew underlines this sentence when, at the end of the Lord's Prayer, he continues: "For if you forgive others their trespasses, your heavenly Father will also forgive you" (Matt 6:14). Christians often tend to include in their estimation of faith and life God's readiness to forgive as if it were a guaranteed and calculable reality. But Matthew gives the name "Heavenly Father" also to the God who is ready to forgive. Even when people experience forgiveness, God's fatherliness is not measurable by earthly standards.

More faithfully than Christians, for whom "Father" is practically the name of God, Jews, who call on God as "our Father," and "our king," hold fast to the conviction that the image of the father cannot encompass God's entire activity.[27] Life-tested Jewish wisdom speaks also in the counsel that Jesus Sirach gives to troubled people. Those who find themselves in a life-threatening situation because of their enemies or through their own fault should call out: "O Lord, Father and Master of my life!" (Sir 23:1; see 51:10).

People who see in God only a father equipped with divine power will be hindered in time of need by their own image of God from even seeking the Father in God. Why should they entrust themselves to someone who, though able to help, does not do so? Sirach counsels people in need to see in God not only the Father but the Master from whom all of life, with its low points and high points, must be taken as God gives it.

This thought is disclosed in the narrative context of another saying about fathers that comes from Jewish wisdom. Tobit was saved from guilt and misery (see ch. 1, section 4 above) and responds with a song of praise in which he interprets his personal story as a confirmation of Israel's experience. He sings: "Acknowledge him before the nations, O children of Israel; for he has scattered you among them. He has shown you his greatness even there" (Tob 13:3). Instead of a useless complaint about Israel's dispersion among the nations we find an insight that spurs to activity: God had scattered Israel because God was planning something new with them. Now Israelites can confess their God everywhere in the world. Tobit continues: ". . . he is our Father and he is God forever" (Tob 13:4). Because the Eternal One is not to be measured with the standards of human time, Israel can confess that God is Father even in those times when God tries the people with evil. As long as Tobit considered himself the sole righteous person, he was also isolated in his family. The one God is not isolated by fatherhood. Rather, God's fatherhood is fully realized only when the "children of Israel" confess their Father both in good times and in the Diaspora.

It is on such sources that Matthew draws when, at the end of the Lord's Prayer, he comments on the petition for forgiveness. People often confuse forgiveness with the release from all responsibility for evil deeds. When the results of their deeds become a heavy load for them to bear, they think they have not been forgiven. Even evil deeds that have been forgiven continue having their bad effects. Whoever accepts this experience from "the heavenly Father" experiences precisely in this what forgiveness is, namely, that the evil past is no longer binding. Even out of a disastrous initial situation there are ways open to good ways of life. For the guilty person, too, God wants to be a Father who needs a capable "son" and helper.

Jewish sages occasionally paraphrased such experiences of God with a saying drawn from family and school life of the time, that is, God "punishes" the one God loves as a father punishes his son. It would be better to translate these words differently. In Prov 31:1 they refer to the loving but firm words that a mother gives her son on his way. One cannot call her words "punishment," for they are "correction." The "correcting" God corrects those whose life-experiences have caused them to lose their way.[28] Whoever trusts that it is the fatherly God who appears even where either one's own guilt or the guilt of others shows its disastrous effects is liberated from the compulsion of continually having to ask how much guilt is to be assigned, and to whom. In place of self-accusations and assignments of blame there comes the courage to look for new possibilities for the future.

Luke passes on as a word of the Crucified the message that Matthew appended to the Lord's Prayer: "Father, forgive them; for they do not know what they are doing" (Luke 23:34). Jesus taught his disciples the Lord's Prayer as a prayer that may be spoken by those who have already forgiven their fellow human beings. In the word of the Crucified it becomes clear what the issue is, namely, that the readiness to forgive is not a preliminary achievement in consideration of which God then in turn replies with forgiveness. It is the work that the capable son does for his father in order that the inheritance be preserved. Jesus even goes through death so that the inheritance of his Father is not lost. It is the inclusive heritage of God that belongs to all humanity, including even those who crucified him.

5. God, a Father with daughters

A remarkable expression in one of Paul's epistles

Only once does the Bible say that God the Father has not only "sons" but also "daughters." The section where this appears, 2 Cor 6:16-18, also has a form of speech that is very exotic within the letters of Paul; within a short space ten or even twelve phrases from the Old Testament are woven into a chain of quotations. Such compositions of sayings were much loved in Qumran, and the theme of the section is also consistent with the characteristic way of life of the people of Qumran, who, remote from other Jews, believed that a holy people with God in their midst must certainly isolate themselves. Yet these verses certainly do not come from Qumran, for no one there would have spoken of daughters of God. There was no place for women in the holy assembly of Qumran.

In 2 Corinthians Paul waxes polemical against a group that was threatening to split the congregation in Corinth. Perhaps these people made use of such chains of quotations in their argumentation, and Paul, who wished to defeat them with their own weapons, had recourse to what was for him an unusual form of discourse in order to convince the congregation to shun them. When considered in the context where they originated, the Scripture verses he uses point only in a general way in the direction of his exhortation. They do not demand self-isolation, but speak about the presence of God with God's people or encourage the deportees to return home.[29]

It may be that Paul was alluding to Isa 43:6-7, where through the prophet of the Exile God promises to "bring my sons from far away and my daughters from the end of the earth—everyone who is called by my name." Thus Deutero-Isaiah renews Isaiah's early creed. Even after the loss of its political freedom Israel is the people of YHWH, called by the divine name. This ancient statement of faith never speaks of God's fatherhood, nor does Isaiah 43, for Israel hopes that YHWH will help more powerfully than a father (see section 2 above).

In 2 Cor 6:18 another word of Scripture sounds out more clearly than Deutero-Isaiah's promise to those who return home. God promises King David divine care for his son: "I will be a father to him, and he shall be a son to me" (2 Sam 7:14). Paul reformulates this statement: "I will be your father, and you shall be my sons and daughters" (2 Cor 6:18). This quotation is hardly suited to the overall message of the composition of sayings. It brings no further "scriptural proof" that the holy people must isolate themselves. In fact, it underscores the chain's origin in Christianity. Christian congregations liked to appeal to the promise to David, which is mentioned in the New Testament with relative frequency. Thus the apostle had chosen an expression that may have been especially dear also to the Corinthians. Paul explains to them that the promise to David applies to the entire congregation, to men and to women. It becomes clear how bold that is when one considers the meaning this saying otherwise had.

Two ways in which God is the Father of the sons of David

In its original setting this text reflects Israel's historical experience. It is a word of God to David. God makes David a promise about what God will do for his son and successor: "I will be a father to him, and he shall be a son to me" (2 Sam 7:14). David had failed in raising his sons. God wants to assume David's place in correcting his son, as would have been the right and duty of fathers (see sections 4 and 8 of ch. 3 above). When Saul failed, Israel had already experienced that God could also act as sovereign over the chosen king (see ch. 2, section 1 above). To the son of David it is promised, however, that God will limit the divine power and treat him "according to human custom," as does a father.

In the New Testament this promise receives a new meaning. Prompted by two psalms, Christians allowed themselves to look far beyond the history of Israel. Psalms 2:7 and 89:27-28 understand the commitment that God assumes in recognizing the king as God's son and bestowing on him the rights of a son. As a son bears responsibility for the hereditary property of his father, so the king assumes it for all that belongs to God, for the whole earth. Early Christian congregations also understood 2 Sam 7:14 in this sense, that is, as a promise of lordship, and heard it as a word referring to Jesus.

Luke, for example, calls David the "father" of Jesus. The angel promises the mother of Jesus that he will inherit the kingdom of this father: "the Lord God will give to him the throne of his ancestor David" (Luke 1:32). Because Luke cannot imagine that an inheritance can be passed on in any other way than through the father he makes a point of stating that Mary was betrothed to Joseph, "of the house of David" (1:27). The male line leads from David through Joseph.[30]

In his chain of quotations, therefore, Paul very unconventionally gives the promise to David a different meaning. Men and women are "sons and daughters" to whom God passes on responsibility to rule. Paul must have had a good reason for weaving this unconventional quotation into the argumentation with which he wants to reach his opponents in Corinth and also for reformulating it so remarkably. It is conceivable that these people not only made use of a way of arguing that had come from Qumran but also sought to exclude women from the assembly of the holy, as was the rigorously practiced custom in Qumran. In the congregation at Corinth, in which women "prophesied" (1 Cor 11:5-6), such demands could cause considerable disquiet. Paul was convinced that women, too, have a part in Jesus' sonship from David. He holds fast to the belief that among those "who were baptized into Christ . . . there is no longer male and female" (Gal 3:27-28).

Had it not been for that argumentation in Corinth that he answers with the composition of sayings in 2 Cor 6:16-18 Paul would not have considered it necessary to say that the Father God also has strong helpers in his daughters, for otherwise he could be sure that he would not be misunderstood when he spoke of "sons" and "brothers," thereby including women. According to the custom of that day, daughters left their father's house when they married. Only brothers and sons were responsible for the father's inheritance. In the congregation, however, women were "sons" of God who did not have to go away, and who helped bear the "brotherly" responsibility. Not until Paul has to fear that this way of speaking could be interpreted to the disadvantage of women does he speak differently. He even alters the famous promise to David so that it becomes clear that God also gives "daughters" kingly responsibility for the divine inheritance.

The "Abba" cry of the early Christians

Christians have become so accustomed to calling God "Father" that they always hear this word when they have "sons and daughters" of God in mind. Paul lived with the Old Testament as his Holy Scripture, in which expressions about God the Father are rare and speak about a final and difficult hope. In his letter to the Galatians he declares that even for those who belong to Christ it is by no means a matter of course to address God as Father: "And because you are children, God has sent the Spirit of his Son into our hearts, crying, 'Abba! Father!' So you are no longer a slave but a child, and if a child then also an heir, through God" (Gal 4:6-7; see Rom 8:15).

Because Jesus alone is a son as God wishes, no one but he should be permitted to call God "Father." When those who are baptized do so together with him, that is a nonnegotiable gift. The Greek-speaking congregation to whom Paul writes took this "together" so seriously that they called on God as Father in Aramaic, Jesus' native language: *ʾabbaʾ*.

Paul emphasizes that whoever calls out *ʾabbaʾ* is not just a son, but also an heir. To the baptized (according to Gal 3:28, men and women) is entrusted the royal inheritance that God had promised to the Son of David. In the letter to the Romans the apostle repeats that the *ʾabbaʾ* cry of Christians is a cry of the Spirit of Christ. However, the beautiful image of the family inheritance collapses: "we are . . . heirs of God and joint heirs with Christ—if, in fact, we suffer with him . . ." (Rom 8:16-17). What do receiving an inheritance and suffering have to do with one another?

It is precisely this word about suffering, so unfitting within the imagery of inheritance, that agrees with the only non-Pauline text that tells of an *ʾabbaʾ* cry, that from the Mount of Olives scene in Mark. What moved the early Christians, to whom we owe the earliest report of the passion, to divulge precisely this confidential and familiar expression? The next section will start from this scene to ask how the relationship of father and son between God and Jesus is understood in the New Testament.

6. God, the Father of Jesus

The "Abba" cry as a witness to Jesus' message about the Father

Jesus spoke to God just as one spoke to the father in the intimate family circle. As representative of the house, as the head of the family responsible for justice and the preservation of the inheritance, the father was the *ʾab*. The Jews called on God as "our father," "our kin," *ʾabenu malkenu*. Jesus, however, used the everyday word *ʾabbaʾ*.

Jesus often takes images out of the everyday routine of families in order to speak of God's activity. He renews the old, festive message of God's fatherhood but, like the narrators of the Old Testament, he demonstrates that justice and peace are at risk when the simple affection for one's fellow men and women demonstrated even by humble people is missing.[31] In the word *ʾabbaʾ,* therefore, Jesus' basic message rings out, that is, that Israel possesses in its faith a wonderful family inheritance. But what is an inheritance worth when the father is considered only as the lord of the inheritance and not as a father with whom it is a joy to live?

The Old Testament does not understand the familiar closeness of father and son simply as a private matter. Jonathan fought at his father's side for Israel's survival and was convinced that no one understood this man as well as he, for "my father does nothing either great or small without disclosing it to me" (1 Sam 20:2). Jonathan, of course, must have understood that in the darkening of his state of mind Saul no longer understood even himself. Nevertheless, he remained true to his father. David sings of the two: "Saul and Jonathan, beloved and lovely! In life and in death they were not divided."[32]

The New Testament understands Jesus' bond with God according to the image of such filial love: "All things have been handed over to me by my Father; and no one knows who the Son is except the Father, or who the Father is except the Son and anyone to whom the Son chooses to reveal him" (Luke 10:22; cf. Matt 11:27). This statement sounds as if it had come out of the latest gospel, the Gospel of John, that theologically sharpens Jesus' message about the Father. It is, nevertheless, a word of earlier origin. Independently from one another, Luke and Matthew took it out of a still older document. Certainly Jesus himself understood his filial relationship to God in this way. He had further developed ancient ideas of the mutual bond between father and son.

From the Old Testament it was known that it was a life-and-death necessity for Israel that fatherly love not be a legally defensible right that always benefits everyone in the same degree. Would the people of Israel ever have been formed out of the twelve sons of Jacob if Judah had not offered himself as a slave in place of the brother privileged by his father (see ch. 3, section 5 above)? In the same way, because of his Father's will Jesus is also ready to give up his life for the "brethren." Jesus, the only and privileged Son, walks even into death for the "kingdom of the Father," just as Jonathan did for his father, King Saul (see ch. 2, section 3 above). The love of a son moves Jesus to work for the God who has called himself "Father of Israel." He wants to bring Israel to repentance so that God can finally approach this "child of delight" (see section 1 above).

The point of departure for the following inquiry about the special filial relationship of Jesus will be the Mount of Olives scene in Mark 14, the only text that tells about Jesus' cry of *ʾabbaʾ*.

Mark 14:36: Jesus alone with the Father

Jesus had begun the renewal of Israel by gathering disciples around himself. This makes the beginning of the Mount of Olives scene especially dramatic: Jesus leaves the disciples behind. Is he abandoning the work of the son for the Father's inheritance? The narrative names only outwardly visible and audible events, simultaneously inviting us with every word to discover what is really going on secretly behind the scenes. Allusions to Old Testament stories are to be heard at the same time, for once more a question was to be decided that had already often affected Israel's history, namely, whether a People of God can exist at all. When Jesus asks the disciples to stay behind, saying "sit here while I pray" (Mark 14:32), one is reminded of the Abraham story from Genesis 22, in which the very future existence of Israel once hung in the balance. Abraham had left his servants behind in the same way: "Stay here with the donkey; the boy and I will go over there; we will worship, and then we will come back to you" (Gen 22:5). With this gesture of worship, by which human beings say to God that they await nothing from themselves and everything from God, Jesus throws himself on the ground when he prays. To "worship," Abraham had taken only his son, who was the personified guarantee that God wanted to give him a future (see ch. 3, section 7 above). Jesus, too, takes along those who are his ultimate guarantee that the renewal of Israel is successful, that is, the first three of his disciples.

Nevertheless, the three leave Jesus alone. He keeps coming back to them—three times—in a vain attempt to share his anguish with them. Asleep, they fail to notice that he is praying: "Abba, Father, for you all things are possible; remove this cup from me; yet, not what I want, but what you want" (Mark 14:36). The scene shows vividly that for Jesus, too, "Father" was the expression of final hope. The three men who embody the last hope of Israel's renewal have left him alone, and there is nothing left for him but the certainty that God is as close to him as a dear father.

Mark did not learn the Mount of Olives prayer from a witness who had heard it. He himself emphasizes that the three disciples go to sleep and hear nothing. In Mark 14:36 the evangelist summarized what was often told and thought through in early congregations, namely, with what extraordinary familiarity Jesus—he alone—had conversed with God. It is just that much more significant that in the Mount of Olives scene Jesus had striven not to be alone. In his prayer he is alone with his dear Father not because he wants it that way but because the disciples leave him alone.

Jesus seeks successors

The narrators are deeply concerned with Jesus' persistent efforts on behalf of the three disciples. They mention it three times in the course of their brief report. This can be understood from a second Old Testament story to which there are allusions in the Mount of

Olives scene: Like Abraham, Elijah would also once have endangered the continued existence of Israel if God had not intervened.

All Israel had fallen away. Only Elijah the prophet remained, and he had gone into the wilderness. "He asked that he might die," says 1 Kings 19:4. In the lament with which Jesus reveals his affliction to the three, he echoes this word: "I am deeply grieved, even to death."[33] In those days God had not permitted that deathly-weary Elijah should die. An angel sent him farther, and Elijah traveled to the mountain of God. But there he had to hear a reproach from God: "What are you doing here, Elijah?" (1 Kings 19:13). A prophet who seeks out his God alone is in the wrong place, and God sends Elijah back. God's priority is that the work for God's people is carried on.

Jesus does not need such an instruction. He is the son who agrees with his Father in all things. In contrast to Elijah, he concerns himself with successors. For this reason he tells the three that he is deeply troubled, and thus he wants to include them in his prayer. When none of this is understood he nevertheless does not give up. "Get up, let us be going. See, my betrayer is at hand" (Mark 14:42). The three are to accompany him on his way to suffering.

How is that done, to accompany Jesus in his suffering? A peculiar scene shows how it cannot be done. It was not as a demonstration of faith that Jesus wants to take the disciples along on the way of suffering. The family of disciples is not to be a substitute for the strong paternal house that protects a man in danger.[34] When the henchmen seize Jesus, "one of those who stood near" strikes with his sword. This valiant man cannot be called a "disciple," for a disciple would have acted differently. But what could Jesus have expected from a disciple? That cannot be determined from the Mount of Olives text, which closes with the flight of the disciples. Nevertheless, to its background belongs also the story that describes how Elijah found a successor. The true disciple, Elisha, did not leave his master alone. When he saw that God meant to "take" Elijah he clung stubbornly to his feet until God allowed him to inherit the spirit of Elijah (see ch. 2, section 8 above). Jesus did not have that kind of disciple, for he died alone.

The Father of Jesus is the incomprehensible God

In all his prayers in the New Testament, Jesus addresses God as "Father." Only in his last prayer does he not call on the Father, but cries out "with a loud voice" to his God: "My God, my God, why have you forsaken me?" (Mark 15:34). On the cross Jesus is led beyond his message that God is Father. Yet he does not allow himself to be led away from God. God has abandoned him, and yet he insists that for him God is "my God." In the chronicles of world history the laments of the many who have been alone in terrible distress and death were seldom recorded. The writers of history prefer to record the shouts of victory, which are louder. Jesus cries out to the silent God humanity's ancient and never-ending lament of abandonment. He does it with the words of a psalm (Ps 22:1) that, for its part, takes up the abandonment complaints of ancient Near Eastern prayers: "My goddess has left me alone and has disappeared; my god has gone away."[35] For thousands of years before Jesus, people had been praying in this way. The poet of Psalm 22 brings his complaint to the right address, to the God of Israel, and Jesus joins him in so doing. Even when he cries in abandonment on the cross, he does not forget his people. Had he wished only to reach his God, a whimper would have been enough, for God hears even quiet groans. Jesus wants people to hear him and it is for this reason that he cries out "with a loud voice."

This last attempt by Jesus to reach his people failed, just as had his efforts on behalf of the three disciples at the Mount of Olives. Those who stood nearby misunderstood his cry. Not until after his death do the narrators mention that there was still a final, weak bond that linked Jesus with his people: "There were also women looking on from a distance" (Mark 15:40). The dead Jesus is not entirely abandoned by his people. As soon as possible the women want to give him at least the final honors that a family gave a dead person. Then it can be seen that for God the thread of personal affection is actually strong enough to renew the People of God. God reconnects the bond that the disciples tore apart when they ran away. The women are to bring the message to the disciples and Peter: "you will see him, just as he told you" (Mark 16:7).

The resurrection message in Mark is formulated only with great reserve, and yet in such a way that every word has great weight as the summary of a long conversation about the faith. "Just as he told you": the last word that Jesus had said to his disciples before his death was "Get up, let us be going. See, my betrayer is at hand." If the disciples had listened more carefully they would have understood that Jesus alone was sentenced to die, and that their flight was unnecessary. Then they would have stayed with him and seen him as he wanted to be seen. Even in death he does not abandon his effort for the People of God. Because three disciples failed, God must intervene and give them a message by the mouth of the women. They will see Jesus in the way he intended, as renewer of the People of God.

Father, for you all things are possible

Only within the entire context can Jesus' "Abba" prayer on the Mount of Olives be correctly heard. In the scene in Gethsemane the story shows how Jesus anticipated the experience of his death. The sadness of death has already seized him, and in the midst of this he prays: "Abba, Father, for you all things are possible; remove this cup from me; yet, not what I want, but what you want" (Mark 14:36).

Though no one overheard this prayer, neither was it thought up by some highly imaginative storyteller in order, perhaps, to praise a Jesus who willingly subjects himself to a Father who sends him to die. In the prayer Jesus shows himself as his disciples knew him. The manner in which he turns to God helps to decipher one of his enigmatic expressions: "whoever does not receive the kingdom of God as a little child will never enter it" (Mark 10:15). Jesus speaks with God in the demanding tone that beloved children employ when they ask trusted parents for what they need: "Remove this cup from me!"

The plea is not granted. Jesus drinks the cup of defeat down to the dregs. But the story provides a clue that in the case of a prayer like this one of Jesus the important thing is not that the petition be fulfilled just as it was spoken. Jesus had explained it to the three disciples: "pray that you may not come into the time of trial" (Mark 14:38). Prayer to God the loving Father does not save from suffering and death, but from temptation. From what temptation?[36]

Just as Jesus anticipates on the Mount of Olives his death on the cross, so his lonely "Abba" prayer anticipates and interprets his final prayer to God. The cry in which he addresses the incomprehensible and silent God, "My God, my God . . . ," goes beyond the message about the Father, yet without departing from it. If Jesus had expected only the deliverance of which he speaks in the form of a child's request, then God would in reality not have been a father to him on the Mount of Olives. Rather, his anxiety would simply have allowed him to feign for a time that God is Father. But the scene in Gethsemane does not portray a Jesus who is fooling himself. God is the dear Father for him even in the midst of the sorrow of death because he recognizes this Father as the incomprehensible God for whom "all things are possible."

Whoever calls on God together with Jesus as Abba, dear Father, as did the early Christians (see section 5 above) does not reduce God to human dimensions. God is Father because God does not impose the divine will with power from above and against all resistance, but carries it through only when that will finds an echo in the heart of a son or daughter. The Father of Jesus is God because the divine will is accomplished even when God's true Son fails in spite of all effort. It is sufficient for God that there are women who do not want to abandon the dead Jesus, and then the "echo" has been heard by which God reveals that God's will is going to be accomplished, the will of the Creator that gives life and does not abandon Jesus to death.

7. Fragmentary images of the Father

In the Old Testament only rare and late voices speak of God as the Father. In addition, they always do so in such a way that this father image emerges through its abrasion against other images: God is namely more than just a father. In human life, too, a good father must be more than just a father, and there is no use having a father who is not like a father.

When only fragments of the image of divine fatherhood appear in the Bible, then that is no error that one needs to correct by supplying the missing parts. For example, that God is like a father does not mean that God is like a man. The only thing that is exclusively male about being a father is the ability to sire a child. But in biblical pictures of the fatherhood of God, the point is not the descent from God but the hope in God. It is a complicated "hope in hope." Israel hopes in God because it trusts that God indeed hopes to be recognized as Father.

The fragility of the New Testament's concept of God as Father can be seen especially in the fact that it continually makes careful distinctions between God as the Father of Jesus and as Father of the company of disciples. The scene on the Mount of Olives describes how this breach came into existence. Jesus wants to include the disciples in his prayer to the Father, but the three leave him alone (see section 6 above). The Christian hope in God depends on God permitting the disciples to see their master as he wished, until the end, to be seen, that is, as the true Son who does God's work and founds Israel anew. For this reason the new People of God are an incomplete family of brothers, sisters, and mothers that receives a Father only through Jesus (see ch. 2, section 10; and section 5 of this chapter).

Though the biblical image of the fatherhood of God is fragmentary, its fragments are not without relation to one another. In the conversation of the traditions its elements constantly develop out of the same roots. Three key points resulted in especially strong motifs:

- The father passes on the inheritance.
- The son works together with the father.
- The hearts of father and son are closely bound together.

It is with the intention of summarizing and expanding what has been said above that this final section will once more give attention to these three motifs.

Fragmentary images of the father's heritage

Among the agricultural and pastoral people of Israel a father was, in the first place, a man who had an inheritance to pass on. In this context "father" is also a word of hope. A man who has a son can hope that he will care for the inheritance as he himself does (see ch. 2, section 5; and ch. 3, section 5 above). Although the Bible speaks only once about "daughters" of God the Father (see section 5 above), that is because "father" and "inheritance" were thought of very closely together. Daughters had no part in the father's inheritance, and therefore women who did not want to give up God's inheritance were glad to let themselves be reckoned to the "sons" of God.

Nevertheless, the Bible knows no single and unified image of God's inheritance. God's inheritance is the land or the people or the whole world. Ancient voices had spoken already of the land as God's heritage.[37] But Jeremiah was the first to speak about God as the father who passes on the inheritance, and for him the image of the inheritance is already shattered. The land is being lost, and the prophet interprets the loss as the result of the fact that Israel is not the kind of son for its God that a father hopes for when he has a good heritage to pass on (see section 1 above).

The ideas of the people as God's "hereditary property" and of God as Father are united only in a late prophetic song of lament. Israel pleads with God to look after the "tribes of Israel," God's "heritage" (Isa 63:17), and calls on God as "our Father." However, God needs to do more for the continuance of Israel than a father does for his inheritance. God must be a creator who shapes withered foliage as a potter does the clay. The scripturally learned poet blends fragments of images of diverse origins one over the other. Only in this way does he discover where sinful Israel still has a basis for hope (see section 3 above).

A parable of Jesus about the people as God's hereditary property speaks much more simply. It tells of a father who sends his son into the vineyard. The "vineyard," Israel, falls into ruin when the will of the father, who wishes to preserve it, fails to find an echo in the hearts of his sons. This picture, too, is incomplete, and must be so for the sake of its message. The parable is to find its echo in the hearts of its hearers, who are themselves to judge what motivates the son who had at first flatly refused to do the work in the inheritance.

The thought that God, the Lord of the entire world, entrusts divine work to human beings appears frequently. The image of the paternal inheritance is thereby often missing, however, for God, the Lord of the world, is never called "father" in the Bible, even though the neighboring peoples' impressive concepts of the divine Father in whose kindness everything is secure would have suggested it (see section 2 above).

The idea of God's universal fatherhood had special weight in the ancient Near Eastern and Egyptian ideology of the king. Kings called the supreme god their father, and understood themselves as his sons who had inherited divine rule over the world and bore responsibility for life in the world. Two biblical texts take this up: the creation story in Genesis 1, and Psalm 2, one of the royal psalms. They are texts very different from one another, and it is just that much more remarkable that both set aside the image elements "father/son." However unusual it may be to go again into individual cases in a closing chapter, the comparison of the two texts will nevertheless have to be carried through a bit more precisely in what follows.

Fragmentary images of divine sonship

Genesis 1:26 tells how God conceives of the human being: "let us make humankind in our image, according to our likeness; and let them have dominion . . . ." God places hope in humankind. The human being is to be a likeness by which can be discerned how God rules. The creation story describes this in detail. God creates living space, awakens the life-forces, and makes available green plants for food. God hopes human beings will rule in the same way. The office of protector and promoter of life, which was the office of kings in the ancient world, becomes the office of all humankind.

Genesis 5:3 repeats words from Gen 1:26: "Adam . . . became the father of a son in his likeness, according to his image." However clearly this statement is related to Gen 1:26, it also differs from it. Among human beings it happens that a son is such an exact image of his father that everyone can see who sired him. The similarity between God and a human being cannot be explained in this way. The report in Gen 1:26 underlines this when it not only avoids the "father-son" image but beyond this in 1:27 when it again speaks differently about the "image." Adam "sired" his likeness, while God "created" his likeness. *Bara'*, create, is a "theological" verb used exclusively to speak of God's activity, and that means that God does what human beings are not able even to imagine.[38]

The significantly complicated relationships between Gen 1:26-27 and Gen 5:3 can once more reveal why, though no conclusive image of God's fatherhood appears in the Bible, this image is nevertheless not excluded. Faith can sustain the tension arising from the fact that the inscrutable God is also the God who is close at hand.

Psalm 2 expresses this tension in its complex linguistic form. The psalmist allows the king to tell what God had said to him.

> "He [YHWH] said to me, "You are my son; today I have begotten
> you.
> Ask of me, and I will make the nations your heritage,
> and the ends of the earth your possession" (Ps 2:7-8).

The image of a son "begotten" just at the moment is so inconceivable that another translation, also possible according to the Hebrew grammar, would fit better: "I have borne you." On the day of his assumption of the throne the king in Israel becomes like a newborn babe.

The psalmist calls God "he who sits in the heavens," "LORD," and "YHWH," but the word "father " is not present. It is simply obvious that a son receives the inheritance from his father. The psalmist, however, wants to proclaim something that cannot be grasped by earthly standards. The king may make his request to God just as do little children who speak with their parents in the demanding tone of command. Then the Lord of heaven will fulfill the king's request and give him the comprehensive inheritance that reaches to the ends of the earth.

If one takes the biblical authors seriously in their remarkable restraint in using the father-son image as part of the ideology concerning the king—and one is forced to do so by the effort they dedicate to citing this image and yet minimizing it—then one may not simply supply what they leave out when another biblical text seems to offer what is missing. Psalm 89, another royal psalm, speaks of God as the Father of the king, alluding, however, not to the royal ideology but to the characteristic idea of God's fatherhood that first appears in Jeremiah. This psalmist, too, choses a complicated form of speech. He anticipates that God already imagines how the king will one day call on him:

> He [the king] shall cry to me, 'You are my Father,
> my God, and the Rock of my salvation' (Ps 89:26).

The great kings of the ancient Near East wished to be called "father" by their vassals. In the Bible, however, it is the king's helper, the good official, who receives the honorable title of "father" (see ch. 2, section 7 above). The poet of Psalm 89 sees God in the servant role of the helper. God would like to be called a helping Father, "strong as a rock."

How does it happen that biblical authors treat with such restraint the beautiful picture of the inheritance of the divine Father with which the ancient Near Eastern ideology of the king reminded the rulers of their responsibility for life on the earth? The great kings of the ancient world liked to believe that they had a right to rule the world. For a king of Israel this would have been criminal day-dreaming. When the creation story in Genesis 1 came into being Israel had long ago lost its land to great and violent powers. Though Psalm 2 may be of earlier origin, it certainly did not belong to the psalter until this much later time. The image of the inclusive fatherly inheritance of God was shattered in the Bible by the sober recognition of the reality that power is easily transformed into violence. In view of a world full of violence, biblical authors neither desire nor are able to demonstrate that God is Father. They show how people who live in a world in which the just are seldom stronger than the unjust can seek their Father in God.

Father and son work together

How is it possible in a world full of injustice to seek the Father in God? Jesus' famous statement about loving one's enemies shows one way: "Love your enemies and pray for those who persecute you, so that you may be children of your Father in heaven; for he makes the sun rise on the evil and on the good, and sends rain on the righteous and on the unrighteous" (Matt 5:44-45). When one hears this saying in isolation it has the effect of a radical demand that can hardly be achieved. It sounds different when one considers that Jesus carries on old biblical themes in his own way. In ancient Israel it was taken for granted that sons work together with their fathers. Jesus, too, grew up in an environment in which sons lived in this way. In Nazareth he was known as "the carpenter's son" (Matt 13:55). He had certainly been seen often in the workshop of his father, Joseph. Sons grew into the work of their fathers, at first imitating them, then as helpers on demand, and finally as their successors.

Jesus often took from the everyday life of ordinary people his parables about life with God. Against this background even the words about loving one's enemies become easily understandable: as a child imitates its father, so the disciples should do the work of God. God is at work everywhere that the rain falls and the sun shines. For this reason the disciples of Jesus are to look out beyond their little company and assume worldwide responsibility, even for those who are their enemies.

The word of Jesus, too, holds fast to the biblical tradition that sees God as the Father of the people Israel, "our Father," not the Father of the world. Jesus calls God "your Father," the Father of the little flock he had gathered to restore the People of God. Already Jeremiah had, for his message about the Father, modified the concept of father and son working together. Because he knew how disheartened the deportees were he proclaimed that it was enough for God's longing to be Father that God's people go as far to meet God as a child can (see section 1 above).

Jesus gives special emphasis to the parable about being a child when he frees the thought about the worldwide "reign of God" from its context in promises about the future king and links it to images of the child. Urgently he admonishes his disciples to seize the reign of God with the same naturalness with which a child takes from its parents what it needs to live (see section 4 above). When one hears this admonition in the context of the command to love one's enemies, not only the enigmatic words about children but also the puzzle of the passage itself are illuminated. God wants to be "Father" for the little flock because God needs "sons" who do God's work in the world. Just as God gives "rain and sun" to everyone who lives, so the disciples of Jesus are not to begrudge to anyone, even their enemies, what they need to live.

The hearts of father and son are close to one another

Images of childhood can be reminiscent of a certain concept of the origin of religious needs that is certainly appropriate when taken for itself. People seek security in a well-disposed divine protective power. The "primeval trust" that a well-loved child acquires in its family has its reflection in such piety. The father, especially, is often experienced as the one who is unshakably powerful and kind. A child must confront and deal with the failures and weaknesses of its mother earlier in its life because it lives more closely together with her.

In Israel, too, people looked to God as the basis for such trust (see section 2 above). Nevertheless, biblical authors warn that this piety is not sufficient. When they speak of God as the provident Father they also emphasize that God is looking for "sons" able to stand up for themselves and even for God. At the same time, they do not forget that the same law applies as in human relations, namely, that justice and righteousness die unless hearty affection brings them to life (see ch. 3, sections 5 and 6 above). Thus faith, too, receives its living power only when it is anchored in feelings.

Jeremiah and Jesus, the two great teachers of the faith, combine profound feeling with the sober knowledge of the world that had been acquired by the little people of Israel, who had often only narrowly escaped destruction. Jeremiah speaks of the destruction of Judah and Jerusalem as if all of it were a story of the inner relation between God and God's people. In Jesus' prayer on the Mount of Olives the question whether a People of God can even exist is directed to the dear Father. Both of them give the trust in God's paternal love a more durable foundation than that which the "primeval trust" acquired in childhood, that is, God is a Father for those who entrust themselves to God with the whole strength of their nature and yet honor God as the Incomprehensible One.

The living power biblical faith obtained from this can be observed in history. Jeremiah does not deny that it was God who abandoned the people, and thereby contributes to the fact that Israel's faith survived the destruction of Judah and Jerusalem. And at the beginning of the history of Christianity stands the faith of Jesus, who, as the true Son, stepped forward for the renewal of the People of God when he had to die forsaken by everyone. In a voice loud enough that the people, too, could hear, he called on the God who had forsaken him.

Notes: Chapter Four

[1] God is like a mother: cf. Isa 49:15; 66:13; Deut 32:18. God loves Israel because it is the son of a friend: Isa 41:8. God is "blood brother." In Exod 24:8 the "blood of the covenant" covers the altar and the people. God is spouse and bridegroom: Hosea 2; Isaiah 54. God is the *go'el* (savior), that is, the rich relative who is committed to saving the family's inheritance when an impoverished member of the family cannot do it: Job 19:25 (cf. also Jer 32:7-8). The OT speaks fifteen times of God as Father, the NT about one hundred seventy times. That in the NT the multiplicity of the OT images of relationships is not quite forgotten is attested by John 1:13; 1 Pet 1:3; Jas 1:17-18, texts that speak of God and even of God the "Father" as of a mother in childbirth.

[2] Cf. Lam 5:3. On the paternal duties to which Jeremiah alludes, cf. ch. 2, section 5 above.

[3] On David, cf. ch. 3, section 8 above; on Jacob see ch. 3, section 5.

[4] In Gen 22:7 the child Isaac addresses his father Abraham in this way.

[5] "Friend of my youth" or "partner of youth" denotes a young husband also in Prov 2:17.

[6] Cf. Hos 2:18. In Gen 29:32, 34; 30:20 "my man/husband" is the term with which Leah expresses her longing to experience Jacob's love.

[7] In Isa 66:13 appears the image of God as the consoling mother.

[8] The meaning of the firstborn is reflected in, among other things, the generational list in Genesis 5: only the firstborn continue the list of fathers and sons. Jeremiah probably takes up a tradition that is alluded to in the prophetically formed statement of God in Exod 4:22, where God calls Israel "my firstborn son."

[9] Hosea 11 relates the history of Israel as the story of a son who, though he has been loved since he was little, is nevertheless a renegade; cf. also Isa 1:2. In Exod 4:22 Israel is called the "firstborn son" of God. According to Num 21:29 Chemosh has "sons and daughters," yet is never called "father" of Moab.

[10] Cf. ch. 2 above, sections 2 and 9, and ch. 3, section 8.

[11] Ignace J. Gelb, *Glossary of Old Akkadian* (Chicago: University of Chicago Press, 1957) *abu.*

[12] Ernst Jenni, ed., *Theologisches Handwörterbuch zum Alten Testament (ThWAT)* (Munich, 1971), *ʾab.* Zeus, too, is named "father of the gods and humans," "father of the universe," cf. Plato, *Timaeus* 28c. Greek-speaking Jewish writers speak in the same way about the God of Israel; for example Josephus, *Ant.* 1, 20, names God *pantōn patēr.*

[13] A. Fallenstein and W. von Soden, *Sumerische und akkadische Hymnen und Gebete* (Zürich, 1953) 223.

[14] This text from the time of Ashurbanipal (a contemporary of Jeremiah) is cited in W.H.Ph. Römer and K. Hecker, *Texte aus der Umwelt des Alten Testaments* (TUAT) II, 5; Otto Kaiser, ed. (Gütersloh: Gerd Mohn, 1989) 754.

[15] Eph 3:14 gives universal validity to a thought that had concrete meaning in the factional conflicts in Corinth: various groups there named themselves after Paul, Apollos, Cephas, and Christ. Self-confidently, Paul declares that the congregation did not have "many fathers," for he alone had "sired" it (1 Cor 4:15), but exhorts them at the same time that they are not to name themselves after anyone, for the congregation is "God's field," "God's building," and "God's people."

[16] Jesus says "your Father" in Matt 5:16, 45, 48; 6:1, 8, 14, 32 and "our Father" in Matt 6:9. Paul speaks of "our Father" in Rom 1:7; 1 Cor 1:3; 2 Cor 1:2; 6:18; Gal 1:3, and elsewhere. In Isa 63:16; 64:8; Tob 13:4, God is addressed as "our Father." Jewish prayers, whose basic form was shaped before the time of Jesus, address God as "our Father, our King" (cf. Pnina Navé-Levinson, *Einführung in die rabbinische Theologie* (Darmstadt: Wissenschaftliche Buchgesellschaft, 1982) 49–50.

[17] On Jeremiah 29 see ch. 1, section 3 above.

[18] Cf. H. Ranke, *Die Ägyptische Personennamen* (Glückstadt, 1952) 2:174, 251, 252; F. Gröndall, *Die Personennamen der Texte aus Ugarit* (Rome, 1967) 54, 55, 86, 109; J. J. Stamm, *Die akkadische Namengebung,* Mitteilungen der vorderasiatisch-ägyptische Gesellschaft (MVAG) 44 (Leipzig, 1939) 312. See also *ThWAT* (n. 12 above).

[19] *TUAT* 5:572 (see n. 14 above).

[20] F. Gröndall, *Personennamen* 46, 90.

[21] Cf. Pss 22:25; 35:18, among others.

[22] Older translations of Deut 32:18 spoke of the father who "begets" (e.g., RSV, "You were unmindful of the Rock that begot you," but with a footnote: "Or bore"). It is more probable that the verse should retain the mother image. Behind the words for "the Rock that bore you" lies the same image found in Jer 2:27: "(They say) to a stone, 'You gave me birth.'" The underlying image may be that of the rock from which water runs forth. Cf. Isa 51:1, where the progenitrix Sarah is called "the quarry from which you were dug."

[23] A. Falkenstein and W. v. Soden, *Sumerische und akkadische Hymnen und Gebete* (Zürich, 1953) 140. In Akkadian personal names *abu* (father) and *banu* (begetter) have the same meaning; cf. *ThWAT* art. *ʾab* (as in section 2, n. 12), "Since my mother bore me you have been my God," was also Israel's prayer (Ps 22:10).

[24] Only in Exod 19:4 does a similar image appear. On "the wings of eagles" God had brought the people to Sinai. Probably Deut 30:11 is quoted there in abbreviated form: God wishes for responsible sons and daughters who "fly" in their own strength. Therefore God brings Israel to Sinai, the place of the Law.

[25] For example, the saga from Genesis 38 tells with what courage the Canaanite woman, Tamar, won life for herself and for the entire tribe. Malachi distorts her into a deterrent example.

[26] How dreadfully extreme poverty can change human beings is described by a motif from OT cursing texts. Hungry mothers and fathers consume their children, and children devour their parents: cf. 2 Kings 6:28-29; Deut 28:53-57; Lev 26:29; Jer 19:9; Ezek 5:10; Lam 2:20; 4:10.

[27] Cf. section 2, n. 16 above.

[28] Cf. Prov 3:12; Deut 8:5; 2 Sam 7:14; Heb 12:7; cf. also ch. 3, section 4 above.

[29] Presence of God: Lev 26:11-12; Ezek 37:27; encouragement to return home: Isa 52:11; Jer 51:45; Ezek 20:34, 41.

[30] Matthew also presents matters in such a way that the sonship of David is passed to Jesus by way of Joseph; cf. ch. 2, section 7 above.

[31] Cf. ch. 3, section 6 above: The king loses his hold on the entire kingdom because he does not love his daughter even as much as a poor man does his lamb.

[32] 2 Sam 1:23; cf. on this ch. 2, section 3 above.

[33] Early Christians understood who Jesus was by the example of Elijah; cf. ch. 2, section 8 above. In a variant text (Luke 22:43-44) Luke cites even more plainly the Elijah story from 1 Kings 19: Jesus is strengthened by an

angel on the Mount of Olives just as Elijah had been strengthened in the wilderness.

[34] Cf. ch. 2, sections 1 and 2 above. Ahitub submits to Saul's judgment with all his men so that the king might see what he was letting himself in for in attacking a man of the famous priestly house. Jesus, on the other hand, surrenders alone to his captors; John 18:8 emphasizes this element of the Mount of Olives scene: "I told you that I am he. So if you are looking for me, let these men go."

[35] Cf. on this H. Vorländer, *Mein Gott. Die Vorstellung vom persönlichen Gott im alten Orient und im Alten Testament.* Kevelaer, 1975.

[36] The Lord's Prayer is passed on only by Matthew and Luke, but in the Markan congregations people prayed in the Spirit of Jesus just as the Lord's Prayer teaches: childlike prayer supports resistance in times of temptation (see section 4 above). An indication that here, too, the Lord's Prayer was taught is, among others, Mark 11:25. There, in connection with Jesus' teaching on prayer, appears the saying with which Matthew especially emphasized the petition for forgiveness in the Lord's Prayer.

[37] Cf. the lament of David in 1 Sam 26:19 that he, distant from his "share in the heritage of the LORD," must serve other gods.

[38] *Bara'* appears seven times in the first creation story, three times in connection with the creation of "heavens and the earth," once in the creation of the "sea monsters," three times in Gen 1:27. The human being is just as great a miracle of creation as the "heavens and the earth." It is also an incomprehensible act of creation that it contains powers of evil, represented by the "sea monsters."

Index

Abba, 198–201
Abiathar, 45
Abraham
  and Ishmael, 133
  different children of, 6
  hospitality of, 21–22
  sacrifice of, 142–147
Absalom, 76–77, 119–120
Ahaz, 79–82
Ahimelech, 43, 47, 58. *See also* Saul

Bible
  a product of its times, 157
  good and bad people in the, xxii, 35, 37, 64, 95, 114, 152, 157, 159, 160
Boaz, 21, 35
Bride price, 116

Cain, 63–64
Child sacrifice. *See* Abraham, sacrifice of
Church patriarchalism, xxiii

Daughters. *See also* Paul in 2 Cor 6:16-18
  absent from genealogies, 91
  destined to leave the father's house, 162
  rarely the object of their fathers' love, 93
  right of inheritance of, 19, 68–69
David. *See also* Jonathan; Saul
  and Absalom, 151
  and Ahimelech, 45–46
  and Bathsheba, 75–77
  and daughter, 117–118
  and his men and parents, 45, 74
  promise to, 196–197
  Son of, 78, 197
Dinah, 137, 149
Divine sonship, 208–210
Doeg, the Edomite, 44–45, 46, 48. *See also* Fatherless men

Eli, 152–153
Eliakim, 72, 73
Elijah, 7, 84–89
Elisha, 84–89, 97
Elkanah, 29, 32, 33
Ezekiel, 63
Ezra, 31

Faith alive in hostile surroundings, 11, 15
"Father and his whole household," 4–5, 6, 8, 9, 10
Father, a title of respect, 73–74
Father, described as,
 a generous host, 21–27
 a preserver of the inheritance, 66, 71, 91, 206
 a protector and helper, 65, 90
Fatherhood, biblical ideas about, xix, xx, xxi, 72, 89–96
Fatherless men, 71–77, 88, 93
Father of the king. *See* Elisha
Fathers and "brothers," 20, 29, 35, 51, 52, 90–91, 125
Fathers and sons, 79, 94–95, 126–130, 132–136, 161
Fathers, failures of, 95, 159, 160
Fathers, grave of the, 67, 99
Father's house, 46–47, 50–52, 80–82, 90, 95
Fathers in public life, xxiv–xxv, 93, 162–163
Fathers, new beginnings without, 101–102
Fathers, not patriarchs, 34–39
Fathers, religious authority of, 29–30
Fathers, renewal of divine blessing without, 94–95
Flood story revised, 13–14
Forgiveness, 194

Gideon, 29, 30, 49
God as father
 addressed thus in Jesus' prayers, 202–203
 a theme cautiously treated in the Bible, xxv
 first called thus by Jeremiah, 170–176, 177
 never seen as father of the world, 207, 210
 seen in many Old Testament names, 180
 still also the Incomprehensible One, 182, 202
God's inheritance, 206–207
Guilty yet just, 113–114

Hagar and Ishmael, 133
Hannah, 32, 33
Hospitality, 21–27. *See also* Abraham, hospitality of
 in the New Testament, 26–27
 in the Old Testament, 21–26

Inheritance
 conflicts over, 92
 given to daughters only in special cases, 68–69
 heritage of the fathers passed on to sons, 65, 89, 134–135, 156
Isaac, 151–152. *See also* Abraham
Isaiah, 80–82, 187–189

Jacob, 108–115, 122, 149–150, 182
Jail official in Philippi, xxiv, 1–4, 10
Jairus, 139–141
Jephthtah, 120–121
Jeremiah
 his letter to fathers in exile, 11, 12
 renounces wife and children, 83
 speaks of God as Father, 170–176
Job, 69–70, 138–139. *See also* Inheritance
John the Baptist. *See* Elijah; Luke; Malachi
Jonathan, 52–57, 199–200. *See also* David; Saul

Joseph, called father to Pharaoh, 73, 136–137

Kings, never called fathers in the Bible, 83

Laban, 109, 110, 115
Leah and Rachel, 109, 114, 115, 116
Levirate marriage, 67
Lord's prayer, the, 190–195
Lot, 25–26, 112–113
Luke
 in Acts 16:23-40, 1–5
 mentions hospitable men and women, 27
 repeats Malachi's closing words, 7

Malachi, 7, 189–190
Mixed marriages, 19, 189. *See also* Nehemiah
Moses, 23–25
Mothers
 named only 220 times in the Bible, 1
 not named in genealogies, 91

Nathan, 75–77
Nehemiah, 31, 38. *See also* Mixed marriages
Noah, 5, 10, 125. *See also* Flood story revised

"Oedipus complex," xviii, 159

Parable of the merciful father, 70–71. *See also* Inheritance
Paternal house. *See* Father's house
"Patriarchalism," 154, 157–159. *See also* Fathers, not patriarchs
Paul and Silas. *See* Jail official in Philippi
Paul in 2 Cor 6:16-18, 195
People of God, 8, 30–31, 33, 38, 70, 157, 203
Pilgrimages, 29, 32
Priests of Nob. *See* Ahimelech

Qumran, 195, 197

Raguel, 23–25, 26
Rape regarded as murder, 119
Raphael, 19–20
Readiness to give mutual help, 35
Rehoboam, 123–124

Samson, 49
Sarah, 22, 25, 35
Saul, xxiv, 42, 79, 83. *See also* David; Jonathan
Solomon, 60–61
Sons
 must respect their fathers, 124
 never shown as defending themselves against powerful fathers, 93–94
 not necessarily imitating their fathers, 126
 punished for the sins of their fathers, 58–62, 63, 95, 161

Tamar, 113, 119, 161. *See also* David, and daughter
Teachers of the Law, 31, 60, 116, 119, 121, 134, 153, 154, 155, 184
Tobit, xxiv, 15–20
Tocqueville, Alexis de, xix–xx

"Will of the Father," 183